THE
REFLECTION
PLANNER

Reflection, Self-Care, and Growth for Moms

KEERA L. ALBERGARIA

WESTBOW
PRESS®
A DIVISION OF THOMAS NELSON
& ZONDERVAN

WestBow Press books may be ordered through booksellers or by contacting:

WestBow Press
A Division of Thomas Nelson & Zondervan
1663 Liberty Drive
Bloomington, IN 47403
www.westbowpress.com
844-714-3454

Scripture quotations are taken from The Holy Bible, English Standard Version® (ESV®), Copyright © 2001 by Crossway, a publishing ministry of Good News Publishers. All rights reserved.

ISBN: 978-1-9736-9675-9 (sc)
ISBN: 978-1-9736-9676-6 (e)

Print information available on the last page.

WestBow Press rev. date: 08/24/2020

This planner is dedicated to my children and husband. THANK YOU for being patient with me while I dedicated this time to help fellow moms along their journey God gave them.

Moms, a special "thank you" goes out to you all for taking part in this journey. Thank you for allowing me to help guide you as well as pray for you.

Welcome Mom!!

I am so proud of you for taking this step towards focusing on YOU! As moms, we tend to put ourselves last, while we put the needs of others first. As the Lord put us on this Earth to love one another, we also need to take the time to fill our cups, in order to pour into other. This is YOUR time to do just that! Now…let's dive right in!!!

How a "reflection planner" works?

Mom, isn't it true that when you think of a planner for mothers, your brain immediately goes to all the things we "must do"? It tends to get overwhelming writing meal planning ideas, grocery shopping lists, kid's activities…the list goes on. That is why the "reflection planner" was designed to take care of what your soul needs. The purpose of this planner is to end the day, putting your mind at ease, and reflecting on how your day went while making your goals for tomorrow. Below, are instructions on how this planner was designed to be filled out each day:

It's the end of your day. Everyone is settled in for the night. It is time to put your "to do" list aside. Why the end of the night? Because this allows you to truly reflect. Mornings can be hectic for a mom. The last thing you want to do is rush through your entry for the day! Before you crawl into bed for the evening is the perfect time to clear your head, reflect on your day, and plan your day ahead. Let us get started!!

Reflection.

Here is where you can reflect on your day…not your children's day and not your husbands. YOURS. Let us start with celebrating something each day. Big or small…You deserve it! Next, lets move onto gratitude. There is no better way to end the day then to give thanks. Now let us move on to something a little more challenging. Let us reflect on a portion of the day that maybe we would do differently. Here is where self- forgiveness comes in. Maybe we snapped at our little one for not getting out the door as quick as we would have liked. Maybe we allowed an abnormally long amount of time for electronics today. Guess what? Let us focus on doing things differently next time and not focusing on the negative. Lastly, how did you use your gift today? We all have gifts. Some can be challenging to recognize in ourselves, but God has given gifts to all of us. Let us not keep these to ourselves! Use them! Celebrate them!

Self-Care.

In this section, you will be putting that "self-forgiveness" to use. We may make plans to spend some alone time each day, however, us moms know that curve balls are thrown our way each day. That is where we need to learn to adjust, not beat ourselves up, and forgive ourselves just as the Lord forgives us. Each day you will be challenged to spend 15 minutes of "YOU" time. Plan it out the night before. That is why you will be asked to write down your 15 minutes plan for tomorrow. If that plan changes, THAT'S OK! Just make sure you do take 15 mins in some other way to celebrate you. Another key component to self-care is to show gratitude for the ability to move! To you, that may mean a 60-minute hard core workout. To others, that may mean you held your newborn while you walked up and down the stairs 10 times. Movement is important for your body as well as our mind. If you are blessed with movement, let us show praise in doing so. Hold yourself accountable!

Growth.

Growth is key to becoming who you were designed to be. We are called to greatness and let us lean into that. Hold yourself accountable to take steps towards your goal each day. Not sure what your goal is? Start small. Maybe it is time you clean out that bathroom closet that needed to get done 6 months ago. Starting small may help you discover what your large goal may be. Already have your large goal in mind? Each day you will be asked what steps you took towards that goal. Being a mom does not mean that is your only identity. God has designed each one of us in His image. Let us dig deep, find that goal, and take a step towards that each day. Each day

Date:_____

Reflection:

Jeremiah 29:11 "For I know the plans I have for you, declares the Lord, plans for welfare and not for evil, to give you a future and a hope."

What am I celebrating today? _____

_____

What am I grateful for today? _____

_____

What do I need to forgive myself for today? _____

_____

How did I use my gifts today?: _____

_____

Self-care:

3 John 1:2 "Beloved, I pray that all may go well with you and that you may be in good health, as it goes well with your soul."

How did I spend my 15 minutes of "me" time today? _____

_____

How will I spend my 15 minutes of "me" time tomorrow? _____

_____

How did I show gratitude for the ability to move my body today? ____

_____

How will I move tomorrow? _____

_____

Growth:

1 Timothy 4:15 "Practice these things, immerse yourself in them, so that all may see your progress."

What steps did I take towards my goal today? _____

_____

What did today teach me that I will bring into tomorrow? _____

_____

Reflection:

Jeremiah 29:11 "For I know the plans I have for you, declares the Lord, plans for welfare and not for evil, to give you a future and a hope."

What am I celebrating today? _____

_____

What am I grateful for today? _____

_____

What do I need to forgive myself for today? _____

_____

How did I use my gifts today?: _____

_____

Self-care:

3 John 1:2 "Beloved, I pray that all may go well with you and that you may be in good health, as it goes well with your soul."

How did I spend my 15 minutes of "me" time today? _____

_____

How will I spend my 15 minutes of "me" time tomorrow? _____

_____

How did I show gratitude for the ability to move my body today? _____

_____

How will I move tomorrow? _____

_____

Growth:

1 Timothy 4:15 "Practice these things, immerse yourself in them, so that all may see your progress."

What steps did I take towards my goal today? _____

_____

What did today teach me that I will bring into tomorrow? _____

_____

Reflection:

Jeremiah 29:11 "For I know the plans I have for you, declares the Lord, plans for welfare and not for evil, to give you a future and a hope."

What am I celebrating today? _____

_____

What am I grateful for today? _____

_____

What do I need to forgive myself for today? _____

_____

How did I use my gifts today?: _____

_____

Self-care:

3 John 1:2 "Beloved, I pray that all may go well with you and that you may be in good health, as it goes well with your soul."

How did I spend my 15 minutes of "me" time today? _____

_____

How will I spend my 15 minutes of "me" time tomorrow? _____

_____

How did I show gratitude for the ability to move my body today? _____

_____

How will I move tomorrow? _____

_____

Growth:

1 Timothy 4:15 "Practice these things, immerse yourself in them, so that all may see your progress."

What steps did I take towards my goal today? _____

_____

What did today teach me that I will bring into tomorrow? _____

_____

Date:_____

Reflection:

Jeremiah 29:11 "For I know the plans I have for you, declares the Lord, plans for welfare and not for evil, to give you a future and a hope."

What am I celebrating today? _____

_____

What am I grateful for today? _____

_____

What do I need to forgive myself for today? _____

_____

How did I use my gifts today?: _____

_____

Self-care:

3 John 1:2 "Beloved, I pray that all may go well with you and that you may be in good health, as it goes well with your soul."

How did I spend my 15 minutes of "me" time today? _____

_____

How will I spend my 15 minutes of "me" time tomorrow? _____

_____

How did I show gratitude for the ability to move my body today? _____

_____

How will I move tomorrow? _____

_____

Growth:

1 Timothy 4:15 "Practice these things, immerse yourself in them, so that all may see your progress."

What steps did I take towards my goal today? _____

_____

What did today teach me that I will bring into tomorrow? _____

_____

Date:_____

Reflection:

Jeremiah 29:11 "For I know the plans I have for you, declares the Lord, plans for welfare and not for evil, to give you a future and a hope."

What am I celebrating today? _____

_____

What am I grateful for today? _____

_____

What do I need to forgive myself for today? _____

_____

How did I use my gifts today?: _____

_____

Self-care:

3 John 1:2 "Beloved, I pray that all may go well with you and that you may be in good health, as it goes well with your soul."

How did I spend my 15 minutes of "me" time today? _____

_____

How will I spend my 15 minutes of "me" time tomorrow? _____

_____

How did I show gratitude for the ability to move my body today? _____

_____

How will I move tomorrow? _____

_____

Growth:

1 Timothy 4:15 "Practice these things, immerse yourself in them, so that all may see your progress."

What steps did I take towards my goal today? _____

_____

What did today teach me that I will bring into tomorrow? _____

_____

Reflection:

Jeremiah 29:11 "For I know the plans I have for you, declares the Lord, plans for welfare and not for evil, to give you a future and a hope."

What am I celebrating today? _____

_____

What am I grateful for today? _____

_____

What do I need to forgive myself for today? _____

_____

How did I use my gifts today?: _____

_____

Self-care:

3 John 1:2 "Beloved, I pray that all may go well with you and that you may be in good health, as it goes well with your soul."

How did I spend my 15 minutes of "me" time today? _____

_____

How will I spend my 15 minutes of "me" time tomorrow? _____

_____

How did I show gratitude for the ability to move my body today? _____

_____

How will I move tomorrow? _____

_____

Growth:

1 Timothy 4:15 "Practice these things, immerse yourself in them, so that all may see your progress."

What steps did I take towards my goal today? _____

_____

What did today teach me that I will bring into tomorrow? _____

_____

Isaiah 66:13 "As one whom his mother comforts, so I will comfort you..."

I remember a time when I was a single mother. I would cry at night because I just wanted that helping hand in the house. That hand to not only help me with my child, but that hand to hold me at night and comfort ME. I never stopped praying for a soul mate, and God answered my prayers. Moms, he hears your cries and knows the desires of your heart. God not only gave me the soul mate I prayed for, but in my time on my knees, He reminded me that He has been my comforter all along. You are NEVER alone.

Let this serve as a reminder to you this week:

He sees you.

He hears you.

He loves you.

Weekly Challenge:

It's time to reflect on your entries from last week. Pray. Meditate. Celebrate.

Date:_____

Reflection:

Jeremiah 29:11 "For I know the plans I have for you, declares the Lord, plans for welfare and not for evil, to give you a future and a hope."

What am I celebrating today? _____

_____

What am I grateful for today? _____

_____

What do I need to forgive myself for today? _____

_____

How did I use my gifts today?: _____

_____

Self-care:

3 John 1:2 "Beloved, I pray that all may go well with you and that you may be in good health, as it goes well with your soul."

How did I spend my 15 minutes of "me" time today? _____

_____

How will I spend my 15 minutes of "me" time tomorrow? _____

_____

How did I show gratitude for the ability to move my body today? _____

_____

How will I move tomorrow? _____

_____

Growth:

1 Timothy 4:15 "Practice these things, immerse yourself in them, so that all may see your progress."

What steps did I take towards my goal today? _____

_____

What did today teach me that I will bring into tomorrow? _____

_____

Date:_____

Reflection:

Jeremiah 29:11 "For I know the plans I have for you, declares the Lord, plans for welfare and not for evil, to give you a future and a hope."

What am I celebrating today? _____

_____

What am I grateful for today? _____

_____

What do I need to forgive myself for today? _____

_____

How did I use my gifts today?: _____

_____

Self-care:

3 John 1:2 "Beloved, I pray that all may go well with you and that you may be in good health, as it goes well with your soul."

How did I spend my 15 minutes of "me" time today? _____

_____

How will I spend my 15 minutes of "me" time tomorrow? _____

_____

How did I show gratitude for the ability to move my body today? _____

_____

How will I move tomorrow? _____

_____

Growth:

1 Timothy 4:15 "Practice these things, immerse yourself in them, so that all may see your progress."

What steps did I take towards my goal today? _____

_____

What did today teach me that I will bring into tomorrow? _____

_____

Date:_____

Reflection:

Jeremiah 29:11 "For I know the plans I have for you, declares the Lord, plans for welfare and not for evil, to give you a future and a hope."

What am I celebrating today? _____

_____

What am I grateful for today? _____

_____

What do I need to forgive myself for today? _____

_____

How did I use my gifts today?: _____

_____

Self-care:

3 John 1:2 "Beloved, I pray that all may go well with you and that you may be in good health, as it goes well with your soul."

How did I spend my 15 minutes of "me" time today? _____

_____

How will I spend my 15 minutes of "me" time tomorrow? _____

_____

How did I show gratitude for the ability to move my body today? _____

_____

How will I move tomorrow? _____

_____

Growth:

1 Timothy 4:15 "Practice these things, immerse yourself in them, so that all may see your progress."

What steps did I take towards my goal today? _____

_____

What did today teach me that I will bring into tomorrow? _____

_____

Date:_____

Reflection:

Jeremiah 29:11 "For I know the plans I have for you, declares the Lord, plans for welfare and not for evil, to give you a future and a hope."

What am I celebrating today? _____
_____

What am I grateful for today? _____
_____

What do I need to forgive myself for today? _____
_____

How did I use my gifts today?: _____
_____

Self-care:

3 John 1:2 "Beloved, I pray that all may go well with you and that you may be in good health, as it goes well with your soul."

How did I spend my 15 minutes of "me" time today? _____
_____

How will I spend my 15 minutes of "me" time tomorrow? _____
_____

How did I show gratitude for the ability to move my body today? _____
_____

How will I move tomorrow? _____
_____

Growth:

1 Timothy 4:15 "Practice these things, immerse yourself in them, so that all may see your progress."

What steps did I take towards my goal today? _____
_____

What did today teach me that I will bring into tomorrow? _____
_____

Date:_____

Reflection:

Jeremiah 29:11 "For I know the plans I have for you, declares the Lord, plans for welfare and not for evil, to give you a future and a hope."

What am I celebrating today? _____

_____

What am I grateful for today? _____

_____

What do I need to forgive myself for today? _____

_____

How did I use my gifts today?: _____

_____

Self-care:

3 John 1:2 "Beloved, I pray that all may go well with you and that you may be in good health, as it goes well with your soul."

How did I spend my 15 minutes of "me" time today? _____

_____

How will I spend my 15 minutes of "me" time tomorrow? _____

_____

How did I show gratitude for the ability to move my body today? _____

_____

How will I move tomorrow? _____

_____

Growth:

1 Timothy 4:15 "Practice these things, immerse yourself in them, so that all may see your progress."

What steps did I take towards my goal today? _____

_____

What did today teach me that I will bring into tomorrow? _____

_____

Date:_____

Reflection:

Jeremiah 29:11 "For I know the plans I have for you, declares the Lord, plans for welfare and not for evil, to give you a future and a hope."

What am I celebrating today? _____
_____

What am I grateful for today? _____
_____

What do I need to forgive myself for today? _____
_____

How did I use my gifts today?: _____
_____

Self-care:

3 John 1:2 "Beloved, I pray that all may go well with you and that you may be in good health, as it goes well with your soul."

How did I spend my 15 minutes of "me" time today? _____
_____

How will I spend my 15 minutes of "me" time tomorrow? _____
_____

How did I show gratitude for the ability to move my body today? _____
_____

How will I move tomorrow? _____
_____

Growth:

1 Timothy 4:15 "Practice these things, immerse yourself in them, so that all may see your progress."

What steps did I take towards my goal today? _____
_____

What did today teach me that I will bring into tomorrow? _____
_____

Date:_____

Reflection:

Jeremiah 29:11 "For I know the plans I have for you, declares the Lord, plans for welfare and not for evil, to give you a future and a hope."

What am I celebrating today? _____
_____

What am I grateful for today? _____
_____

What do I need to forgive myself for today? _____
_____

How did I use my gifts today?: _____
_____

Self-care:

3 John 1:2 "Beloved, I pray that all may go well with you and that you may be in good health, as it goes well with your soul."

How did I spend my 15 minutes of "me" time today? _____
_____

How will I spend my 15 minutes of "me" time tomorrow? _____
_____

How did I show gratitude for the ability to move my body today? _____
_____

How will I move tomorrow? _____
_____

Growth:

1 Timothy 4:15 "Practice these things, immerse yourself in them, so that all may see your progress."

What steps did I take towards my goal today? _____
_____

What did today teach me that I will bring into tomorrow? _____
_____

Proverbs 31:25 "Strength and dignity are her clothing, and she laughs at the time to come"

One of the hardest things we can do as mothers is let our children see us cry. Moms, I am here to tell you that one of the strongest things you can do is allow yourself to feel emotions around your children. Why? Because that is giving them permission to show emotions as well. Let your children know what they are feeling and allow them to show those emotions properly. When you have one of those moments, it can be a great lesson for our children. Show them they can lean on the Lord during those vulnerable times. Show them our strength comes from HIM. That is the greatest example you could allow them to see. When we are weak, HE is strong.

Let this serve as a reminder to you this week:

He sees you.

He hears you.

He loves you.

Weekly Challenge:

It's time to reflect on your entries from last week. Pray. Meditate. Celebrate.

Date:_____

Reflection:

Jeremiah 29:11 "For I know the plans I have for you, declares the Lord, plans for welfare and not for evil, to give you a future and a hope."

What am I celebrating today? _____

_____

What am I grateful for today? _____

_____

What do I need to forgive myself for today? _____

_____

How did I use my gifts today?: _____

_____

Self-care:

3 John 1:2 "Beloved, I pray that all may go well with you and that you may be in good health, as it goes well with your soul."

How did I spend my 15 minutes of "me" time today? _____

_____

How will I spend my 15 minutes of "me" time tomorrow? _____

_____

How did I show gratitude for the ability to move my body today? _____

_____

How will I move tomorrow? _____

_____

Growth:

1 Timothy 4:15 "Practice these things, immerse yourself in them, so that all may see your progress."

What steps did I take towards my goal today? _____

_____

What did today teach me that I will bring into tomorrow? _____

_____

Date:_____

Reflection:

Jeremiah 29:11 "For I know the plans I have for you, declares the Lord, plans for welfare and not for evil, to give you a future and a hope."

What am I celebrating today? _____
_____

What am I grateful for today? _____
_____

What do I need to forgive myself for today? _____
_____

How did I use my gifts today?: _____
_____

Self-care:

3 John 1:2 "Beloved, I pray that all may go well with you and that you may be in good health, as it goes well with your soul."

How did I spend my 15 minutes of "me" time today? _____
_____

How will I spend my 15 minutes of "me" time tomorrow? _____
_____

How did I show gratitude for the ability to move my body today? _____
_____

How will I move tomorrow? _____
_____

Growth:

1 Timothy 4:15 "Practice these things, immerse yourself in them, so that all may see your progress."

What steps did I take towards my goal today? _____
_____

What did today teach me that I will bring into tomorrow? _____
_____

Date:_____

Reflection:

Jeremiah 29:11 "For I know the plans I have for you, declares the Lord, plans for welfare and not for evil, to give you a future and a hope."

What am I celebrating today? _____

_____

What am I grateful for today? _____

_____

What do I need to forgive myself for today? _____

_____

How did I use my gifts today?: _____

_____

Self-care:

3 John 1:2 "Beloved, I pray that all may go well with you and that you may be in good health, as it goes well with your soul."

How did I spend my 15 minutes of "me" time today? _____

_____

How will I spend my 15 minutes of "me" time tomorrow? _____

_____

How did I show gratitude for the ability to move my body today? _____

_____

How will I move tomorrow? _____

_____

Growth:

1 Timothy 4:15 "Practice these things, immerse yourself in them, so that all may see your progress."

What steps did I take towards my goal today? _____

_____

What did today teach me that I will bring into tomorrow? _____

_____

Date:_____

Reflection:

Jeremiah 29:11 "For I know the plans I have for you, declares the Lord, plans for welfare and not for evil, to give you a future and a hope."

What am I celebrating today? _____

_____

What am I grateful for today? _____

_____

What do I need to forgive myself for today? _____

_____

How did I use my gifts today?: _____

_____

Self-care:

3 John 1:2 "Beloved, I pray that all may go well with you and that you may be in good health, as it goes well with your soul."

How did I spend my 15 minutes of "me" time today? _____

_____

How will I spend my 15 minutes of "me" time tomorrow? _____

_____

How did I show gratitude for the ability to move my body today? _____

_____

How will I move tomorrow? _____

_____

Growth:

1 Timothy 4:15 "Practice these things, immerse yourself in them, so that all may see your progress."

What steps did I take towards my goal today? _____

_____

What did today teach me that I will bring into tomorrow? _____

_____

Date:_____

Reflection:

Jeremiah 29:11 "For I know the plans I have for you, declares the Lord, plans for welfare and not for evil, to give you a future and a hope."

What am I celebrating today? _____

_____

What am I grateful for today? _____

_____

What do I need to forgive myself for today? _____

_____

How did I use my gifts today?: _____

_____

Self-care:

3 John 1:2 "Beloved, I pray that all may go well with you and that you may be in good health, as it goes well with your soul."

How did I spend my 15 minutes of "me" time today? _____

_____

How will I spend my 15 minutes of "me" time tomorrow? _____

_____

How did I show gratitude for the ability to move my body today? _____

_____

How will I move tomorrow? _____

_____

Growth:

1 Timothy 4:15 "Practice these things, immerse yourself in them, so that all may see your progress."

What steps did I take towards my goal today? _____

_____

What did today teach me that I will bring into tomorrow? _____

_____

Date:_____

Reflection:

Jeremiah 29:11 "For I know the plans I have for you, declares the Lord, plans for welfare and not for evil, to give you a future and a hope."

What am I celebrating today? _____
_____

What am I grateful for today? _____
_____

What do I need to forgive myself for today? _____
_____

How did I use my gifts today?: _____
_____

Self-care:

3 John 1:2 "Beloved, I pray that all may go well with you and that you may be in good health, as it goes well with your soul."

How did I spend my 15 minutes of "me" time today? _____
_____

How will I spend my 15 minutes of "me" time tomorrow? _____
_____

How did I show gratitude for the ability to move my body today? _____
_____

How will I move tomorrow? _____
_____

Growth:

1 Timothy 4:15 "Practice these things, immerse yourself in them, so that all may see your progress."

What steps did I take towards my goal today? _____
_____

What did today teach me that I will bring into tomorrow? _____
_____

Date:_____

Reflection:

Jeremiah 29:11 "For I know the plans I have for you, declares the Lord, plans for welfare and not for evil, to give you a future and a hope."

What am I celebrating today? _____

_____

What am I grateful for today? _____

_____

What do I need to forgive myself for today? _____

_____

How did I use my gifts today?: _____

_____

Self-care:

3 John 1:2 "Beloved, I pray that all may go well with you and that you may be in good health, as it goes well with your soul."

How did I spend my 15 minutes of "me" time today? _____

_____

How will I spend my 15 minutes of "me" time tomorrow? _____

_____

How did I show gratitude for the ability to move my body today? _____

_____

How will I move tomorrow? _____

_____

Growth:

1 Timothy 4:15 "Practice these things, immerse yourself in them, so that all may see your progress."

What steps did I take towards my goal today? _____

_____

What did today teach me that I will bring into tomorrow? _____

_____

Genesis 3:20 "The man called his wife's name Eve, because she was the mother of all living"

This is your reminder that GOD chose YOU to be the mother of your child(ren). He chose YOU because no one else was qualified for the job. He chose YOU because He set you apart to raise your little one(s) in His image, because they were created in His image. Mom…give thanks. Do not beat yourself up. You are doing a great job…Just as HE knew you would.

Let this serve as a reminder to you this week:

He sees you.

He hears you.

He loves you.

Weekly Challenge:

It's time to reflect on your entries from last week. Pray. Meditate. Celebrate.

Date:_____

Reflection:

Jeremiah 29:11 "For I know the plans I have for you, declares the Lord, plans for welfare and not for evil, to give you a future and a hope."

What am I celebrating today? _____

_____

What am I grateful for today? _____

_____

What do I need to forgive myself for today? _____

_____

How did I use my gifts today?: _____

_____

Self-care:

3 John 1:2 "Beloved, I pray that all may go well with you and that you may be in good health, as it goes well with your soul."

How did I spend my 15 minutes of "me" time today? _____

_____

How will I spend my 15 minutes of "me" time tomorrow? _____

_____

How did I show gratitude for the ability to move my body today? _____

_____

How will I move tomorrow? _____

_____

Growth:

1 Timothy 4:15 "Practice these things, immerse yourself in them, so that all may see your progress."

What steps did I take towards my goal today? _____

_____

What did today teach me that I will bring into tomorrow? _____

_____

Date:_____

Reflection:

Jeremiah 29:11 "For I know the plans I have for you, declares the Lord, plans for welfare and not for evil, to give you a future and a hope."

What am I celebrating today? _____

_____

What am I grateful for today? _____

_____

What do I need to forgive myself for today? _____

_____

How did I use my gifts today?: _____

_____

Self-care:

3 John 1:2 "Beloved, I pray that all may go well with you and that you may be in good health, as it goes well with your soul."

How did I spend my 15 minutes of "me" time today? _____

_____

How will I spend my 15 minutes of "me" time tomorrow? _____

_____

How did I show gratitude for the ability to move my body today? _____

_____

How will I move tomorrow? _____

_____

Growth:

1 Timothy 4:15 "Practice these things, immerse yourself in them, so that all may see your progress."

What steps did I take towards my goal today? _____

_____

What did today teach me that I will bring into tomorrow? _____

_____

Date:_____

Reflection:

Jeremiah 29:11 "For I know the plans I have for you, declares the Lord, plans for welfare and not for evil, to give you a future and a hope."

What am I celebrating today? _____

_____

What am I grateful for today? _____

_____

What do I need to forgive myself for today? _____

_____

How did I use my gifts today?: _____

_____

Self-care:

3 John 1:2 "Beloved, I pray that all may go well with you and that you may be in good health, as it goes well with your soul."

How did I spend my 15 minutes of "me" time today? _____

_____

How will I spend my 15 minutes of "me" time tomorrow? _____

_____

How did I show gratitude for the ability to move my body today? _____

_____

How will I move tomorrow? _____

_____

Growth:

1 Timothy 4:15 "Practice these things, immerse yourself in them, so that all may see your progress."

What steps did I take towards my goal today? _____

_____

What did today teach me that I will bring into tomorrow? _____

_____

Reflection:

Jeremiah 29:11 "For I know the plans I have for you, declares the Lord, plans for welfare and not for evil, to give you a future and a hope."

What am I celebrating today? _____

_____

What am I grateful for today? _____

_____

What do I need to forgive myself for today? _____

_____

How did I use my gifts today?: _____

_____

Self-care:

3 John 1:2 "Beloved, I pray that all may go well with you and that you may be in good health, as it goes well with your soul."

How did I spend my 15 minutes of "me" time today? _____

_____

How will I spend my 15 minutes of "me" time tomorrow? _____

_____

How did I show gratitude for the ability to move my body today? _____

_____

How will I move tomorrow? _____

_____

Growth:

1 Timothy 4:15 "Practice these things, immerse yourself in them, so that all may see your progress."

What steps did I take towards my goal today? _____

_____

What did today teach me that I will bring into tomorrow? _____

_____

Reflection:

Jeremiah 29:11 "For I know the plans I have for you, declares the Lord, plans for welfare and not for evil, to give you a future and a hope."

What am I celebrating today? _____

_____

What am I grateful for today? _____

_____

What do I need to forgive myself for today? _____

_____

How did I use my gifts today?: _____

_____

Self-care:

3 John 1:2 "Beloved, I pray that all may go well with you and that you may be in good health, as it goes well with your soul."

How did I spend my 15 minutes of "me" time today? _____

_____

How will I spend my 15 minutes of "me" time tomorrow? _____

_____

How did I show gratitude for the ability to move my body today? _____

_____

How will I move tomorrow? _____

_____

Growth:

1 Timothy 4:15 "Practice these things, immerse yourself in them, so that all may see your progress."

What steps did I take towards my goal today? _____

_____

What did today teach me that I will bring into tomorrow? _____

_____

Date:_____

Reflection:

Jeremiah 29:11 "For I know the plans I have for you, declares the Lord, plans for welfare and not for evil, to give you a future and a hope."

What am I celebrating today? _____
_____

What am I grateful for today? _____
_____

What do I need to forgive myself for today? _____
_____

How did I use my gifts today?: _____
_____

Self-care:

3 John 1:2 "Beloved, I pray that all may go well with you and that you may be in good health, as it goes well with your soul."

How did I spend my 15 minutes of "me" time today? _____
_____

How will I spend my 15 minutes of "me" time tomorrow? _____
_____

How did I show gratitude for the ability to move my body today? _____
_____

How will I move tomorrow? _____
_____

Growth:

1 Timothy 4:15 "Practice these things, immerse yourself in them, so that all may see your progress."

What steps did I take towards my goal today? _____
_____

What did today teach me that I will bring into tomorrow? _____
_____

Reflection:

Jeremiah 29:11 "For I know the plans I have for you, declares the Lord, plans for welfare and not for evil, to give you a future and a hope."

What am I celebrating today? _____

_____

What am I grateful for today? _____

_____

What do I need to forgive myself for today? _____

_____

How did I use my gifts today?: _____

_____

Self-care:

3 John 1:2 "Beloved, I pray that all may go well with you and that you may be in good health, as it goes well with your soul."

How did I spend my 15 minutes of "me" time today? _____

_____

How will I spend my 15 minutes of "me" time tomorrow? _____

_____

How did I show gratitude for the ability to move my body today? _____

_____

How will I move tomorrow? _____

_____

Growth:

1 Timothy 4:15 "Practice these things, immerse yourself in them, so that all may see your progress."

What steps did I take towards my goal today? _____

_____

What did today teach me that I will bring into tomorrow? _____

_____

1 John 4:19 "We love because He first loved us"

When our child was first placed in our arms, our whole life changed. Didn't it? Sometimes I try to imagine what my boys will be like when they are older. What will their careers be? Will they move away? Will they get married and have lots of children? How many children? These are just some of the questions I find myself playing in my mind. Now, take that love we have for our children and times it by infinity (that is what my oldest boy always says). That is how much our Father loves us. That can be hard to imagine but think of this…He loves us so much that He allowed us to feel real, true love. We feel that every time we look into the eyes of our children. What greater gift could we have received?! We get to love these children because HE loved us first. Thank you, Lord!

Let this serve as a reminder to you this week:

He sees you.

He hears you.

He loves you.

<u>**Weekly Challenge:**</u>

It's time to reflect on your entries from last week. Pray. Meditate. Celebrate.

Date:_____

Reflection:

Jeremiah 29:11 "For I know the plans I have for you, declares the Lord, plans for welfare and not for evil, to give you a future and a hope."

What am I celebrating today? _____

_____

What am I grateful for today? _____

_____

What do I need to forgive myself for today? _____

_____

How did I use my gifts today?: _____

_____

Self-care:

3 John 1:2 "Beloved, I pray that all may go well with you and that you may be in good health, as it goes well with your soul."

How did I spend my 15 minutes of "me" time today? _____

_____

How will I spend my 15 minutes of "me" time tomorrow? _____

_____

How did I show gratitude for the ability to move my body today? _____

_____

How will I move tomorrow? _____

_____

Growth:

1 Timothy 4:15 "Practice these things, immerse yourself in them, so that all may see your progress."

What steps did I take towards my goal today? _____

_____

What did today teach me that I will bring into tomorrow? _____

_____

Date:_____

Reflection:

Jeremiah 29:11 "For I know the plans I have for you, declares the Lord, plans for welfare and not for evil, to give you a future and a hope."

What am I celebrating today? _____
_____

What am I grateful for today? _____
_____

What do I need to forgive myself for today? _____
_____

How did I use my gifts today?: _____
_____

Self-care:

3 John 1:2 "Beloved, I pray that all may go well with you and that you may be in good health, as it goes well with your soul."

How did I spend my 15 minutes of "me" time today? _____
_____

How will I spend my 15 minutes of "me" time tomorrow? _____
_____

How did I show gratitude for the ability to move my body today? _____
_____

How will I move tomorrow? _____
_____

Growth:

1 Timothy 4:15 "Practice these things, immerse yourself in them, so that all may see your progress."

What steps did I take towards my goal today? _____
_____

What did today teach me that I will bring into tomorrow? _____
_____

Date:_____

Reflection:

Jeremiah 29:11 "For I know the plans I have for you, declares the Lord, plans for welfare and not for evil, to give you a future and a hope."

What am I celebrating today? _____

_____

What am I grateful for today? _____

_____

What do I need to forgive myself for today? _____

_____

How did I use my gifts today?: _____

_____

Self-care:

3 John 1:2 "Beloved, I pray that all may go well with you and that you may be in good health, as it goes well with your soul."

How did I spend my 15 minutes of "me" time today? _____

_____

How will I spend my 15 minutes of "me" time tomorrow? _____

_____

How did I show gratitude for the ability to move my body today? _____

_____

How will I move tomorrow? _____

_____

Growth:

1 Timothy 4:15 "Practice these things, immerse yourself in them, so that all may see your progress."

What steps did I take towards my goal today? _____

_____

What did today teach me that I will bring into tomorrow? _____

_____

Date:_____

Reflection:

Jeremiah 29:11 "For I know the plans I have for you, declares the Lord, plans for welfare and not for evil, to give you a future and a hope."

What am I celebrating today? _____

_____

What am I grateful for today? _____

_____

What do I need to forgive myself for today? _____

_____

How did I use my gifts today?: _____

_____

Self-care:

3 John 1:2 "Beloved, I pray that all may go well with you and that you may be in good health, as it goes well with your soul."

How did I spend my 15 minutes of "me" time today? _____

_____

How will I spend my 15 minutes of "me" time tomorrow? _____

_____

How did I show gratitude for the ability to move my body today? _____

_____

How will I move tomorrow? _____

_____

Growth:

1 Timothy 4:15 "Practice these things, immerse yourself in them, so that all may see your progress."

What steps did I take towards my goal today? _____

_____

What did today teach me that I will bring into tomorrow? _____

_____

Date:_____

Reflection:

Jeremiah 29:11 "For I know the plans I have for you, declares the Lord, plans for welfare and not for evil, to give you a future and a hope."

What am I celebrating today? _____
_____

What am I grateful for today? _____
_____

What do I need to forgive myself for today? _____
_____

How did I use my gifts today?: _____
_____

Self-care:

3 John 1:2 "Beloved, I pray that all may go well with you and that you may be in good health, as it goes well with your soul."

How did I spend my 15 minutes of "me" time today? _____
_____

How will I spend my 15 minutes of "me" time tomorrow? _____
_____

How did I show gratitude for the ability to move my body today? _____
_____

How will I move tomorrow? _____
_____

Growth:

1 Timothy 4:15 "Practice these things, immerse yourself in them, so that all may see your progress."

What steps did I take towards my goal today? _____
_____

What did today teach me that I will bring into tomorrow? _____
_____

Date:_____

Reflection:

Jeremiah 29:11 "For I know the plans I have for you, declares the Lord, plans for welfare and not for evil, to give you a future and a hope."

What am I celebrating today? _____
_____

What am I grateful for today? _____
_____

What do I need to forgive myself for today? _____
_____

How did I use my gifts today?: _____
_____

Self-care:

3 John 1:2 "Beloved, I pray that all may go well with you and that you may be in good health, as it goes well with your soul."

How did I spend my 15 minutes of "me" time today? _____
_____

How will I spend my 15 minutes of "me" time tomorrow? _____
_____

How did I show gratitude for the ability to move my body today? _____
_____

How will I move tomorrow? _____
_____

Growth:

1 Timothy 4:15 "Practice these things, immerse yourself in them, so that all may see your progress."

What steps did I take towards my goal today? _____
_____

What did today teach me that I will bring into tomorrow? _____
_____

Date:_____

Reflection:

Jeremiah 29:11 "For I know the plans I have for you, declares the Lord, plans for welfare and not for evil, to give you a future and a hope."

What am I celebrating today? _____

_____

What am I grateful for today? _____

_____

What do I need to forgive myself for today? _____

_____

How did I use my gifts today?: _____

_____

Self-care:

3 John 1:2 "Beloved, I pray that all may go well with you and that you may be in good health, as it goes well with your soul."

How did I spend my 15 minutes of "me" time today? _____

_____

How will I spend my 15 minutes of "me" time tomorrow? _____

_____

How did I show gratitude for the ability to move my body today? _____

_____

How will I move tomorrow? _____

_____

Growth:

1 Timothy 4:15 "Practice these things, immerse yourself in them, so that all may see your progress."

What steps did I take towards my goal today? _____

_____

What did today teach me that I will bring into tomorrow? _____

_____

Proverbs 31:26 "She opens her mouth with wisdom, and the teaching of kindness is on her tongue"

I will never forget the day I was working outdoors with my oldest son. I was personal training a couple clients and decided to take my son with me to enjoy the sunshine on that beautiful day. As we were walking up the stairs to go back into the building, I began to walk ahead of him because he was safe while walking with my husband. As soon as my foot reached the top stairs of that indoor hallway, I heard my name being screamed from my husband's mouth. In that moment, my heart sank. Isn't it funny how our "mother's intuition" kicks in a split second? I turned around to find my son in my husband's arms. He had fallen outside before he even reached the front door. My son was not paying attention to where he was going, and he tripped. He fell on the corner of the outdoor steps. He had cut his head badly. I rushed him into the nearby hospital where they administered stiches to the wound. He was ok….just a wound that needed to be sewn. Sitting in that ER room, I mentally beat myself up. How could I have taken my eye off him? How could I have been so careless that I allowed my son to get injured? Moms, how many times do we beat ourselves up over something that we just cannot control? It is natural for us to blame ourselves. However, this is where grace comes in. God has given us grace which needs to be an example of the grace we need to bestow upon ourselves! I could not have stopped my son from falling. Maybe I could have caught him, but I learned that I cannot live in that "what if" state of mind. Instead, in that moment, I realized that I needed to give thanks to the Lord for protecting my son and give myself grace.

In what area of your life do you need to give yourself more grace?

Let this serve as a reminder to you this week:

He sees you.

He hears you.

He loves you.

<u>Weekly Challenge:</u>

It's time to reflect on your entries from last week. Pray. Meditate. Celebrate.

Reflection:

Jeremiah 29:11 "For I know the plans I have for you, declares the Lord, plans for welfare and not for evil, to give you a future and a hope."

What am I celebrating today? _____

_____

What am I grateful for today? _____

_____

What do I need to forgive myself for today? _____

_____

How did I use my gifts today?: _____

_____

Self-care:

3 John 1:2 "Beloved, I pray that all may go well with you and that you may be in good health, as it goes well with your soul."

How did I spend my 15 minutes of "me" time today? _____

_____

How will I spend my 15 minutes of "me" time tomorrow? _____

_____

How did I show gratitude for the ability to move my body today? _____

_____

How will I move tomorrow? _____

_____

Growth:

1 Timothy 4:15 "Practice these things, immerse yourself in them, so that all may see your progress."

What steps did I take towards my goal today? _____

_____

What did today teach me that I will bring into tomorrow? _____

_____

Date:_____

Reflection:

Jeremiah 29:11 "For I know the plans I have for you, declares the Lord, plans for welfare and not for evil, to give you a future and a hope."

What am I celebrating today? _____

_____

What am I grateful for today? _____

_____

What do I need to forgive myself for today? _____

_____

How did I use my gifts today?: _____

_____

Self-care:

3 John 1:2 "Beloved, I pray that all may go well with you and that you may be in good health, as it goes well with your soul."

How did I spend my 15 minutes of "me" time today? _____

_____

How will I spend my 15 minutes of "me" time tomorrow? _____

_____

How did I show gratitude for the ability to move my body today? _____

_____

How will I move tomorrow? _____

_____

Growth:

1 Timothy 4:15 "Practice these things, immerse yourself in them, so that all may see your progress."

What steps did I take towards my goal today? _____

_____

What did today teach me that I will bring into tomorrow? _____

_____

Date:_____

Reflection:

Jeremiah 29:11 "For I know the plans I have for you, declares the Lord, plans for welfare and not for evil, to give you a future and a hope."

What am I celebrating today? _____

_____

What am I grateful for today? _____

_____

What do I need to forgive myself for today? _____

_____

How did I use my gifts today?: _____

_____

Self-care:

3 John 1:2 "Beloved, I pray that all may go well with you and that you may be in good health, as it goes well with your soul."

How did I spend my 15 minutes of "me" time today? _____

_____

How will I spend my 15 minutes of "me" time tomorrow? _____

_____

How did I show gratitude for the ability to move my body today? _____

_____

How will I move tomorrow? _____

_____

Growth:

1 Timothy 4:15 "Practice these things, immerse yourself in them, so that all may see your progress."

What steps did I take towards my goal today? _____

_____

What did today teach me that I will bring into tomorrow? _____

_____

Date:_____

Reflection:

Jeremiah 29:11 "For I know the plans I have for you, declares the Lord, plans for welfare and not for evil, to give you a future and a hope."

What am I celebrating today? _____

_____

What am I grateful for today? _____

_____

What do I need to forgive myself for today? _____

_____

How did I use my gifts today?: _____

_____

Self-care:

3 John 1:2 "Beloved, I pray that all may go well with you and that you may be in good health, as it goes well with your soul."

How did I spend my 15 minutes of "me" time today? _____

_____

How will I spend my 15 minutes of "me" time tomorrow? _____

_____

How did I show gratitude for the ability to move my body today? _____

_____

How will I move tomorrow? _____

_____

Growth:

1 Timothy 4:15 "Practice these things, immerse yourself in them, so that all may see your progress."

What steps did I take towards my goal today? _____

_____

What did today teach me that I will bring into tomorrow? _____

_____

Date:_____

Reflection:

Jeremiah 29:11 "For I know the plans I have for you, declares the Lord, plans for welfare and not for evil, to give you a future and a hope."

What am I celebrating today? _____
_____

What am I grateful for today? _____
_____

What do I need to forgive myself for today? _____
_____

How did I use my gifts today?: _____
_____

Self-care:

3 John 1:2 "Beloved, I pray that all may go well with you and that you may be in good health, as it goes well with your soul."

How did I spend my 15 minutes of "me" time today? _____
_____

How will I spend my 15 minutes of "me" time tomorrow? _____
_____

How did I show gratitude for the ability to move my body today? _____
_____

How will I move tomorrow? _____
_____

Growth:

1 Timothy 4:15 "Practice these things, immerse yourself in them, so that all may see your progress."

What steps did I take towards my goal today? _____
_____

What did today teach me that I will bring into tomorrow? _____
_____

Date:_____

Reflection:

Jeremiah 29:11 "For I know the plans I have for you, declares the Lord, plans for welfare and not for evil, to give you a future and a hope."

What am I celebrating today? _____

_____

What am I grateful for today? _____

_____

What do I need to forgive myself for today? _____

_____

How did I use my gifts today?: _____

_____

Self-care:

3 John 1:2 "Beloved, I pray that all may go well with you and that you may be in good health, as it goes well with your soul."

How did I spend my 15 minutes of "me" time today? _____

_____

How will I spend my 15 minutes of "me" time tomorrow? _____

_____

How did I show gratitude for the ability to move my body today? _____

_____

How will I move tomorrow? _____

_____

Growth:

1 Timothy 4:15 "Practice these things, immerse yourself in them, so that all may see your progress."

What steps did I take towards my goal today? _____

_____

What did today teach me that I will bring into tomorrow? _____

_____

Date:_____

Reflection:

Jeremiah 29:11 "For I know the plans I have for you, declares the Lord, plans for welfare and not for evil, to give you a future and a hope."

What am I celebrating today? _____

_____

What am I grateful for today? _____

_____

What do I need to forgive myself for today? _____

_____

How did I use my gifts today?: _____

_____

Self-care:

3 John 1:2 "Beloved, I pray that all may go well with you and that you may be in good health, as it goes well with your soul."

How did I spend my 15 minutes of "me" time today? _____

_____

How will I spend my 15 minutes of "me" time tomorrow? _____

_____

How did I show gratitude for the ability to move my body today? _____

_____

How will I move tomorrow? _____

_____

Growth:

1 Timothy 4:15 "Practice these things, immerse yourself in them, so that all may see your progress."

What steps did I take towards my goal today? _____

_____

What did today teach me that I will bring into tomorrow? _____

_____

1 Corinthians 13:13 "So now faith, hope, and love abide, these three; but the greatest of these is love"

After having given birth to my second son, I was diagnosed with postpartum depression. I was not shocked due to the sleep deprivation I was experiencing. My son would only sleep twenty minutes a night for the first four months of his life!! Twenty minutes of sleep would effect anyone mentally! Although this was not a shock, I still took this diagnosis in a rough way. There is a stigma around postpartum depression that gives the illusion that we, as moms, must resent or despise our child in order to be diagnosed with the dreaded PPD. A part of me could not comprehend WHY I would be diagnosed with this PPD if I loved and adored my son. Once I began to vocalize my diagnosis to other moms, as well as began to help other moms deal with the same label, I realized that God turned a blessing out of my storm. I began to realize that the blessing came in the form of helping other moms… and I was helped in return by acknowledging that I was not alone! I loved my son the moment I was chosen to be his mother. I was not a bad mom. I was not a "sick" mom. I was a tired mom that needed God to guide me to the place He called me to be…right here…guiding you.

Let this serve as a reminder to you this week:

He sees you.

He hears you.

He loves you.

<u>Weekly Challenge:</u>

It's time to reflect on your entries from last week. Pray. Meditate. Celebrate.

Date:_____

Reflection:

Jeremiah 29:11 "For I know the plans I have for you, declares the Lord, plans for welfare and not for evil, to give you a future and a hope."

What am I celebrating today? _____

_____

What am I grateful for today? _____

_____

What do I need to forgive myself for today? _____

_____

How did I use my gifts today?: _____

_____

Self-care:

3 John 1:2 "Beloved, I pray that all may go well with you and that you may be in good health, as it goes well with your soul."

How did I spend my 15 minutes of "me" time today? _____

_____

How will I spend my 15 minutes of "me" time tomorrow? _____

_____

How did I show gratitude for the ability to move my body today? _____

_____

How will I move tomorrow? _____

_____

Growth:

1 Timothy 4:15 "Practice these things, immerse yourself in them, so that all may see your progress."

What steps did I take towards my goal today? _____

_____

What did today teach me that I will bring into tomorrow? _____

_____

Date:_____

Reflection:

Jeremiah 29:11 "For I know the plans I have for you, declares the Lord, plans for welfare and not for evil, to give you a future and a hope."

What am I celebrating today? _____

_____

What am I grateful for today? _____

_____

What do I need to forgive myself for today? _____

_____

How did I use my gifts today?: _____

_____

Self-care:

3 John 1:2 "Beloved, I pray that all may go well with you and that you may be in good health, as it goes well with your soul."

How did I spend my 15 minutes of "me" time today? _____

_____

How will I spend my 15 minutes of "me" time tomorrow? _____

_____

How did I show gratitude for the ability to move my body today? _____

_____

How will I move tomorrow? _____

_____

Growth:

1 Timothy 4:15 "Practice these things, immerse yourself in them, so that all may see your progress."

What steps did I take towards my goal today? _____

_____

What did today teach me that I will bring into tomorrow? _____

_____

Reflection:

Jeremiah 29:11 "For I know the plans I have for you, declares the Lord, plans for welfare and not for evil, to give you a future and a hope."

What am I celebrating today? _____
_____

What am I grateful for today? _____
_____

What do I need to forgive myself for today? _____
_____

How did I use my gifts today?: _____
_____

Self-care:

3 John 1:2 "Beloved, I pray that all may go well with you and that you may be in good health, as it goes well with your soul."

How did I spend my 15 minutes of "me" time today? _____
_____

How will I spend my 15 minutes of "me" time tomorrow? _____
_____

How did I show gratitude for the ability to move my body today? _____

_____

How will I move tomorrow? _____
_____

Growth:

1 Timothy 4:15 "Practice these things, immerse yourself in them, so that all may see your progress."

What steps did I take towards my goal today? _____
_____

What did today teach me that I will bring into tomorrow? _____
_____

Date:_____

Reflection:

Jeremiah 29:11 "For I know the plans I have for you, declares the Lord, plans for welfare and not for evil, to give you a future and a hope."

What am I celebrating today? _____

_____

What am I grateful for today? _____

_____

What do I need to forgive myself for today? _____

_____

How did I use my gifts today?: _____

_____

Self-care:

3 John 1:2 "Beloved, I pray that all may go well with you and that you may be in good health, as it goes well with your soul."

How did I spend my 15 minutes of "me" time today? _____

_____

How will I spend my 15 minutes of "me" time tomorrow? _____

_____

How did I show gratitude for the ability to move my body today? _____

_____

How will I move tomorrow? _____

_____

Growth:

1 Timothy 4:15 "Practice these things, immerse yourself in them, so that all may see your progress."

What steps did I take towards my goal today? _____

_____

What did today teach me that I will bring into tomorrow? _____

_____

Reflection:

Jeremiah 29:11 "For I know the plans I have for you, declares the Lord, plans for welfare and not for evil, to give you a future and a hope."

What am I celebrating today? _____

_____

What am I grateful for today? _____

_____

What do I need to forgive myself for today? _____

_____

How did I use my gifts today?: _____

_____

Self-care:

3 John 1:2 "Beloved, I pray that all may go well with you and that you may be in good health, as it goes well with your soul."

How did I spend my 15 minutes of "me" time today? _____

_____

How will I spend my 15 minutes of "me" time tomorrow? _____

_____

How did I show gratitude for the ability to move my body today? _____

_____

How will I move tomorrow? _____

_____

Growth:

1 Timothy 4:15 "Practice these things, immerse yourself in them, so that all may see your progress."

What steps did I take towards my goal today? _____

_____

What did today teach me that I will bring into tomorrow? _____

_____

Date:_____

Reflection:

Jeremiah 29:11 "For I know the plans I have for you, declares the Lord, plans for welfare and not for evil, to give you a future and a hope."

What am I celebrating today? _____

_____

What am I grateful for today? _____

_____

What do I need to forgive myself for today? _____

_____

How did I use my gifts today?: _____

_____

Self-care:

3 John 1:2 "Beloved, I pray that all may go well with you and that you may be in good health, as it goes well with your soul."

How did I spend my 15 minutes of "me" time today? _____

_____

How will I spend my 15 minutes of "me" time tomorrow? _____

_____

How did I show gratitude for the ability to move my body today? ___

_____

How will I move tomorrow? _____

_____

Growth:

1 Timothy 4:15 "Practice these things, immerse yourself in them, so that all may see your progress."

What steps did I take towards my goal today? _____

_____

What did today teach me that I will bring into tomorrow? _____

_____

Date:_____

Reflection:

Jeremiah 29:11 "For I know the plans I have for you, declares the Lord, plans for welfare and not for evil, to give you a future and a hope."

What am I celebrating today? _____

_____

What am I grateful for today? _____

_____

What do I need to forgive myself for today? _____

_____

How did I use my gifts today?: _____

_____

Self-care:

3 John 1:2 "Beloved, I pray that all may go well with you and that you may be in good health, as it goes well with your soul."

How did I spend my 15 minutes of "me" time today? _____

_____

How will I spend my 15 minutes of "me" time tomorrow? _____

_____

How did I show gratitude for the ability to move my body today? _____

_____

How will I move tomorrow? _____

_____

Growth:

1 Timothy 4:15 "Practice these things, immerse yourself in them, so that all may see your progress."

What steps did I take towards my goal today? _____

_____

What did today teach me that I will bring into tomorrow? _____

_____

John 16:21 "when a woman is giving birth, she has sorrow because her hour has come, but when she has delivered the baby, she no longer remembers the anguish, for the joy that a human being has been born into the world"

We all have a unique birth story. It is a story that we, as moms, will never forget. However, the pain of childbirth is a "forgetful pain." Do you ever stop and think why that is? We probably will never know the real reason, but I will share with you what I like to think it is. Our God is such a loving God. He cares for us as his own child. When we see our children hurt, we want to take the pain away ourselves. I like to think that is God's way of taking the pain away from his children. Due to Eve sinning against the Lord, we must endure the pain of childbirth. But how beautiful is it that our Father, our God wants to take that pain away from His children. Therefore, he has made the pain of childbirth a "forgetful pain." Let us celebrate that next time we tell our birth story. You may be a testimony to others.

Let this serve as a reminder to you this week:

He sees you.

He hears you.

He loves you.

Weekly Challenge:

It's time to reflect on your entries from last week. Pray. Meditate. Celebrate.

Date:_____

Reflection:

Jeremiah 29:11 "For I know the plans I have for you, declares the Lord, plans for welfare and not for evil, to give you a future and a hope."

What am I celebrating today? _____
_____

What am I grateful for today? _____
_____

What do I need to forgive myself for today? _____
_____

How did I use my gifts today?: _____
_____

Self-care:

3 John 1:2 "Beloved, I pray that all may go well with you and that you may be in good health, as it goes well with your soul."

How did I spend my 15 minutes of "me" time today? _____
_____

How will I spend my 15 minutes of "me" time tomorrow? _____
_____

How did I show gratitude for the ability to move my body today? ____
_____

How will I move tomorrow? _____
_____

Growth:

1 Timothy 4:15 "Practice these things, immerse yourself in them, so that all may see your progress."

What steps did I take towards my goal today? _____
_____

What did today teach me that I will bring into tomorrow? _____
_____

Date:_____

Reflection:

Jeremiah 29:11 "For I know the plans I have for you, declares the Lord, plans for welfare and not for evil, to give you a future and a hope."

What am I celebrating today? _____

_____

What am I grateful for today? _____

_____

What do I need to forgive myself for today? _____

_____

How did I use my gifts today?: _____

_____

Self-care:

3 John 1:2 "Beloved, I pray that all may go well with you and that you may be in good health, as it goes well with your soul."

How did I spend my 15 minutes of "me" time today? _____

_____

How will I spend my 15 minutes of "me" time tomorrow? _____

_____

How did I show gratitude for the ability to move my body today? ___

_____

How will I move tomorrow? _____

_____

Growth:

1 Timothy 4:15 "Practice these things, immerse yourself in them, so that all may see your progress."

What steps did I take towards my goal today? _____

_____

What did today teach me that I will bring into tomorrow? _____

_____

Date:_____

Reflection:

Jeremiah 29:11 "For I know the plans I have for you, declares the Lord, plans for welfare and not for evil, to give you a future and a hope."

What am I celebrating today? _____

_____

What am I grateful for today? _____

_____

What do I need to forgive myself for today? _____

_____

How did I use my gifts today?: _____

_____

Self-care:

3 John 1:2 "Beloved, I pray that all may go well with you and that you may be in good health, as it goes well with your soul."

How did I spend my 15 minutes of "me" time today? _____

_____

How will I spend my 15 minutes of "me" time tomorrow? _____

_____

How did I show gratitude for the ability to move my body today? _____

_____

How will I move tomorrow? _____

_____

Growth:

1 Timothy 4:15 "Practice these things, immerse yourself in them, so that all may see your progress."

What steps did I take towards my goal today? _____

_____

What did today teach me that I will bring into tomorrow? _____

_____

Date:_____

Reflection:

Jeremiah 29:11 "For I know the plans I have for you, declares the Lord, plans for welfare and not for evil, to give you a future and a hope."

What am I celebrating today? _____

_____

What am I grateful for today? _____

_____

What do I need to forgive myself for today? _____

_____

How did I use my gifts today?: _____

_____

Self-care:

3 John 1:2 "Beloved, I pray that all may go well with you and that you may be in good health, as it goes well with your soul."

How did I spend my 15 minutes of "me" time today? _____

_____

How will I spend my 15 minutes of "me" time tomorrow? _____

_____

How did I show gratitude for the ability to move my body today? _____

_____

How will I move tomorrow? _____

_____

Growth:

1 Timothy 4:15 "Practice these things, immerse yourself in them, so that all may see your progress."

What steps did I take towards my goal today? _____

_____

What did today teach me that I will bring into tomorrow? _____

_____

Date:_____

Reflection:

Jeremiah 29:11 "For I know the plans I have for you, declares the Lord, plans for welfare and not for evil, to give you a future and a hope."

What am I celebrating today? _____

_____

What am I grateful for today? _____

_____

What do I need to forgive myself for today? _____

_____

How did I use my gifts today?: _____

_____

Self-care:

3 John 1:2 "Beloved, I pray that all may go well with you and that you may be in good health, as it goes well with your soul."

How did I spend my 15 minutes of "me" time today? _____

_____

How will I spend my 15 minutes of "me" time tomorrow? _____

_____

How did I show gratitude for the ability to move my body today? _____

_____

How will I move tomorrow? _____

_____

Growth:

1 Timothy 4:15 "Practice these things, immerse yourself in them, so that all may see your progress."

What steps did I take towards my goal today? _____

_____

What did today teach me that I will bring into tomorrow? _____

_____

Date:_____

Reflection:

Jeremiah 29:11 "For I know the plans I have for you, declares the Lord, plans for welfare and not for evil, to give you a future and a hope."

What am I celebrating today? _____

_____

What am I grateful for today? _____

_____

What do I need to forgive myself for today? _____

_____

How did I use my gifts today?: _____

_____

Self-care:

3 John 1:2 "Beloved, I pray that all may go well with you and that you may be in good health, as it goes well with your soul."

How did I spend my 15 minutes of "me" time today? _____

_____

How will I spend my 15 minutes of "me" time tomorrow? _____

_____

How did I show gratitude for the ability to move my body today? ____

_____

How will I move tomorrow? _____

_____

Growth:

1 Timothy 4:15 "Practice these things, immerse yourself in them, so that all may see your progress."

What steps did I take towards my goal today? _____

_____

What did today teach me that I will bring into tomorrow? _____

_____

Date:_____

Reflection:

Jeremiah 29:11 "For I know the plans I have for you, declares the Lord, plans for welfare and not for evil, to give you a future and a hope."

What am I celebrating today? _____

_____

What am I grateful for today? _____

_____

What do I need to forgive myself for today? _____

_____

How did I use my gifts today?: _____

_____

Self-care:

3 John 1:2 "Beloved, I pray that all may go well with you and that you may be in good health, as it goes well with your soul."

How did I spend my 15 minutes of "me" time today? _____

_____

How will I spend my 15 minutes of "me" time tomorrow? _____

_____

How did I show gratitude for the ability to move my body today? _____

_____

How will I move tomorrow? _____

_____

Growth:

1 Timothy 4:15 "Practice these things, immerse yourself in them, so that all may see your progress."

What steps did I take towards my goal today? _____

_____

What did today teach me that I will bring into tomorrow? _____

_____

Proverbs 31:28-29 "Her children rise up and call her blessed; her husband also, and he praises her: Many women have done excellently, but you surpass them all"

I know you have had some difficult days along this journey of motherhood. I know you have fought hard to be the mom you envisioned yourself to be. I know you stay up some nights arguing with yourself whether you made the right chose when it came to decisions about your children or not. I am here to remind you that it will not be easy…not every single moment is not only worth it, but it is a blessing. "Her children rise up and call her blessed." God sees you. He hears your cries. He will not leave you. You are NEVER alone.

Let this serve as a reminder to you this week:

He sees you.

He hears you.

He loves you.

Weekly Challenge:

It's time to reflect on your entries from last week. Pray. Meditate. Celebrate.

Date:_____

Reflection:

Jeremiah 29:11 "For I know the plans I have for you, declares the Lord, plans for welfare and not for evil, to give you a future and a hope."

What am I celebrating today? _____

_____

What am I grateful for today? _____

_____

What do I need to forgive myself for today? _____

_____

How did I use my gifts today?: _____

_____

Self-care:

3 John 1:2 "Beloved, I pray that all may go well with you and that you may be in good health, as it goes well with your soul."

How did I spend my 15 minutes of "me" time today? _____

_____

How will I spend my 15 minutes of "me" time tomorrow? _____

_____

How did I show gratitude for the ability to move my body today? _____

_____

How will I move tomorrow? _____

_____

Growth:

1 Timothy 4:15 "Practice these things, immerse yourself in them, so that all may see your progress."

What steps did I take towards my goal today? _____

_____

What did today teach me that I will bring into tomorrow? _____

_____

Date:_____

Reflection:

Jeremiah 29:11 "For I know the plans I have for you, declares the Lord, plans for welfare and not for evil, to give you a future and a hope."

What am I celebrating today? _____

_____

What am I grateful for today? _____

_____

What do I need to forgive myself for today? _____

_____

How did I use my gifts today?: _____

_____

Self-care:

3 John 1:2 "Beloved, I pray that all may go well with you and that you may be in good health, as it goes well with your soul."

How did I spend my 15 minutes of "me" time today? _____

_____

How will I spend my 15 minutes of "me" time tomorrow? _____

_____

How did I show gratitude for the ability to move my body today? _____

_____

How will I move tomorrow? _____

_____

Growth:

1 Timothy 4:15 "Practice these things, immerse yourself in them, so that all may see your progress."

What steps did I take towards my goal today? _____

_____

What did today teach me that I will bring into tomorrow? _____

_____

Date:_____

Reflection:

Jeremiah 29:11 "For I know the plans I have for you, declares the Lord, plans for welfare and not for evil, to give you a future and a hope."

What am I celebrating today? _____
_____

What am I grateful for today? _____
_____

What do I need to forgive myself for today? _____
_____

How did I use my gifts today?: _____
_____

Self-care:

3 John 1:2 "Beloved, I pray that all may go well with you and that you may be in good health, as it goes well with your soul."

How did I spend my 15 minutes of "me" time today? _____
_____

How will I spend my 15 minutes of "me" time tomorrow? _____
_____

How did I show gratitude for the ability to move my body today? _____
_____

How will I move tomorrow? _____
_____

Growth:

1 Timothy 4:15 "Practice these things, immerse yourself in them, so that all may see your progress."

What steps did I take towards my goal today? _____
_____

What did today teach me that I will bring into tomorrow? _____
_____

Date:_____

Reflection:

Jeremiah 29:11 "For I know the plans I have for you, declares the Lord, plans for welfare and not for evil, to give you a future and a hope."

What am I celebrating today? _____

_____

What am I grateful for today? _____

_____

What do I need to forgive myself for today? _____

_____

How did I use my gifts today?: _____

_____

Self-care:

3 John 1:2 "Beloved, I pray that all may go well with you and that you may be in good health, as it goes well with your soul."

How did I spend my 15 minutes of "me" time today? _____

_____

How will I spend my 15 minutes of "me" time tomorrow? _____

_____

How did I show gratitude for the ability to move my body today? _____

_____

How will I move tomorrow? _____

_____

Growth:

1 Timothy 4:15 "Practice these things, immerse yourself in them, so that all may see your progress."

What steps did I take towards my goal today? _____

_____

What did today teach me that I will bring into tomorrow? _____

_____

Date:_____

Reflection:

Jeremiah 29:11 "For I know the plans I have for you, declares the Lord, plans for welfare and not for evil, to give you a future and a hope."

What am I celebrating today? _____
_____

What am I grateful for today? _____
_____

What do I need to forgive myself for today? _____
_____

How did I use my gifts today?: _____
_____

Self-care:

3 John 1:2 "Beloved, I pray that all may go well with you and that you may be in good health, as it goes well with your soul."

How did I spend my 15 minutes of "me" time today? _____
_____

How will I spend my 15 minutes of "me" time tomorrow? _____
_____

How did I show gratitude for the ability to move my body today? ____
_____

How will I move tomorrow? _____
_____

Growth:

1 Timothy 4:15 "Practice these things, immerse yourself in them, so that all may see your progress."

What steps did I take towards my goal today? _____
_____

What did today teach me that I will bring into tomorrow? _____
_____

Reflection:

Jeremiah 29:11 "For I know the plans I have for you, declares the Lord, plans for welfare and not for evil, to give you a future and a hope."

What am I celebrating today? _____

_____

What am I grateful for today? _____

_____

What do I need to forgive myself for today? _____

_____

How did I use my gifts today?: _____

_____

Self-care:

3 John 1:2 "Beloved, I pray that all may go well with you and that you may be in good health, as it goes well with your soul."

How did I spend my 15 minutes of "me" time today? _____

_____

How will I spend my 15 minutes of "me" time tomorrow? _____

_____

How did I show gratitude for the ability to move my body today? _____

_____

How will I move tomorrow? _____

_____

Growth:

1 Timothy 4:15 "Practice these things, immerse yourself in them, so that all may see your progress."

What steps did I take towards my goal today? _____

_____

What did today teach me that I will bring into tomorrow? _____

_____

Date:_____

Reflection:

Jeremiah 29:11 "For I know the plans I have for you, declares the Lord, plans for welfare and not for evil, to give you a future and a hope."

What am I celebrating today? _____

_____

What am I grateful for today? _____

_____

What do I need to forgive myself for today? _____

_____

How did I use my gifts today?: _____

_____

Self-care:

3 John 1:2 "Beloved, I pray that all may go well with you and that you may be in good health, as it goes well with your soul."

How did I spend my 15 minutes of "me" time today? _____

_____

How will I spend my 15 minutes of "me" time tomorrow? _____

_____

How did I show gratitude for the ability to move my body today? _____

_____

How will I move tomorrow? _____

_____

Growth:

1 Timothy 4:15 "Practice these things, immerse yourself in them, so that all may see your progress."

What steps did I take towards my goal today? _____

_____

What did today teach me that I will bring into tomorrow? _____

_____

Proverbs 22:6 "Train up a child in the way he should go; even when he is old he will not depart from it"

Growing up, my mother use to have little sayings that she would say to me. These were so special to me then and now. I felt as though we almost had a secret code that no one knew about. These became OUR sayings. After becoming a mom, myself, I continued this tradition. One way is when I drop my son off at school in the mornings. Each morning as he climbs out of the car, he turns around to say "I love you, mommy" to which I respond, "I love you, bubba! Remember, you can do anything through God!" His typical response to this is "I know, mom. You tell me every day." I am glad he recognizes that I speak those words into his life daily. Words are such a powerful tool. I want you to take note at the words you speak into the life of your child(ren) this week. Maybe you too can come up with something special just between you and your little one(s).

Let this serve as a reminder to you this week:

He sees you.

He hears you.

He loves you.

<u>Weekly Challenge:</u>

It's time to reflect on your entries from last week. Pray. Meditate. Celebrate.

Date:_____

Reflection:

Jeremiah 29:11 "For I know the plans I have for you, declares the Lord, plans for welfare and not for evil, to give you a future and a hope."

What am I celebrating today? _____

_____

What am I grateful for today? _____

_____

What do I need to forgive myself for today? _____

_____

How did I use my gifts today?: _____

_____

Self-care:

3 John 1:2 "Beloved, I pray that all may go well with you and that you may be in good health, as it goes well with your soul."

How did I spend my 15 minutes of "me" time today? _____

_____

How will I spend my 15 minutes of "me" time tomorrow? _____

_____

How did I show gratitude for the ability to move my body today? _____

_____

How will I move tomorrow? _____

_____

Growth:

1 Timothy 4:15 "Practice these things, immerse yourself in them, so that all may see your progress."

What steps did I take towards my goal today? _____

_____

What did today teach me that I will bring into tomorrow? _____

_____

Date:_____

Reflection:

Jeremiah 29:11 "For I know the plans I have for you, declares the Lord, plans for welfare and not for evil, to give you a future and a hope."

What am I celebrating today? _____

_____

What am I grateful for today? _____

_____

What do I need to forgive myself for today? _____

_____

How did I use my gifts today?: _____

_____

Self-care:

3 John 1:2 "Beloved, I pray that all may go well with you and that you may be in good health, as it goes well with your soul."

How did I spend my 15 minutes of "me" time today? _____

_____

How will I spend my 15 minutes of "me" time tomorrow? _____

_____

How did I show gratitude for the ability to move my body today? _____

_____

How will I move tomorrow? _____

_____

Growth:

1 Timothy 4:15 "Practice these things, immerse yourself in them, so that all may see your progress."

What steps did I take towards my goal today? _____

_____

What did today teach me that I will bring into tomorrow? _____

_____

Date:_____

Reflection:

Jeremiah 29:11 "For I know the plans I have for you, declares the Lord, plans for welfare and not for evil, to give you a future and a hope."

What am I celebrating today? _____
_____

What am I grateful for today? _____
_____

What do I need to forgive myself for today? _____
_____

How did I use my gifts today?: _____
_____

Self-care:

3 John 1:2 "Beloved, I pray that all may go well with you and that you may be in good health, as it goes well with your soul."

How did I spend my 15 minutes of "me" time today? _____
_____

How will I spend my 15 minutes of "me" time tomorrow? _____
_____

How did I show gratitude for the ability to move my body today? _____
_____

How will I move tomorrow? _____
_____

Growth:

1 Timothy 4:15 "Practice these things, immerse yourself in them, so that all may see your progress."

What steps did I take towards my goal today? _____
_____

·What did today teach me that I will bring into tomorrow? _____
_____

Date:_____

Reflection:

Jeremiah 29:11 "For I know the plans I have for you, declares the Lord, plans for welfare and not for evil, to give you a future and a hope."

What am I celebrating today? _____

_____

What am I grateful for today? _____

_____

What do I need to forgive myself for today? _____

_____

How did I use my gifts today?: _____

_____

Self-care:

3 John 1:2 "Beloved, I pray that all may go well with you and that you may be in good health, as it goes well with your soul."

How did I spend my 15 minutes of "me" time today? _____

_____

How will I spend my 15 minutes of "me" time tomorrow? _____

_____

How did I show gratitude for the ability to move my body today? _____

_____

How will I move tomorrow? _____

_____

Growth:

1 Timothy 4:15 "Practice these things, immerse yourself in them, so that all may see your progress."

What steps did I take towards my goal today? _____

_____

What did today teach me that I will bring into tomorrow? _____

_____

Date:_____

Reflection:

Jeremiah 29:11 "For I know the plans I have for you, declares the Lord, plans for welfare and not for evil, to give you a future and a hope."

What am I celebrating today? _____
_____

What am I grateful for today? _____
_____

What do I need to forgive myself for today? _____
_____

How did I use my gifts today?: _____
_____

Self-care:

3 John 1:2 "Beloved, I pray that all may go well with you and that you may be in good health, as it goes well with your soul."

How did I spend my 15 minutes of "me" time today? _____
_____

How will I spend my 15 minutes of "me" time tomorrow? _____
_____

How did I show gratitude for the ability to move my body today? _____
_____

How will I move tomorrow? _____
_____

Growth:

1 Timothy 4:15 "Practice these things, immerse yourself in them, so that all may see your progress."

What steps did I take towards my goal today? _____
_____

What did today teach me that I will bring into tomorrow? _____
_____

Date:_____

Reflection:

Jeremiah 29:11 "For I know the plans I have for you, declares the Lord, plans for welfare and not for evil, to give you a future and a hope."

What am I celebrating today? _____

_____

What am I grateful for today? _____

_____

What do I need to forgive myself for today? _____

_____

How did I use my gifts today?: _____

_____

Self-care:

3 John 1:2 "Beloved, I pray that all may go well with you and that you may be in good health, as it goes well with your soul."

How did I spend my 15 minutes of "me" time today? _____

_____

How will I spend my 15 minutes of "me" time tomorrow? _____

_____

How did I show gratitude for the ability to move my body today? _____

_____

How will I move tomorrow? _____

_____

Growth:

1 Timothy 4:15 "Practice these things, immerse yourself in them, so that all may see your progress."

What steps did I take towards my goal today? _____

_____

What did today teach me that I will bring into tomorrow? _____

_____

Date:_____

Reflection:

Jeremiah 29:11 "For I know the plans I have for you, declares the Lord, plans for welfare and not for evil, to give you a future and a hope."

What am I celebrating today? _____
_____

What am I grateful for today? _____
_____

What do I need to forgive myself for today? _____
_____

How did I use my gifts today?: _____
_____

Self-care:

3 John 1:2 "Beloved, I pray that all may go well with you and that you may be in good health, as it goes well with your soul."

How did I spend my 15 minutes of "me" time today? _____
_____

How will I spend my 15 minutes of "me" time tomorrow? _____
_____

How did I show gratitude for the ability to move my body today? _____
_____

How will I move tomorrow? _____
_____

Growth:

1 Timothy 4:15 "Practice these things, immerse yourself in them, so that all may see your progress."

What steps did I take towards my goal today? _____
_____

What did today teach me that I will bring into tomorrow? _____
_____

Philippians 4:6-7 "Do not be anxious about anything, but in everything by prayer and supplication with thanksgiving let your requests be made known to God. And the peace of God, which surpasses all understanding, will guard your hearts and your minds in Christ Jesus."

Is it just me, or did you suddenly become a worrier once you had your first born? Things I never gave a thought to before such as organic milk or store brand? Too much tv or just enough? Rocking my child to sleep or letting him cry it out? It can be so overwhelming at times. Whatever your belief is on these topics might work for you but may not work for the next mom. That is why when you leave the hospital with your little one after birth, you are not sent home with a manual on "how to raise a child." God has guided us in His Word, however. Worry changes nothing! There is a saying that goes "worry never robs tomorrow of its sorrow, it only saps today of its joy" -Leo Buscaglia. When you begin to worry, take that time to stop and make your requests known to Him. Pray that His will be done. Pray or guidance in your decision making. Most importantly, pray for PEACE. Worry will not change what is happening, but God can change where your mindset is at.

Let this serve as a reminder to you this week:

He sees you.

He hears you.

He loves you.

Weekly Challenge:

It's time to reflect on your entries from last week. Pray. Meditate. Celebrate.

Date:_____

Reflection:

Jeremiah 29:11 "For I know the plans I have for you, declares the Lord, plans for welfare and not for evil, to give you a future and a hope."

What am I celebrating today? _____

_____

What am I grateful for today? _____

_____

What do I need to forgive myself for today? _____

_____

How did I use my gifts today?: _____

_____

Self-care:

3 John 1:2 "Beloved, I pray that all may go well with you and that you may be in good health, as it goes well with your soul."

How did I spend my 15 minutes of "me" time today? _____

_____

How will I spend my 15 minutes of "me" time tomorrow? _____

_____

How did I show gratitude for the ability to move my body today? _____

_____

How will I move tomorrow? _____

_____

Growth:

1 Timothy 4:15 "Practice these things, immerse yourself in them, so that all may see your progress."

What steps did I take towards my goal today? _____

_____

What did today teach me that I will bring into tomorrow? _____

_____

Date:_____

Reflection:

Jeremiah 29:11 "For I know the plans I have for you, declares the Lord, plans for welfare and not for evil, to give you a future and a hope."

What am I celebrating today? _____

_____

What am I grateful for today? _____

_____

What do I need to forgive myself for today? _____

_____

How did I use my gifts today?: _____

_____

Self-care:

3 John 1:2 "Beloved, I pray that all may go well with you and that you may be in good health, as it goes well with your soul."

How did I spend my 15 minutes of "me" time today? _____

_____

How will I spend my 15 minutes of "me" time tomorrow? _____

_____

How did I show gratitude for the ability to move my body today? ____

_____

How will I move tomorrow? _____

_____

Growth:

1 Timothy 4:15 "Practice these things, immerse yourself in them, so that all may see your progress."

What steps did I take towards my goal today? _____

_____

What did today teach me that I will bring into tomorrow? _____

_____

Date:_____

Reflection:

Jeremiah 29:11 "For I know the plans I have for you, declares the Lord, plans for welfare and not for evil, to give you a future and a hope."

What am I celebrating today? _____
_____

What am I grateful for today? _____
_____

What do I need to forgive myself for today? _____
_____

How did I use my gifts today?: _____
_____

Self-care:

3 John 1:2 "Beloved, I pray that all may go well with you and that you may be in good health, as it goes well with your soul."

How did I spend my 15 minutes of "me" time today? _____
_____

How will I spend my 15 minutes of "me" time tomorrow? _____
_____

How did I show gratitude for the ability to move my body today? _____
_____

How will I move tomorrow? _____
_____

Growth:

1 Timothy 4:15 "Practice these things, immerse yourself in them, so that all may see your progress."

What steps did I take towards my goal today? _____
_____

What did today teach me that I will bring into tomorrow? _____
_____

Date:_____

Reflection:

Jeremiah 29:11 "For I know the plans I have for you, declares the Lord, plans for welfare and not for evil, to give you a future and a hope."

What am I celebrating today? _____

_____

What am I grateful for today? _____

_____

What do I need to forgive myself for today? _____

_____

How did I use my gifts today?: _____

_____

Self-care:

3 John 1:2 "Beloved, I pray that all may go well with you and that you may be in good health, as it goes well with your soul."

How did I spend my 15 minutes of "me" time today? _____

_____

How will I spend my 15 minutes of "me" time tomorrow? _____

_____

How did I show gratitude for the ability to move my body today? _____

_____

How will I move tomorrow? _____

_____

Growth:

1 Timothy 4:15 "Practice these things, immerse yourself in them, so that all may see your progress."

What steps did I take towards my goal today? _____

_____

What did today teach me that I will bring into tomorrow? _____

_____

Date:_____

Reflection:

Jeremiah 29:11 "For I know the plans I have for you, declares the Lord, plans for welfare and not for evil, to give you a future and a hope."

What am I celebrating today? _____

_____

What am I grateful for today? _____

_____

What do I need to forgive myself for today? _____

_____

How did I use my gifts today?: _____

_____

Self-care:

3 John 1:2 "Beloved, I pray that all may go well with you and that you may be in good health, as it goes well with your soul."

How did I spend my 15 minutes of "me" time today? _____

_____

How will I spend my 15 minutes of "me" time tomorrow? _____

_____

How did I show gratitude for the ability to move my body today? _____

_____

How will I move tomorrow? _____

_____

Growth:

1 Timothy 4:15 "Practice these things, immerse yourself in them, so that all may see your progress."

What steps did I take towards my goal today? _____

_____

What did today teach me that I will bring into tomorrow? _____

_____

Date:_____

Reflection:

Jeremiah 29:11 "For I know the plans I have for you, declares the Lord, plans for welfare and not for evil, to give you a future and a hope."

What am I celebrating today? _____

_____

What am I grateful for today? _____

_____

What do I need to forgive myself for today? _____

_____

How did I use my gifts today?: _____

_____

Self-care:

3 John 1:2 "Beloved, I pray that all may go well with you and that you may be in good health, as it goes well with your soul."

How did I spend my 15 minutes of "me" time today? _____

_____

How will I spend my 15 minutes of "me" time tomorrow? _____

_____

How did I show gratitude for the ability to move my body today? _____

_____

How will I move tomorrow? _____

_____

Growth:

1 Timothy 4:15 "Practice these things, immerse yourself in them, so that all may see your progress."

What steps did I take towards my goal today? _____

_____

What did today teach me that I will bring into tomorrow? _____

_____

Reflection:

Jeremiah 29:11 "For I know the plans I have for you, declares the Lord, plans for welfare and not for evil, to give you a future and a hope."

What am I celebrating today? _____
_____

What am I grateful for today? _____
_____

What do I need to forgive myself for today? _____
_____

How did I use my gifts today?: _____
_____

Self-care:

3 John 1:2 "Beloved, I pray that all may go well with you and that you may be in good health, as it goes well with your soul."

How did I spend my 15 minutes of "me" time today? _____
_____

How will I spend my 15 minutes of "me" time tomorrow? _____
_____

How did I show gratitude for the ability to move my body today? _____
_____

How will I move tomorrow? _____
_____

Growth:

1 Timothy 4:15 "Practice these things, immerse yourself in them, so that all may see your progress."

What steps did I take towards my goal today? _____
_____

What did today teach me that I will bring into tomorrow? _____
_____

Psalms 139:14 "I praise you, for I am fearfully and wonderfully made. Wonderful are your works; my soul knows it very well."

Mom, when is the last time you celebrated yourself?? I mean, really celebrated yourself! You should be doing this daily in this Reflection Planner (if you are not, start that now). Outside of physically writing it down, celebrate yourself daily by looking at yourself in the mirror and tell yourself how proud you have made yourself. Celebrate the little victories. Maybe your toddler ate his cereal for breakfast without putting up a fight. Maybe you got a raise at your job. Whatever it may be, it is not selfish to celebrate. Celebrating your victories gives glory to God. He created you and it brings him joy when you grow. Celebrate that growth! Promise yourself that starting this week, you WILL celebrate the big and the small victories!

Let this serve as a reminder to you this week:

He sees you.

He hears you.

He loves you.

<u>Weekly Challenge:</u>

It's time to reflect on your entries from last week. Pray. Meditate. Celebrate.

Date:_____

Reflection:

Jeremiah 29:11 "For I know the plans I have for you, declares the Lord, plans for welfare and not for evil, to give you a future and a hope."

What am I celebrating today? _____
_____

What am I grateful for today? _____
_____

What do I need to forgive myself for today? _____
_____

How did I use my gifts today?: _____
_____

Self-care:

3 John 1:2 "Beloved, I pray that all may go well with you and that you may be in good health, as it goes well with your soul."

How did I spend my 15 minutes of "me" time today? _____
_____

How will I spend my 15 minutes of "me" time tomorrow? _____
_____

How did I show gratitude for the ability to move my body today? _____
_____

How will I move tomorrow? _____
_____

Growth:

1 Timothy 4:15 "Practice these things, immerse yourself in them, so that all may see your progress."

What steps did I take towards my goal today? _____
_____

What did today teach me that I will bring into tomorrow? _____
_____

Date:_____

Reflection:

Jeremiah 29:11 "For I know the plans I have for you, declares the Lord, plans for welfare and not for evil, to give you a future and a hope."

What am I celebrating today? _____

_____

What am I grateful for today? _____

_____

What do I need to forgive myself for today? _____

_____

How did I use my gifts today?: _____

_____

Self-care:

3 John 1:2 "Beloved, I pray that all may go well with you and that you may be in good health, as it goes well with your soul."

How did I spend my 15 minutes of "me" time today? _____

_____

How will I spend my 15 minutes of "me" time tomorrow? _____

_____

How did I show gratitude for the ability to move my body today? _____

_____

How will I move tomorrow? _____

_____

Growth:

1 Timothy 4:15 "Practice these things, immerse yourself in them, so that all may see your progress."

What steps did I take towards my goal today? _____

_____

What did today teach me that I will bring into tomorrow? _____

_____

Date:_____

Reflection:

Jeremiah 29:11 "For I know the plans I have for you, declares the Lord, plans for welfare and not for evil, to give you a future and a hope."

What am I celebrating today? _____
_____

What am I grateful for today? _____
_____

What do I need to forgive myself for today? _____
_____

How did I use my gifts today?: _____
_____

Self-care:

3 John 1:2 "Beloved, I pray that all may go well with you and that you may be in good health, as it goes well with your soul."

How did I spend my 15 minutes of "me" time today? _____
_____

How will I spend my 15 minutes of "me" time tomorrow? _____
_____

How did I show gratitude for the ability to move my body today? _____
_____

How will I move tomorrow? _____
_____

Growth:

1 Timothy 4:15 "Practice these things, immerse yourself in them, so that all may see your progress."

What steps did I take towards my goal today? _____
_____

What did today teach me that I will bring into tomorrow? _____
_____

Date:_____

Reflection:

Jeremiah 29:11 "For I know the plans I have for you, declares the Lord, plans for welfare and not for evil, to give you a future and a hope."

What am I celebrating today? _____

_____

What am I grateful for today? _____

_____

What do I need to forgive myself for today? _____

_____

How did I use my gifts today?: _____

_____

Self-care:

3 John 1:2 "Beloved, I pray that all may go well with you and that you may be in good health, as it goes well with your soul."

How did I spend my 15 minutes of "me" time today? _____

_____

How will I spend my 15 minutes of "me" time tomorrow? _____

_____

How did I show gratitude for the ability to move my body today? ___

_____

How will I move tomorrow? _____

_____

Growth:

1 Timothy 4:15 "Practice these things, immerse yourself in them, so that all may see your progress."

What steps did I take towards my goal today? _____

_____

What did today teach me that I will bring into tomorrow? _____

_____

Date:_____

Reflection:

Jeremiah 29:11 "For I know the plans I have for you, declares the Lord, plans for welfare and not for evil, to give you a future and a hope."

What am I celebrating today? _____
_____

What am I grateful for today? _____
_____

What do I need to forgive myself for today? _____
_____

How did I use my gifts today?: _____
_____

Self-care:

3 John 1:2 "Beloved, I pray that all may go well with you and that you may be in good health, as it goes well with your soul."

How did I spend my 15 minutes of "me" time today? _____
_____

How will I spend my 15 minutes of "me" time tomorrow? _____
_____

How did I show gratitude for the ability to move my body today? _____
_____

How will I move tomorrow? _____
_____

Growth:

1 Timothy 4:15 "Practice these things, immerse yourself in them, so that all may see your progress."

What steps did I take towards my goal today? _____
_____

What did today teach me that I will bring into tomorrow? _____
_____

Date:_____

Reflection:

Jeremiah 29:11 "For I know the plans I have for you, declares the Lord, plans for welfare and not for evil, to give you a future and a hope."

What am I celebrating today? _____

_____

What am I grateful for today? _____

_____

What do I need to forgive myself for today? _____

_____

How did I use my gifts today?: _____

_____

Self-care:

3 John 1:2 "Beloved, I pray that all may go well with you and that you may be in good health, as it goes well with your soul."

How did I spend my 15 minutes of "me" time today? _____

_____

How will I spend my 15 minutes of "me" time tomorrow? _____

_____

How did I show gratitude for the ability to move my body today? _____

_____

How will I move tomorrow? _____

_____

Growth:

1 Timothy 4:15 "Practice these things, immerse yourself in them, so that all may see your progress."

What steps did I take towards my goal today? _____

_____

What did today teach me that I will bring into tomorrow? _____

_____

Date:_____

Reflection:

Jeremiah 29:11 "For I know the plans I have for you, declares the Lord, plans for welfare and not for evil, to give you a future and a hope."

What am I celebrating today? _____

_____

What am I grateful for today? _____

_____

What do I need to forgive myself for today? _____

_____

How did I use my gifts today?: _____

_____

Self-care:

3 John 1:2 "Beloved, I pray that all may go well with you and that you may be in good health, as it goes well with your soul."

How did I spend my 15 minutes of "me" time today? _____

_____

How will I spend my 15 minutes of "me" time tomorrow? _____

_____

How did I show gratitude for the ability to move my body today? _____

_____

How will I move tomorrow? _____

_____

Growth:

1 Timothy 4:15 "Practice these things, immerse yourself in them, so that all may see your progress."

What steps did I take towards my goal today? _____

_____

What did today teach me that I will bring into tomorrow? _____

_____

Philippians 4:13 "I can do all things through him who strengthens me."

Self-worth. How do we measure our self-worth? Do we measure it with how many "likes" we get on social media? Do we measure it by something we see in ourselves that we may not like? Most of the time, there are outside factors that effect our view on our self-worth. We will never be consistent on how we feel about ourselves and view ourselves. It is in those times where we begin to either allow outside forces or our own little voice in our head to begin to devalue us, that we need to recognize what our souls need. Reflection goes hand in hand with self-worth. If we take a moment to reflect on the moments that may have brought us to where we are, we can usually find a way to bring us back to how we value ourselves the way the Lord values us. It's ok to have a moment where we don't feel as good as we would like. It's not ok to stay there. Reflect and grow.

Let this serve as a reminder to you this week:

He sees you.

He hears you.

He loves you.

<u>Weekly Challenge:</u>

It's time to reflect on your entries from last week. Pray. Meditate. Celebrate.

Date:_____

Reflection:

Jeremiah 29:11 "For I know the plans I have for you, declares the Lord, plans for welfare and not for evil, to give you a future and a hope."

What am I celebrating today? _____

_____

What am I grateful for today? _____

_____

What do I need to forgive myself for today? _____

_____

How did I use my gifts today?: _____

_____

Self-care:

3 John 1:2 "Beloved, I pray that all may go well with you and that you may be in good health, as it goes well with your soul."

How did I spend my 15 minutes of "me" time today? _____

_____

How will I spend my 15 minutes of "me" time tomorrow? _____

_____

How did I show gratitude for the ability to move my body today? _____

_____

How will I move tomorrow? _____

_____

Growth:

1 Timothy 4:15 "Practice these things, immerse yourself in them, so that all may see your progress."

What steps did I take towards my goal today? _____

_____

What did today teach me that I will bring into tomorrow? _____

_____

Date:_____

Reflection:

Jeremiah 29:11 "For I know the plans I have for you, declares the Lord, plans for welfare and not for evil, to give you a future and a hope."

What am I celebrating today? _____

_____

What am I grateful for today? _____

_____

What do I need to forgive myself for today? _____

_____

How did I use my gifts today?: _____

_____

Self-care:

3 John 1:2 "Beloved, I pray that all may go well with you and that you may be in good health, as it goes well with your soul."

How did I spend my 15 minutes of "me" time today? _____

_____

How will I spend my 15 minutes of "me" time tomorrow? _____

_____

How did I show gratitude for the ability to move my body today? _____

_____

How will I move tomorrow? _____

_____

Growth:

1 Timothy 4:15 "Practice these things, immerse yourself in them, so that all may see your progress."

What steps did I take towards my goal today? _____

_____

What did today teach me that I will bring into tomorrow? _____

_____

Date:_____

Reflection:

Jeremiah 29:11 "For I know the plans I have for you, declares the Lord, plans for welfare and not for evil, to give you a future and a hope."

What am I celebrating today? _____

_____

What am I grateful for today? _____

_____

What do I need to forgive myself for today? _____

_____

How did I use my gifts today?: _____

_____

Self-care:

3 John 1:2 "Beloved, I pray that all may go well with you and that you may be in good health, as it goes well with your soul."

How did I spend my 15 minutes of "me" time today? _____

_____

How will I spend my 15 minutes of "me" time tomorrow? _____

_____

How did I show gratitude for the ability to move my body today? _____

_____

How will I move tomorrow? _____

_____

Growth:

1 Timothy 4:15 "Practice these things, immerse yourself in them, so that all may see your progress."

What steps did I take towards my goal today? _____

_____

What did today teach me that I will bring into tomorrow? _____

_____

Date:_____

Reflection:

Jeremiah 29:11 "For I know the plans I have for you, declares the Lord, plans for welfare and not for evil, to give you a future and a hope."

What am I celebrating today? _____

_____

What am I grateful for today? _____

_____

What do I need to forgive myself for today? _____

_____

How did I use my gifts today?: _____

_____

Self-care:

3 John 1:2 "Beloved, I pray that all may go well with you and that you may be in good health, as it goes well with your soul."

How did I spend my 15 minutes of "me" time today? _____

_____

How will I spend my 15 minutes of "me" time tomorrow? _____

_____

How did I show gratitude for the ability to move my body today? _____

_____

How will I move tomorrow? _____

_____

Growth:

1 Timothy 4:15 "Practice these things, immerse yourself in them, so that all may see your progress."

What steps did I take towards my goal today? _____

_____

What did today teach me that I will bring into tomorrow? _____

_____

Date:_____

Reflection:

Jeremiah 29:11 "For I know the plans I have for you, declares the Lord, plans for welfare and not for evil, to give you a future and a hope."

What am I celebrating today? _____

_____

What am I grateful for today? _____

_____

What do I need to forgive myself for today? _____

_____

How did I use my gifts today?: _____

_____

Self-care:

3 John 1:2 "Beloved, I pray that all may go well with you and that you may be in good health, as it goes well with your soul."

How did I spend my 15 minutes of "me" time today? _____

_____

How will I spend my 15 minutes of "me" time tomorrow? _____

_____

How did I show gratitude for the ability to move my body today? _____

_____

How will I move tomorrow? _____

_____

Growth:

1 Timothy 4:15 "Practice these things, immerse yourself in them, so that all may see your progress."

What steps did I take towards my goal today? _____

_____

What did today teach me that I will bring into tomorrow? _____

_____

Date:_____

Reflection:

Jeremiah 29:11 "For I know the plans I have for you, declares the Lord, plans for welfare and not for evil, to give you a future and a hope."

What am I celebrating today? _____

_____

What am I grateful for today? _____

_____

What do I need to forgive myself for today? _____

_____

How did I use my gifts today?: _____

_____

Self-care:

3 John 1:2 "Beloved, I pray that all may go well with you and that you may be in good health, as it goes well with your soul."

How did I spend my 15 minutes of "me" time today? _____

_____

How will I spend my 15 minutes of "me" time tomorrow? _____

_____

How did I show gratitude for the ability to move my body today? _____

_____

How will I move tomorrow? _____

_____

Growth:

1 Timothy 4:15 "Practice these things, immerse yourself in them, so that all may see your progress."

What steps did I take towards my goal today? _____

_____

What did today teach me that I will bring into tomorrow? _____

_____

Date:_____

Reflection:

Jeremiah 29:11 "For I know the plans I have for you, declares the Lord, plans for welfare and not for evil, to give you a future and a hope."

What am I celebrating today? _____
_____

What am I grateful for today? _____
_____

What do I need to forgive myself for today? _____
_____

How did I use my gifts today?: _____
_____

Self-care:

3 John 1:2 "Beloved, I pray that all may go well with you and that you may be in good health, as it goes well with your soul."

How did I spend my 15 minutes of "me" time today? _____
_____

How will I spend my 15 minutes of "me" time tomorrow? _____
_____

How did I show gratitude for the ability to move my body today? _____
_____

How will I move tomorrow? _____
_____

Growth:

1 Timothy 4:15 "Practice these things, immerse yourself in them, so that all may see your progress."

What steps did I take towards my goal today? _____
_____

What did today teach me that I will bring into tomorrow? _____
_____

Nehemiah 8:10 "….And do not be grieved,
for the joy of the Lord is your strength."

Mom, have you ever had a moment where you sit back and just think to yourself, "WOW?!" That moment where everything you have gone through, your past struggles, your past victories, all of it, has brought you to this moment right here?! Have you ever just thought "Thank you, God, for any storm I've encountered because now I see the blessing you were bringing me?!" If you have not experienced a moment like that in some time, right here, right now is your time to pray. Whatever you are going through, He hears your cries and He sees your tears. Allow God to be your strength right now. He created you to be a mom, therefore His plan for you is great. Do not feel discouraged. Rest in the knowledge that no matter where you are in your "storm", He sees your way out.

Let this serve as a reminder to you this week:

He sees you.

He hears you.

He loves you.

Weekly Challenge:

It's time to reflect on your entries from last
week. Pray. Meditate. Celebrate.

Date:_____

Reflection:

Jeremiah 29:11 "For I know the plans I have for you, declares the Lord, plans for welfare and not for evil, to give you a future and a hope."

What am I celebrating today? _____

_____

What am I grateful for today? _____

_____

What do I need to forgive myself for today? _____

_____

How did I use my gifts today?: _____

_____

Self-care:

3 John 1:2 "Beloved, I pray that all may go well with you and that you may be in good health, as it goes well with your soul."

How did I spend my 15 minutes of "me" time today? _____

_____

How will I spend my 15 minutes of "me" time tomorrow? _____

_____

How did I show gratitude for the ability to move my body today? _____

_____

How will I move tomorrow? _____

_____

Growth:

1 Timothy 4:15 "Practice these things, immerse yourself in them, so that all may see your progress."

What steps did I take towards my goal today? _____

_____

What did today teach me that I will bring into tomorrow? _____

_____

Date:_____

Reflection:

Jeremiah 29:11 "For I know the plans I have for you, declares the Lord, plans for welfare and not for evil, to give you a future and a hope."

What am I celebrating today? _____

_____

What am I grateful for today? _____

_____

What do I need to forgive myself for today? _____

_____

How did I use my gifts today?: _____

_____

Self-care:

3 John 1:2 "Beloved, I pray that all may go well with you and that you may be in good health, as it goes well with your soul."

How did I spend my 15 minutes of "me" time today? _____

_____

How will I spend my 15 minutes of "me" time tomorrow? _____

_____

How did I show gratitude for the ability to move my body today? _____

_____

How will I move tomorrow? _____

_____

Growth:

1 Timothy 4:15 "Practice these things, immerse yourself in them, so that all may see your progress."

What steps did I take towards my goal today? _____

_____

What did today teach me that I will bring into tomorrow? _____

_____

Date:_____

Reflection:

Jeremiah 29:11 "For I know the plans I have for you, declares the Lord, plans for welfare and not for evil, to give you a future and a hope."

What am I celebrating today? _____

_____

What am I grateful for today? _____

_____

What do I need to forgive myself for today? _____

_____

How did I use my gifts today?: _____

_____

Self-care:

3 John 1:2 "Beloved, I pray that all may go well with you and that you may be in good health, as it goes well with your soul."

How did I spend my 15 minutes of "me" time today? _____

_____

How will I spend my 15 minutes of "me" time tomorrow? _____

_____

How did I show gratitude for the ability to move my body today? _____

_____

How will I move tomorrow? _____

_____

Growth:

1 Timothy 4:15 "Practice these things, immerse yourself in them, so that all may see your progress."

What steps did I take towards my goal today? _____

_____

What did today teach me that I will bring into tomorrow? _____

_____

Date:_____

Reflection:

Jeremiah 29:11 "For I know the plans I have for you, declares the Lord, plans for welfare and not for evil, to give you a future and a hope."

What am I celebrating today? _____

_____

What am I grateful for today? _____

_____

What do I need to forgive myself for today? _____

_____

How did I use my gifts today?: _____

_____

Self-care:

3 John 1:2 "Beloved, I pray that all may go well with you and that you may be in good health, as it goes well with your soul."

How did I spend my 15 minutes of "me" time today? _____

_____

How will I spend my 15 minutes of "me" time tomorrow? _____

_____

How did I show gratitude for the ability to move my body today? _____

_____

How will I move tomorrow? _____

_____

Growth:

1 Timothy 4:15 "Practice these things, immerse yourself in them, so that all may see your progress."

What steps did I take towards my goal today? _____

_____

What did today teach me that I will bring into tomorrow? _____

_____

Date:_____

Reflection:

Jeremiah 29:11 "For I know the plans I have for you, declares the Lord, plans for welfare and not for evil, to give you a future and a hope."

What am I celebrating today? _____
_____

What am I grateful for today? _____
_____

What do I need to forgive myself for today? _____
_____

How did I use my gifts today?: _____
_____

Self-care:

3 John 1:2 "Beloved, I pray that all may go well with you and that you may be in good health, as it goes well with your soul."

How did I spend my 15 minutes of "me" time today? _____
_____

How will I spend my 15 minutes of "me" time tomorrow? _____
_____

How did I show gratitude for the ability to move my body today? ____
_____

How will I move tomorrow? _____
_____

Growth:

1 Timothy 4:15 "Practice these things, immerse yourself in them, so that all may see your progress."

What steps did I take towards my goal today? _____
_____

What did today teach me that I will bring into tomorrow? _____
_____

Reflection:

Jeremiah 29:11 "For I know the plans I have for you, declares the Lord, plans for welfare and not for evil, to give you a future and a hope."

What am I celebrating today? _____

_____

What am I grateful for today? _____

_____

What do I need to forgive myself for today? _____

_____

How did I use my gifts today?: _____

_____

Self-care:

3 John 1:2 "Beloved, I pray that all may go well with you and that you may be in good health, as it goes well with your soul."

How did I spend my 15 minutes of "me" time today? _____

_____

How will I spend my 15 minutes of "me" time tomorrow? _____

_____

How did I show gratitude for the ability to move my body today? _____

_____

How will I move tomorrow? _____

_____

Growth:

1 Timothy 4:15 "Practice these things, immerse yourself in them, so that all may see your progress."

What steps did I take towards my goal today? _____

_____

What did today teach me that I will bring into tomorrow? _____

_____

Date:_____

Reflection:

Jeremiah 29:11 "For I know the plans I have for you, declares the Lord, plans for welfare and not for evil, to give you a future and a hope."

What am I celebrating today? _____

_____

What am I grateful for today? _____

_____

What do I need to forgive myself for today? _____

_____

How did I use my gifts today?: _____

_____

Self-care:

3 John 1:2 "Beloved, I pray that all may go well with you and that you may be in good health, as it goes well with your soul."

How did I spend my 15 minutes of "me" time today? _____

_____

How will I spend my 15 minutes of "me" time tomorrow? _____

_____

How did I show gratitude for the ability to move my body today? _____

_____

How will I move tomorrow? _____

_____

Growth:

1 Timothy 4:15 "Practice these things, immerse yourself in them, so that all may see your progress."

What steps did I take towards my goal today? _____

_____

What did today teach me that I will bring into tomorrow? _____

_____

1 Samuel 1:27 "For this child I prayed, and the Lord has granted me my petition that I made to Him."

Each year on my birthday, I plant a flower garden. My birthday is during springtime. I also share my birthday with my first "born." My first "born" may not have been born into my arms many years ago, but that precious little one was born into the arms of the one who created him/her. My little one was "born" into heaven and never made it to day one on this Earth. Therefore, on my birthday I chose to plant a garden in remembrance. Not to mourn, but to bring life into this world on a day that a life came to an end. One year was a little different. It was my first birthday that I was unable to plant a memorial garden because I was flying with my family on a family vacation. At first, I was upset that I was going to miss my yearly ritual. However, this was the perfect way to spend that special day. I never felt closer to my little one as I did that year, flying above the clouds. No matter how many years pass, one truly is never the same after an experience like the one I endured. I know I share this experience with many other women on this Earth. Let me tell you this....no matter how much you talk about it, if that is what helps you, TALK! Everyday if you need to. Allow yourself to feel. If you do not relate to an experience such as this, fill this in with another experience you may have encountered that weighs heavy on your heart. Healing will come. God is our strength and our healer. Cry if you need to. Celebrate when the tears end.

Let this serve as a reminder to you this week:

He sees you.

He hears you.

He loves you.

<u>Weekly Challenge:</u>

It's time to reflect on your entries from last week. Pray. Meditate. Celebrate.

Date:_____

Reflection:

Jeremiah 29:11 "For I know the plans I have for you, declares the Lord, plans for welfare and not for evil, to give you a future and a hope."

What am I celebrating today? _____

_____

What am I grateful for today? _____

_____

What do I need to forgive myself for today? _____

_____

How did I use my gifts today?: _____

_____

Self-care:

3 John 1:2 "Beloved, I pray that all may go well with you and that you may be in good health, as it goes well with your soul."

How did I spend my 15 minutes of "me" time today? _____

_____

How will I spend my 15 minutes of "me" time tomorrow? _____

_____

How did I show gratitude for the ability to move my body today? ____

_____

How will I move tomorrow? _____

_____

Growth:

1 Timothy 4:15 "Practice these things, immerse yourself in them, so that all may see your progress."

What steps did I take towards my goal today? _____

_____

What did today teach me that I will bring into tomorrow? _____

_____

Date:_____

Reflection:

Jeremiah 29:11 "For I know the plans I have for you, declares the Lord, plans for welfare and not for evil, to give you a future and a hope."

What am I celebrating today? _____
_____

What am I grateful for today? _____
_____

What do I need to forgive myself for today? _____
_____

How did I use my gifts today?: _____
_____

Self-care:

3 John 1:2 "Beloved, I pray that all may go well with you and that you may be in good health, as it goes well with your soul."

How did I spend my 15 minutes of "me" time today? _____
_____

How will I spend my 15 minutes of "me" time tomorrow? _____
_____

How did I show gratitude for the ability to move my body today? _____
_____

How will I move tomorrow? _____
_____

Growth:

1 Timothy 4:15 "Practice these things, immerse yourself in them, so that all may see your progress."

What steps did I take towards my goal today? _____
_____

What did today teach me that I will bring into tomorrow? _____
_____

Reflection:

Jeremiah 29:11 "For I know the plans I have for you, declares the Lord, plans for welfare and not for evil, to give you a future and a hope."

What am I celebrating today? _____

_____

What am I grateful for today? _____

_____

What do I need to forgive myself for today? _____

_____

How did I use my gifts today?: _____

_____

Self-care:

3 John 1:2 "Beloved, I pray that all may go well with you and that you may be in good health, as it goes well with your soul."

How did I spend my 15 minutes of "me" time today? _____

_____

How will I spend my 15 minutes of "me" time tomorrow? _____

_____

How did I show gratitude for the ability to move my body today? _____

_____

How will I move tomorrow? _____

_____

Growth:

1 Timothy 4:15 "Practice these things, immerse yourself in them, so that all may see your progress."

What steps did I take towards my goal today? _____

_____

What did today teach me that I will bring into tomorrow? _____

_____

Date:_____

Reflection:

Jeremiah 29:11 "For I know the plans I have for you, declares the Lord, plans for welfare and not for evil, to give you a future and a hope."

What am I celebrating today? _____
_____

What am I grateful for today? _____
_____

What do I need to forgive myself for today? _____
_____

How did I use my gifts today?: _____
_____

Self-care:

3 John 1:2 "Beloved, I pray that all may go well with you and that you may be in good health, as it goes well with your soul."

How did I spend my 15 minutes of "me" time today? _____
_____

How will I spend my 15 minutes of "me" time tomorrow? _____
_____

How did I show gratitude for the ability to move my body today? _____
_____

How will I move tomorrow? _____
_____

Growth:

1 Timothy 4:15 "Practice these things, immerse yourself in them, so that all may see your progress."

What steps did I take towards my goal today? _____
_____

What did today teach me that I will bring into tomorrow? _____
_____

Date:_____

Reflection:

Jeremiah 29:11 "For I know the plans I have for you, declares the Lord, plans for welfare and not for evil, to give you a future and a hope."

What am I celebrating today? _____

_____

What am I grateful for today? _____

_____

What do I need to forgive myself for today? _____

_____

How did I use my gifts today?: _____

_____

Self-care:

3 John 1:2 "Beloved, I pray that all may go well with you and that you may be in good health, as it goes well with your soul."

How did I spend my 15 minutes of "me" time today? _____

_____

How will I spend my 15 minutes of "me" time tomorrow? _____

_____

How did I show gratitude for the ability to move my body today? _____

_____

How will I move tomorrow? _____

_____

Growth:

1 Timothy 4:15 "Practice these things, immerse yourself in them, so that all may see your progress."

What steps did I take towards my goal today? _____

_____

What did today teach me that I will bring into tomorrow? _____

_____

Date:_____

Reflection:

Jeremiah 29:11 "For I know the plans I have for you, declares the Lord, plans for welfare and not for evil, to give you a future and a hope."

What am I celebrating today? _____

_____

What am I grateful for today? _____

_____

What do I need to forgive myself for today? _____

_____

How did I use my gifts today?: _____

_____

Self-care:

3 John 1:2 "Beloved, I pray that all may go well with you and that you may be in good health, as it goes well with your soul."

How did I spend my 15 minutes of "me" time today? _____

_____

How will I spend my 15 minutes of "me" time tomorrow? _____

_____

How did I show gratitude for the ability to move my body today? _____

_____

How will I move tomorrow? _____

_____

Growth:

1 Timothy 4:15 "Practice these things, immerse yourself in them, so that all may see your progress."

What steps did I take towards my goal today? _____

_____

What did today teach me that I will bring into tomorrow? _____

_____

Date:_____

Reflection:

Jeremiah 29:11 "For I know the plans I have for you, declares the Lord, plans for welfare and not for evil, to give you a future and a hope."

What am I celebrating today? _____

_____

What am I grateful for today? _____

_____

What do I need to forgive myself for today? _____

_____

How did I use my gifts today?: _____

_____

Self-care:

3 John 1:2 "Beloved, I pray that all may go well with you and that you may be in good health, as it goes well with your soul."

How did I spend my 15 minutes of "me" time today? _____

_____

How will I spend my 15 minutes of "me" time tomorrow? _____

_____

How did I show gratitude for the ability to move my body today? _____

_____

How will I move tomorrow? _____

_____

Growth:

1 Timothy 4:15 "Practice these things, immerse yourself in them, so that all may see your progress."

What steps did I take towards my goal today? _____

_____

What did today teach me that I will bring into tomorrow? _____

_____

1 Peter 5:7 "Casting all your anxieties
on him, because he cares for you."

Mom, how many times have you beat yourself up over a situation? Now you can look back at that moment and think…hmmm…it really was not so bad! How many times have you not had the "perfect" day? Maybe you did not accomplish EVERYTHING on your list. Maybe you caught your child(ren) licking raw cookie dough from the spoon. Maybe you ate something off your meal plan because you were rushing to get the baby ready for the day. Guess what? It is ok. It is as simple as that! When you can forgive yourself, that is truly your freeing moment. Being HONEST with yourself and limiting your abilities throughout the day is not a bad thing! Sometimes as moms, we hold ourselves to expectations that we HAVE to get things done, however, when you begin to celebrate the little moments, that is when you see how much you are actually accomplishing in the day. Therefore, celebrating you each day is so important. Don't be so hard on yourself, ok?

Let this serve as a reminder to you this week:

He sees you.

He hears you.

He loves you.

Weekly Challenge:

It's time to reflect on your entries from last week. Pray. Meditate. Celebrate.

Date:_____

Reflection:

Jeremiah 29:11 "For I know the plans I have for you, declares the Lord, plans for welfare and not for evil, to give you a future and a hope."

What am I celebrating today? _____

_____

What am I grateful for today? _____

_____

What do I need to forgive myself for today? _____

_____

How did I use my gifts today?: _____

_____

Self-care:

3 John 1:2 "Beloved, I pray that all may go well with you and that you may be in good health, as it goes well with your soul."

How did I spend my 15 minutes of "me" time today? _____

_____

How will I spend my 15 minutes of "me" time tomorrow? _____

_____

How did I show gratitude for the ability to move my body today? _____

_____

How will I move tomorrow? _____

_____

Growth:

1 Timothy 4:15 "Practice these things, immerse yourself in them, so that all may see your progress."

What steps did I take towards my goal today? _____

_____

What did today teach me that I will bring into tomorrow? _____

_____

Date:_____

Reflection:

Jeremiah 29:11 "For I know the plans I have for you, declares the Lord, plans for welfare and not for evil, to give you a future and a hope."

What am I celebrating today? _____
_____

What am I grateful for today? _____
_____

What do I need to forgive myself for today? _____
_____

How did I use my gifts today?: _____
_____

Self-care:

3 John 1:2 "Beloved, I pray that all may go well with you and that you may be in good health, as it goes well with your soul."

How did I spend my 15 minutes of "me" time today? _____
_____

How will I spend my 15 minutes of "me" time tomorrow? _____
_____

How did I show gratitude for the ability to move my body today? _____
_____

How will I move tomorrow? _____
_____

Growth:

1 Timothy 4:15 "Practice these things, immerse yourself in them, so that all may see your progress."

What steps did I take towards my goal today? _____
_____

What did today teach me that I will bring into tomorrow? _____
_____

Date:_____

Reflection:

Jeremiah 29:11 "For I know the plans I have for you, declares the Lord, plans for welfare and not for evil, to give you a future and a hope."

What am I celebrating today? _____

_____

What am I grateful for today? _____

_____

What do I need to forgive myself for today? _____

_____

How did I use my gifts today?: _____

_____

Self-care:

3 John 1:2 "Beloved, I pray that all may go well with you and that you may be in good health, as it goes well with your soul."

How did I spend my 15 minutes of "me" time today? _____

_____

How will I spend my 15 minutes of "me" time tomorrow? _____

_____

How did I show gratitude for the ability to move my body today? _____

_____

How will I move tomorrow? _____

_____

Growth:

1 Timothy 4:15 "Practice these things, immerse yourself in them, so that all may see your progress."

What steps did I take towards my goal today? _____

_____

What did today teach me that I will bring into tomorrow? _____

_____

Date:_____

Reflection:

Jeremiah 29:11 "For I know the plans I have for you, declares the Lord, plans for welfare and not for evil, to give you a future and a hope."

What am I celebrating today? _____

_____

What am I grateful for today? _____

_____

What do I need to forgive myself for today? _____

_____

How did I use my gifts today?: _____

_____

Self-care:

3 John 1:2 "Beloved, I pray that all may go well with you and that you may be in good health, as it goes well with your soul."

How did I spend my 15 minutes of "me" time today? _____

_____

How will I spend my 15 minutes of "me" time tomorrow? _____

_____

How did I show gratitude for the ability to move my body today? _____

_____

How will I move tomorrow? _____

_____

Growth:

1 Timothy 4:15 "Practice these things, immerse yourself in them, so that all may see your progress."

What steps did I take towards my goal today? _____

_____

What did today teach me that I will bring into tomorrow? _____

_____

Date:_____

Reflection:

Jeremiah 29:11 "For I know the plans I have for you, declares the Lord, plans for welfare and not for evil, to give you a future and a hope."

What am I celebrating today? _____

_____

What am I grateful for today? _____

_____

What do I need to forgive myself for today? _____

_____

How did I use my gifts today?: _____

_____

Self-care:

3 John 1:2 "Beloved, I pray that all may go well with you and that you may be in good health, as it goes well with your soul."

How did I spend my 15 minutes of "me" time today? _____

_____

How will I spend my 15 minutes of "me" time tomorrow? _____

_____

How did I show gratitude for the ability to move my body today? _____

_____

How will I move tomorrow? _____

_____

Growth:

1 Timothy 4:15 "Practice these things, immerse yourself in them, so that all may see your progress."

What steps did I take towards my goal today? _____

_____

What did today teach me that I will bring into tomorrow? _____

_____

Date:_____

Reflection:

Jeremiah 29:11 "For I know the plans I have for you, declares the Lord, plans for welfare and not for evil, to give you a future and a hope."

What am I celebrating today? _____

_____

What am I grateful for today? _____

_____

What do I need to forgive myself for today? _____

_____

How did I use my gifts today?: _____

_____

Self-care:

3 John 1:2 "Beloved, I pray that all may go well with you and that you may be in good health, as it goes well with your soul."

How did I spend my 15 minutes of "me" time today? _____

_____

How will I spend my 15 minutes of "me" time tomorrow? _____

_____

How did I show gratitude for the ability to move my body today? _____

_____

How will I move tomorrow? _____

_____

Growth:

1 Timothy 4:15 "Practice these things, immerse yourself in them, so that all may see your progress."

What steps did I take towards my goal today? _____

_____

What did today teach me that I will bring into tomorrow? _____

_____

Reflection:

Jeremiah 29:11 "For I know the plans I have for you, declares the Lord, plans for welfare and not for evil, to give you a future and a hope."

What am I celebrating today? _____

_____

What am I grateful for today? _____

_____

What do I need to forgive myself for today? _____

_____

How did I use my gifts today?: _____

_____

Self-care:

3 John 1:2 "Beloved, I pray that all may go well with you and that you may be in good health, as it goes well with your soul."

How did I spend my 15 minutes of "me" time today? _____

_____

How will I spend my 15 minutes of "me" time tomorrow? _____

_____

How did I show gratitude for the ability to move my body today? _____

_____

How will I move tomorrow? _____

_____

Growth:

1 Timothy 4:15 "Practice these things, immerse yourself in them, so that all may see your progress."

What steps did I take towards my goal today? _____

_____

What did today teach me that I will bring into tomorrow? _____

_____

***Proverbs 29:11 "A fool gives vent to his spirit,
but a wise man quietly hold it back."***

Raise your hand if you have ever felt as though you were just going to
snap. I am sure that hand went up because you are human. I vividly
remember a day that I let that feeling get the best of me. To tell you
a little about myself, I feel emotions in a big way. That is just who I
am. When others hurt me, I feel it in a big way. This day, I logged
into social media. As I began to scroll, I realized my emotions were
getting the best of me. I was so effected by what I read from others
that day. Arguing, opinions, mom shaming...I saw it all. My head
began to spin. That is when I realized I needed to clear my head.
I stepped away and was able to gather my thoughts. That is when
it all dawned on me. I could not condone what I had been seeing;
therefore, I was able to change what I was viewing. In that moment,
I decided to do what was best for my mental health. I decided to stay
away from social media for the time being. It's what my soul needed.

My point is this: if something is not sitting right with you, or if
something is costing you your mental health, take a break from that
instigator. Take care of YOU. To be able to pour into your children
and your family, your cup must be full. Your soul will thank you.

Let this serve as a reminder to you this week:

He sees you.

He hears you.

He loves you.

Weekly Challenge:

It's time to reflect on your entries from last
week. Pray. Meditate. Celebrate.

Date:_____

Reflection:

Jeremiah 29:11 "For I know the plans I have for you, declares the Lord, plans for welfare and not for evil, to give you a future and a hope."

What am I celebrating today? _____

_____

What am I grateful for today? _____

_____

What do I need to forgive myself for today? _____

_____

How did I use my gifts today?: _____

_____

Self-care:

3 John 1:2 "Beloved, I pray that all may go well with you and that you may be in good health, as it goes well with your soul."

How did I spend my 15 minutes of "me" time today? _____

_____

How will I spend my 15 minutes of "me" time tomorrow? _____

_____

How did I show gratitude for the ability to move my body today? _____

_____

How will I move tomorrow? _____

_____

Growth:

1 Timothy 4:15 "Practice these things, immerse yourself in them, so that all may see your progress."

What steps did I take towards my goal today? _____

_____

What did today teach me that I will bring into tomorrow? _____

_____

Date:_____

Reflection:

Jeremiah 29:11 "For I know the plans I have for you, declares the Lord, plans for welfare and not for evil, to give you a future and a hope."

What am I celebrating today? _____
_____

What am I grateful for today? _____
_____

What do I need to forgive myself for today? _____
_____

How did I use my gifts today?: _____
_____

Self-care:

3 John 1:2 "Beloved, I pray that all may go well with you and that you may be in good health, as it goes well with your soul."

How did I spend my 15 minutes of "me" time today? _____
_____

How will I spend my 15 minutes of "me" time tomorrow? _____
_____

How did I show gratitude for the ability to move my body today? ___
_____

How will I move tomorrow? _____
_____

Growth:

1 Timothy 4:15 "Practice these things, immerse yourself in them, so that all may see your progress."

What steps did I take towards my goal today? _____
_____

What did today teach me that I will bring into tomorrow? _____
_____

Date:_____

Reflection:

Jeremiah 29:11 "For I know the plans I have for you, declares the Lord, plans for welfare and not for evil, to give you a future and a hope."

What am I celebrating today? _____

_____

What am I grateful for today? _____

_____

What do I need to forgive myself for today? _____

_____

How did I use my gifts today?: _____

_____

Self-care:

3 John 1:2 "Beloved, I pray that all may go well with you and that you may be in good health, as it goes well with your soul."

How did I spend my 15 minutes of "me" time today? _____

_____

How will I spend my 15 minutes of "me" time tomorrow? _____

_____

How did I show gratitude for the ability to move my body today? _____

_____

How will I move tomorrow? _____

_____

Growth:

1 Timothy 4:15 "Practice these things, immerse yourself in them, so that all may see your progress."

What steps did I take towards my goal today? _____

_____

What did today teach me that I will bring into tomorrow? _____

_____

Date:_____

Reflection:

Jeremiah 29:11 "For I know the plans I have for you, declares the Lord, plans for welfare and not for evil, to give you a future and a hope."

What am I celebrating today? _____

_____

What am I grateful for today? _____

_____

What do I need to forgive myself for today? _____

_____

How did I use my gifts today?: _____

_____

Self-care:

3 John 1:2 "Beloved, I pray that all may go well with you and that you may be in good health, as it goes well with your soul."

How did I spend my 15 minutes of "me" time today? _____

_____

How will I spend my 15 minutes of "me" time tomorrow? _____

_____

How did I show gratitude for the ability to move my body today? _____

_____

How will I move tomorrow? _____

_____

Growth:

1 Timothy 4:15 "Practice these things, immerse yourself in them, so that all may see your progress."

What steps did I take towards my goal today? _____

_____

What did today teach me that I will bring into tomorrow? _____

_____

Date:_____

Reflection:

Jeremiah 29:11 "For I know the plans I have for you, declares the Lord, plans for welfare and not for evil, to give you a future and a hope."

What am I celebrating today? _____
_____

What am I grateful for today? _____
_____

What do I need to forgive myself for today? _____
_____

How did I use my gifts today?: _____
_____

Self-care:

3 John 1:2 "Beloved, I pray that all may go well with you and that you may be in good health, as it goes well with your soul."

How did I spend my 15 minutes of "me" time today? _____
_____

How will I spend my 15 minutes of "me" time tomorrow? _____
_____

How did I show gratitude for the ability to move my body today? _____
_____

How will I move tomorrow? _____
_____

Growth:

1 Timothy 4:15 "Practice these things, immerse yourself in them, so that all may see your progress."

What steps did I take towards my goal today? _____
_____

What did today teach me that I will bring into tomorrow? _____
_____

Date:_____

Reflection:

Jeremiah 29:11 "For I know the plans I have for you, declares the Lord, plans for welfare and not for evil, to give you a future and a hope."

What am I celebrating today? _____
_____

What am I grateful for today? _____
_____

What do I need to forgive myself for today? _____
_____

How did I use my gifts today?: _____
_____

Self-care:

3 John 1:2 "Beloved, I pray that all may go well with you and that you may be in good health, as it goes well with your soul."

How did I spend my 15 minutes of "me" time today? _____
_____

How will I spend my 15 minutes of "me" time tomorrow? _____
_____

How did I show gratitude for the ability to move my body today? _____
_____

How will I move tomorrow? _____
_____

Growth:

1 Timothy 4:15 "Practice these things, immerse yourself in them, so that all may see your progress."

What steps did I take towards my goal today? _____
_____

What did today teach me that I will bring into tomorrow? _____
_____

Date:_____

Reflection:

Jeremiah 29:11 "For I know the plans I have for you, declares the Lord, plans for welfare and not for evil, to give you a future and a hope."

What am I celebrating today? _____

_____

What am I grateful for today? _____

_____

What do I need to forgive myself for today? _____

_____

How did I use my gifts today?: _____

_____

Self-care:

3 John 1:2 "Beloved, I pray that all may go well with you and that you may be in good health, as it goes well with your soul."

How did I spend my 15 minutes of "me" time today? _____

_____

How will I spend my 15 minutes of "me" time tomorrow? _____

_____

How did I show gratitude for the ability to move my body today? _____

_____

How will I move tomorrow? _____

_____

Growth:

1 Timothy 4:15 "Practice these things, immerse yourself in them, so that all may see your progress."

What steps did I take towards my goal today? _____

_____

What did today teach me that I will bring into tomorrow? _____

_____

1 Peter 4:8-9 "Above all, keep loving one another earnestly, since love covers a multitude of sins. Show hospitality to one another without grumbling."

My family and I recently moved into a new home. Let me tell you, packing up all our belongings, moving into new surroundings, and settling into a new forever home stirs up a LOT of emotions! What is it about changing our surroundings that truly makes or breaks us?! Before this move, I had a lot of "healing" that needed to be done. I had past wounds that I struggled with. It was not until recently, that I realized the first four letters of HEALTH are so significant. Those first four letters spell HEAL. I have spoken time and time about loving others, ALL others. That is what we are here for. However, to love those who may have wounded us…that is where healing comes in. I am going to share a tool that has helped me love those who may have hurt me. Instead of praying for them, or wishing them well, change your prayers. Pray that God helps YOU to see them the way He has asked us to do. It is harder for us because we are human and not perfect by any means. Remind yourself of that! You are human, THEY are human. NOT perfect. God still loves them even if YOU have a hard time doing so. That prayer has truly helped me in seeing those who have wounded me, in a different light. I know I have unintentionally hurt others. I pray that those I have hurt can see me as the Father sees me as well. Mom, if saying this prayer is your celebration today, I am proud of you.

Let this serve as a reminder to you this week:

He sees you.

He hears you.

He loves you.

<u>Weekly Challenge:</u>

It's time to reflect on your entries from last week. Pray. Meditate. Celebrate.

Date:_____

Reflection:

Jeremiah 29:11 "For I know the plans I have for you, declares the Lord, plans for welfare and not for evil, to give you a future and a hope."

What am I celebrating today? _____
_____

What am I grateful for today? _____
_____

What do I need to forgive myself for today? _____
_____

How did I use my gifts today?: _____
_____

Self-care:

3 John 1:2 "Beloved, I pray that all may go well with you and that you may be in good health, as it goes well with your soul."

How did I spend my 15 minutes of "me" time today? _____
_____

How will I spend my 15 minutes of "me" time tomorrow? _____
_____

How did I show gratitude for the ability to move my body today? _____
_____

How will I move tomorrow? _____
_____

Growth:

1 Timothy 4:15 "Practice these things, immerse yourself in them, so that all may see your progress."

What steps did I take towards my goal today? _____
_____

What did today teach me that I will bring into tomorrow? _____
_____

Date:_____

Reflection:

Jeremiah 29:11 "For I know the plans I have for you, declares the Lord, plans for welfare and not for evil, to give you a future and a hope."

What am I celebrating today? _____

_____

What am I grateful for today? _____

_____

What do I need to forgive myself for today? _____

_____

How did I use my gifts today?: _____

_____

Self-care:

3 John 1:2 "Beloved, I pray that all may go well with you and that you may be in good health, as it goes well with your soul."

How did I spend my 15 minutes of "me" time today? _____

_____

How will I spend my 15 minutes of "me" time tomorrow? _____

_____

How did I show gratitude for the ability to move my body today? _____

_____

How will I move tomorrow? _____

_____

Growth:

1 Timothy 4:15 "Practice these things, immerse yourself in them, so that all may see your progress."

What steps did I take towards my goal today? _____

_____

What did today teach me that I will bring into tomorrow? _____

_____

Date:_____

Reflection:

Jeremiah 29:11 "For I know the plans I have for you, declares the Lord, plans for welfare and not for evil, to give you a future and a hope."

What am I celebrating today? _____

_____

What am I grateful for today? _____

_____

What do I need to forgive myself for today? _____

_____

How did I use my gifts today?: _____

_____

Self-care:

3 John 1:2 "Beloved, I pray that all may go well with you and that you may be in good health, as it goes well with your soul."

How did I spend my 15 minutes of "me" time today? _____

_____

How will I spend my 15 minutes of "me" time tomorrow? _____

_____

How did I show gratitude for the ability to move my body today? _____

_____

How will I move tomorrow? _____

_____

Growth:

1 Timothy 4:15 "Practice these things, immerse yourself in them, so that all may see your progress."

What steps did I take towards my goal today? _____

_____

What did today teach me that I will bring into tomorrow? _____

_____

Reflection:

Jeremiah 29:11 "For I know the plans I have for you, declares the Lord, plans for welfare and not for evil, to give you a future and a hope."

What am I celebrating today? _____

_____

What am I grateful for today? _____

_____

What do I need to forgive myself for today? _____

_____

How did I use my gifts today?: _____

_____

Self-care:

3 John 1:2 "Beloved, I pray that all may go well with you and that you may be in good health, as it goes well with your soul."

How did I spend my 15 minutes of "me" time today? _____

_____

How will I spend my 15 minutes of "me" time tomorrow? _____

_____

How did I show gratitude for the ability to move my body today? _____

_____

How will I move tomorrow? _____

_____

Growth:

1 Timothy 4:15 "Practice these things, immerse yourself in them, so that all may see your progress."

What steps did I take towards my goal today? _____

_____

What did today teach me that I will bring into tomorrow? _____

_____

Date:_____

Reflection:

Jeremiah 29:11 "For I know the plans I have for you, declares the Lord, plans for welfare and not for evil, to give you a future and a hope."

What am I celebrating today? _____

What am I grateful for today? _____

What do I need to forgive myself for today? _____

How did I use my gifts today?: _____

Self-care:

3 John 1:2 "Beloved, I pray that all may go well with you and that you may be in good health, as it goes well with your soul."

How did I spend my 15 minutes of "me" time today? _____

How will I spend my 15 minutes of "me" time tomorrow? _____

How did I show gratitude for the ability to move my body today? _____

How will I move tomorrow? _____

Growth:

1 Timothy 4:15 "Practice these things, immerse yourself in them, so that all may see your progress."

What steps did I take towards my goal today? _____

What did today teach me that I will bring into tomorrow? _____

Reflection:

Jeremiah 29:11 "For I know the plans I have for you, declares the Lord, plans for welfare and not for evil, to give you a future and a hope."

What am I celebrating today? _____

_____

What am I grateful for today? _____

_____

What do I need to forgive myself for today? _____

_____

How did I use my gifts today?: _____

_____

Self-care:

3 John 1:2 "Beloved, I pray that all may go well with you and that you may be in good health, as it goes well with your soul."

How did I spend my 15 minutes of "me" time today? _____

_____

How will I spend my 15 minutes of "me" time tomorrow? _____

_____

How did I show gratitude for the ability to move my body today? _____

_____

How will I move tomorrow? _____

_____

Growth:

1 Timothy 4:15 "Practice these things, immerse yourself in them, so that all may see your progress."

What steps did I take towards my goal today? _____

_____

What did today teach me that I will bring into tomorrow? _____

_____

Date:_____

Reflection:

Jeremiah 29:11 "For I know the plans I have for you, declares the Lord, plans for welfare and not for evil, to give you a future and a hope."

What am I celebrating today? _____

_____

What am I grateful for today? _____

_____

What do I need to forgive myself for today? _____

_____

How did I use my gifts today?: _____

_____

Self-care:

3 John 1:2 "Beloved, I pray that all may go well with you and that you may be in good health, as it goes well with your soul."

How did I spend my 15 minutes of "me" time today? _____

_____

How will I spend my 15 minutes of "me" time tomorrow? _____

_____

How did I show gratitude for the ability to move my body today? _____

_____

How will I move tomorrow? _____

_____

Growth:

1 Timothy 4:15 "Practice these things, immerse yourself in them, so that all may see your progress."

What steps did I take towards my goal today? _____

_____

What did today teach me that I will bring into tomorrow? _____

_____

1 Thessalonians 5:11 "Therefore encourage one another and build one another up, just as you are doing."

As a mom, when things pile up, I feel as though it is so important to fill your cup when it is getting low, in order to pour out into your own family. There was a time, for 8 months, I was dealing with some medical "issues." Some I was open about to others, and some I was silently dealing with. As mothers, we tend to downplay our own struggles because we may be so used to putting other first. We are used to taking care of our little ones even when we might have a cold. We may tend to make sure we are still carrying our babies around even if we have a sore back. It just becomes first nature to "hide" our own sufferings when someone asks us "how are you?" We may tend to nod and say "I am great, how are YOU?" Mom, lets take time to PLEASE look around at our fellow sisters and begin to lean on each other? We ALL need someone to rely on and why not someone who GETS IT...a fellow mom! Let us strive to break this trend once and for all. For me, those 8 months of medical testing were painful and draining. The unknown answers were scary at that time. Do you know what is even scarier? Leaving your own cup empty during times such as I endured, where I was longing for it to be filled. We may not know what another mom is going through. Let us begin to ask one another "how are you" with genuine concern and appreciation of one another. If the other person responds with "I'm good," it is ok to ask them again. Sometimes (especially moms) someone may need to be asked twice. We need to know it is ok to not be ok sometimes. It is always ok to lean on someone else, while you are also leaning on the Lord. You are not weak. You, mom, are so very strong.

Let this serve as a reminder to you this week:

He sees you.

He hears you.

He loves you.

Weekly Challenge:

It's time to reflect on your entries from last week. Pray. Meditate. Celebrate.

Date:_____

Reflection:

Jeremiah 29:11 "For I know the plans I have for you, declares the Lord, plans for welfare and not for evil, to give you a future and a hope."

What am I celebrating today? _____

_____

What am I grateful for today? _____

_____

What do I need to forgive myself for today? _____

_____

How did I use my gifts today?: _____

_____

Self-care:

3 John 1:2 "Beloved, I pray that all may go well with you and that you may be in good health, as it goes well with your soul."

How did I spend my 15 minutes of "me" time today? _____

_____

How will I spend my 15 minutes of "me" time tomorrow? _____

_____

How did I show gratitude for the ability to move my body today? _____

_____

How will I move tomorrow? _____

_____

Growth:

1 Timothy 4:15 "Practice these things, immerse yourself in them, so that all may see your progress."

What steps did I take towards my goal today? _____

_____

What did today teach me that I will bring into tomorrow? _____

_____

Date:_____

Reflection:

Jeremiah 29:11 "For I know the plans I have for you, declares the Lord, plans for welfare and not for evil, to give you a future and a hope."

What am I celebrating today? _____

_____

What am I grateful for today? _____

_____

What do I need to forgive myself for today? _____

_____

How did I use my gifts today?: _____

_____

Self-care:

3 John 1:2 "Beloved, I pray that all may go well with you and that you may be in good health, as it goes well with your soul."

How did I spend my 15 minutes of "me" time today? _____

_____

How will I spend my 15 minutes of "me" time tomorrow? _____

_____

How did I show gratitude for the ability to move my body today? _____

_____

How will I move tomorrow? _____

_____

Growth:

1 Timothy 4:15 "Practice these things, immerse yourself in them, so that all may see your progress."

What steps did I take towards my goal today? _____

_____

What did today teach me that I will bring into tomorrow? _____

_____

Date:_____

Reflection:

Jeremiah 29:11 "For I know the plans I have for you, declares the Lord, plans for welfare and not for evil, to give you a future and a hope."

What am I celebrating today? _____

_____

What am I grateful for today? _____

_____

What do I need to forgive myself for today? _____

_____

How did I use my gifts today?: _____

_____

Self-care:

3 John 1:2 "Beloved, I pray that all may go well with you and that you may be in good health, as it goes well with your soul."

How did I spend my 15 minutes of "me" time today? _____

_____

How will I spend my 15 minutes of "me" time tomorrow? _____

_____

How did I show gratitude for the ability to move my body today? _____

_____

How will I move tomorrow? _____

_____

Growth:

1 Timothy 4:15 "Practice these things, immerse yourself in them, so that all may see your progress."

What steps did I take towards my goal today? _____

_____

What did today teach me that I will bring into tomorrow? _____

_____

Date:_____

Reflection:

Jeremiah 29:11 "For I know the plans I have for you, declares the Lord, plans for welfare and not for evil, to give you a future and a hope."

What am I celebrating today? _____

_____

What am I grateful for today? _____

_____

What do I need to forgive myself for today? _____

_____

How did I use my gifts today?: _____

_____

Self-care:

3 John 1:2 "Beloved, I pray that all may go well with you and that you may be in good health, as it goes well with your soul."

How did I spend my 15 minutes of "me" time today? _____

_____

How will I spend my 15 minutes of "me" time tomorrow? _____

_____

How did I show gratitude for the ability to move my body today? _____

_____

How will I move tomorrow? _____

_____

Growth:

1 Timothy 4:15 "Practice these things, immerse yourself in them, so that all may see your progress."

What steps did I take towards my goal today? _____

_____

What did today teach me that I will bring into tomorrow? _____

_____

Date:_____

Reflection:

Jeremiah 29:11 "For I know the plans I have for you, declares the Lord, plans for welfare and not for evil, to give you a future and a hope."

What am I celebrating today? _____

_____

What am I grateful for today? _____

_____

What do I need to forgive myself for today? _____

_____

How did I use my gifts today?: _____

_____

Self-care:

3 John 1:2 "Beloved, I pray that all may go well with you and that you may be in good health, as it goes well with your soul."

How did I spend my 15 minutes of "me" time today? _____

_____

How will I spend my 15 minutes of "me" time tomorrow? _____

_____

How did I show gratitude for the ability to move my body today? _____

_____

How will I move tomorrow? _____

_____

Growth:

1 Timothy 4:15 "Practice these things, immerse yourself in them, so that all may see your progress."

What steps did I take towards my goal today? _____

_____

What did today teach me that I will bring into tomorrow? _____

_____

Date:_____

Reflection:

Jeremiah 29:11 "For I know the plans I have for you, declares the Lord, plans for welfare and not for evil, to give you a future and a hope."

What am I celebrating today? _____

_____

What am I grateful for today? _____

_____

What do I need to forgive myself for today? _____

_____

How did I use my gifts today?: _____

_____

Self-care:

3 John 1:2 "Beloved, I pray that all may go well with you and that you may be in good health, as it goes well with your soul."

How did I spend my 15 minutes of "me" time today? _____

_____

How will I spend my 15 minutes of "me" time tomorrow? _____

_____

How did I show gratitude for the ability to move my body today? _____

_____

How will I move tomorrow? _____

_____

Growth:

1 Timothy 4:15 "Practice these things, immerse yourself in them, so that all may see your progress."

What steps did I take towards my goal today? _____

_____

What did today teach me that I will bring into tomorrow? _____

_____

Date:_____

Reflection:

Jeremiah 29:11 "For I know the plans I have for you, declares the Lord, plans for welfare and not for evil, to give you a future and a hope."

What am I celebrating today? _____

_____

What am I grateful for today? _____

_____

What do I need to forgive myself for today? _____

_____

How did I use my gifts today?: _____

_____

Self-care:

3 John 1:2 "Beloved, I pray that all may go well with you and that you may be in good health, as it goes well with your soul."

How did I spend my 15 minutes of "me" time today? _____

_____

How will I spend my 15 minutes of "me" time tomorrow? _____

_____

How did I show gratitude for the ability to move my body today? _____

_____

How will I move tomorrow? _____

_____

Growth:

1 Timothy 4:15 "Practice these things, immerse yourself in them, so that all may see your progress."

What steps did I take towards my goal today? _____

_____

What did today teach me that I will bring into tomorrow? _____

_____

***Isaiah 41:10 "Fear not, for I am with you;
be not dismayed, for I am your God; I will
strengthen you, I will help you, I will uphold
you with my righteous right hand."***

Mom, have you let out a little cry today? If you answered yes, I'm here to say GOOD FOR YOU! If you thought I would tell you to "move forward! Do not let your emotions get the best of you", you are so very wrong. I am here to celebrate you and the release of your emotions. Here is a list of what letting out a cry does NOT mean: 1) it does NOT mean you are weak. 2) it does NOT mean you are ungrateful for the things you have. 3) it does NOT mean you have postpartum depression. 4) it does NOT mean your children will think less of you. That is just to name a few. Here is a list of what letting out a cry DOES mean: 1) it means you have endured something heavy and instead of making whatever that is make you feel weak, you chose to embrace the difficult emotions of it. 2) it means you are showing gratitude for the ability to have feelings. You have been blessed with the ability to have emotions and what better way to show gratitude than to express that ability. 3) a cry here and there does not mean you should self-diagnose yourself with postpartum depression. You probably have enough going on. If the crying does not stop, however, I do recommend seeing someone who can guide you in the right direction to help yourself. 4) it means your children will look at you with respect. We never want our children to "get over it.", right? There is no better way than to lead by example and let them see it is OK to be vulnerable.

It is so important to remember that strength shows in many ways. Sometimes gaining strength may mean you shed a tear here and there. I will even share a secret with you. I cry before noon some days! There was a time I even cried over spilt apples! I dropped my son's apples all over the floor after I had the wonderful adventure of making him three separate lunches, all of which he refused to eat. I dropped his apples and I cried. I do not feel less of myself and my infant certainly did not think less of me while he watched me cry. Find comfort in the Lord.

Let this serve as a reminder to you this week:

He sees you.

He hears you.

He loves you.

<u>Weekly Challenge:</u>

It's time to reflect on your entries from last week. Pray. Meditate. Celebrate.

Date:_____

Reflection:

Jeremiah 29:11 "For I know the plans I have for you, declares the Lord, plans for welfare and not for evil, to give you a future and a hope."

What am I celebrating today? _____
_____

What am I grateful for today? _____
_____

What do I need to forgive myself for today? _____
_____

How did I use my gifts today?: _____
_____

Self-care:

3 John 1:2 "Beloved, I pray that all may go well with you and that you may be in good health, as it goes well with your soul."

How did I spend my 15 minutes of "me" time today? _____
_____

How will I spend my 15 minutes of "me" time tomorrow? _____
_____

How did I show gratitude for the ability to move my body today? _____
_____

How will I move tomorrow? _____
_____

Growth:

1 Timothy 4:15 "Practice these things, immerse yourself in them, so that all may see your progress."

What steps did I take towards my goal today? _____
_____

What did today teach me that I will bring into tomorrow? _____
_____

Date:_____

Reflection:

Jeremiah 29:11 "For I know the plans I have for you, declares the Lord, plans for welfare and not for evil, to give you a future and a hope."

What am I celebrating today? _____

_____

What am I grateful for today? _____

_____

What do I need to forgive myself for today? _____

_____

How did I use my gifts today?: _____

_____

Self-care:

3 John 1:2 "Beloved, I pray that all may go well with you and that you may be in good health, as it goes well with your soul."

How did I spend my 15 minutes of "me" time today? _____

_____

How will I spend my 15 minutes of "me" time tomorrow? _____

_____

How did I show gratitude for the ability to move my body today? _____

_____

How will I move tomorrow? _____

_____

Growth:

1 Timothy 4:15 "Practice these things, immerse yourself in them, so that all may see your progress."

What steps did I take towards my goal today? _____

_____

What did today teach me that I will bring into tomorrow? _____

_____

Date:_____

Reflection:

Jeremiah 29:11 "For I know the plans I have for you, declares the Lord, plans for welfare and not for evil, to give you a future and a hope."

What am I celebrating today? _____

_____

What am I grateful for today? _____

_____

What do I need to forgive myself for today? _____

_____

How did I use my gifts today?: _____

_____

Self-care:

3 John 1:2 "Beloved, I pray that all may go well with you and that you may be in good health, as it goes well with your soul."

How did I spend my 15 minutes of "me" time today? _____

_____

How will I spend my 15 minutes of "me" time tomorrow? _____

_____

How did I show gratitude for the ability to move my body today? _____

_____

How will I move tomorrow? _____

_____

Growth:

1 Timothy 4:15 "Practice these things, immerse yourself in them, so that all may see your progress."

What steps did I take towards my goal today? _____

_____

What did today teach me that I will bring into tomorrow? _____

_____

Date:_____

Reflection:

Jeremiah 29:11 "For I know the plans I have for you, declares the Lord, plans for welfare and not for evil, to give you a future and a hope."

What am I celebrating today? _____

_____

What am I grateful for today? _____

_____

What do I need to forgive myself for today? _____

_____

How did I use my gifts today?: _____

_____

Self-care:

3 John 1:2 "Beloved, I pray that all may go well with you and that you may be in good health, as it goes well with your soul."

How did I spend my 15 minutes of "me" time today? _____

_____

How will I spend my 15 minutes of "me" time tomorrow? _____

_____

How did I show gratitude for the ability to move my body today? ____

_____

How will I move tomorrow? _____

_____

Growth:

1 Timothy 4:15 "Practice these things, immerse yourself in them, so that all may see your progress."

What steps did I take towards my goal today? _____

_____

What did today teach me that I will bring into tomorrow? _____

_____

Reflection:

Jeremiah 29:11 "For I know the plans I have for you, declares the Lord, plans for welfare and not for evil, to give you a future and a hope."

What am I celebrating today? _____

_____

What am I grateful for today? _____

_____

What do I need to forgive myself for today? _____

_____

How did I use my gifts today?: _____

_____

Self-care:

3 John 1:2 "Beloved, I pray that all may go well with you and that you may be in good health, as it goes well with your soul."

How did I spend my 15 minutes of "me" time today? _____

_____

How will I spend my 15 minutes of "me" time tomorrow? _____

_____

How did I show gratitude for the ability to move my body today? _____

_____

How will I move tomorrow? _____

_____

Growth:

1 Timothy 4:15 "Practice these things, immerse yourself in them, so that all may see your progress."

What steps did I take towards my goal today? _____

_____

What did today teach me that I will bring into tomorrow? _____

_____

Date:_____

Reflection:

Jeremiah 29:11 "For I know the plans I have for you, declares the Lord, plans for welfare and not for evil, to give you a future and a hope."

What am I celebrating today? _____

_____

What am I grateful for today? _____

_____

What do I need to forgive myself for today? _____

_____

How did I use my gifts today?: _____

_____

Self-care:

3 John 1:2 "Beloved, I pray that all may go well with you and that you may be in good health, as it goes well with your soul."

How did I spend my 15 minutes of "me" time today? _____

_____

How will I spend my 15 minutes of "me" time tomorrow? _____

_____

How did I show gratitude for the ability to move my body today? _____

_____

How will I move tomorrow? _____

_____

Growth:

1 Timothy 4:15 "Practice these things, immerse yourself in them, so that all may see your progress."

What steps did I take towards my goal today? _____

_____

What did today teach me that I will bring into tomorrow? _____

_____

Date:_____

Reflection:

Jeremiah 29:11 "For I know the plans I have for you, declares the Lord, plans for welfare and not for evil, to give you a future and a hope."

What am I celebrating today? _____
_____

What am I grateful for today? _____
_____

What do I need to forgive myself for today? _____
_____

How did I use my gifts today?: _____
_____

Self-care:

3 John 1:2 "Beloved, I pray that all may go well with you and that you may be in good health, as it goes well with your soul."

How did I spend my 15 minutes of "me" time today? _____
_____

How will I spend my 15 minutes of "me" time tomorrow? _____
_____

How did I show gratitude for the ability to move my body today? _____
_____

How will I move tomorrow? _____
_____

Growth:

1 Timothy 4:15 "Practice these things, immerse yourself in them, so that all may see your progress."

What steps did I take towards my goal today? _____
_____

What did today teach me that I will bring into tomorrow? _____
_____

Matthew 6:14-15 "For if you forgive others their trespasses, your heavenly father will also forgive you, but if you do not forgive others their trespasses, neither will your Father forgive your trespasses."

I want to speak about time. Time to US is so short. There may be moments where we feel as though time is standing still. When we look back at it, time was passing us by. What is important to us one moment, is nonsense the next. As a mother I find myself clinging to the moments that bring me so much joy, while trying to forget the moments I feel anxious and irritable. My instinct is to love and protect my young ones. My instinct is to cheer on my little ones through every single mundane moment. I say time and time again, we are put on this Earth to love one another, just as Christ loves us. The old African saying is true "it takes a village to raise a child." Our instincts should not only be to love and protect our own, but to also love and protect those around us. I am very blessed to have had the opportunity to travel to other countries to help mothers who rely on a "village" of others for simple practices such as dental and medical supplies and care, as well as building a roof over a family's head. Tragedies around us leave us weeping and yearning to hug our loved ones. At times, it leaves us yearning to do the same for others who may not be our own. Time for us is short. Let us not waste a single second with pettiness. Let us not waste a single second with competitive nature. Let us not waste a single second throwing a dagger towards another mother. Instead, let us put down our petty ways and reach out to that fellow mom. Love on her. Love on all, mom, man, woman, and child. There will be times we fail on this aspect. Do not let that draw you backwards. Pick up exactly where you were, forgive and forget, and move on. I challenge you this week if you are holding a grudge on anyone…. DROP IT. There may be no need to sit down with the person to go over what he or she did, or how you responded. Send a simple letter even. Just say these words, "It's dropped." Remember, we are ALL in this together.

Let this serve as a reminder to you this week:

He sees you.

He hears you.

He loves you.

Weekly Challenge:

It's time to reflect on your entries from last week. Pray. Meditate. Celebrate.

Date:_____

Reflection:

Jeremiah 29:11 "For I know the plans I have for you, declares the Lord, plans for welfare and not for evil, to give you a future and a hope."

What am I celebrating today? _____

_____

What am I grateful for today? _____

_____

What do I need to forgive myself for today? _____

_____

How did I use my gifts today?: _____

_____

Self-care:

3 John 1:2 "Beloved, I pray that all may go well with you and that you may be in good health, as it goes well with your soul."

How did I spend my 15 minutes of "me" time today? _____

_____

How will I spend my 15 minutes of "me" time tomorrow? _____

_____

How did I show gratitude for the ability to move my body today? _____

_____

How will I move tomorrow? _____

_____

Growth:

1 Timothy 4:15 "Practice these things, immerse yourself in them, so that all may see your progress."

What steps did I take towards my goal today? _____

_____

What did today teach me that I will bring into tomorrow? _____

_____

Date:_____

Reflection:

Jeremiah 29:11 "For I know the plans I have for you, declares the Lord, plans for welfare and not for evil, to give you a future and a hope."

What am I celebrating today? _____

_____

What am I grateful for today? _____

_____

What do I need to forgive myself for today? _____

_____

How did I use my gifts today?: _____

_____

Self-care:

3 John 1:2 "Beloved, I pray that all may go well with you and that you may be in good health, as it goes well with your soul."

How did I spend my 15 minutes of "me" time today? _____

_____

How will I spend my 15 minutes of "me" time tomorrow? _____

_____

How did I show gratitude for the ability to move my body today? _____

_____

How will I move tomorrow? _____

_____

Growth:

1 Timothy 4:15 "Practice these things, immerse yourself in them, so that all may see your progress."

What steps did I take towards my goal today? _____

_____

What did today teach me that I will bring into tomorrow? _____

_____

Date:_____

Reflection:

Jeremiah 29:11 "For I know the plans I have for you, declares the Lord, plans for welfare and not for evil, to give you a future and a hope."

What am I celebrating today? _____

_____

What am I grateful for today? _____

_____

What do I need to forgive myself for today? _____

_____

How did I use my gifts today?: _____

_____

Self-care:

3 John 1:2 "Beloved, I pray that all may go well with you and that you may be in good health, as it goes well with your soul."

How did I spend my 15 minutes of "me" time today? _____

_____

How will I spend my 15 minutes of "me" time tomorrow? _____

_____

How did I show gratitude for the ability to move my body today? _____

_____

How will I move tomorrow? _____

_____

Growth:

1 Timothy 4:15 "Practice these things, immerse yourself in them, so that all may see your progress."

What steps did I take towards my goal today? _____

_____

What did today teach me that I will bring into tomorrow? _____

_____

Date:_____

Reflection:

Jeremiah 29:11 "For I know the plans I have for you, declares the Lord, plans for welfare and not for evil, to give you a future and a hope."

What am I celebrating today? _____

_____

What am I grateful for today? _____

_____

What do I need to forgive myself for today? _____

_____

How did I use my gifts today?: _____

_____

Self-care:

3 John 1:2 "Beloved, I pray that all may go well with you and that you may be in good health, as it goes well with your soul."

How did I spend my 15 minutes of "me" time today? _____

_____

How will I spend my 15 minutes of "me" time tomorrow? _____

_____

How did I show gratitude for the ability to move my body today? _____

_____

How will I move tomorrow? _____

_____

Growth:

1 Timothy 4:15 "Practice these things, immerse yourself in them, so that all may see your progress."

What steps did I take towards my goal today? _____

_____

What did today teach me that I will bring into tomorrow? _____

_____

Date:_____

Reflection:

Jeremiah 29:11 "For I know the plans I have for you, declares the Lord, plans for welfare and not for evil, to give you a future and a hope."

What am I celebrating today? _____

_____

What am I grateful for today? _____

_____

What do I need to forgive myself for today? _____

_____

How did I use my gifts today?: _____

_____

Self-care:

3 John 1:2 "Beloved, I pray that all may go well with you and that you may be in good health, as it goes well with your soul."

How did I spend my 15 minutes of "me" time today? _____

_____

How will I spend my 15 minutes of "me" time tomorrow? _____

_____

How did I show gratitude for the ability to move my body today? _____

_____

How will I move tomorrow? _____

_____

Growth:

1 Timothy 4:15 "Practice these things, immerse yourself in them, so that all may see your progress."

What steps did I take towards my goal today? _____

_____

What did today teach me that I will bring into tomorrow? _____

_____

Date:_____

Reflection:

Jeremiah 29:11 "For I know the plans I have for you, declares the Lord, plans for welfare and not for evil, to give you a future and a hope."

What am I celebrating today? _____

_____

What am I grateful for today? _____

_____

What do I need to forgive myself for today? _____

_____

How did I use my gifts today?: _____

_____

Self-care:

3 John 1:2 "Beloved, I pray that all may go well with you and that you may be in good health, as it goes well with your soul."

How did I spend my 15 minutes of "me" time today? _____

_____

How will I spend my 15 minutes of "me" time tomorrow? _____

_____

How did I show gratitude for the ability to move my body today? _____

_____

How will I move tomorrow? _____

_____

Growth:

1 Timothy 4:15 "Practice these things, immerse yourself in them, so that all may see your progress."

What steps did I take towards my goal today? _____

_____

What did today teach me that I will bring into tomorrow? _____

_____

Date:_____

Reflection:

Jeremiah 29:11 "For I know the plans I have for you, declares the Lord, plans for welfare and not for evil, to give you a future and a hope."

What am I celebrating today? _____

_____

What am I grateful for today? _____

_____

What do I need to forgive myself for today? _____

_____

How did I use my gifts today?: _____

_____

Self-care:

3 John 1:2 "Beloved, I pray that all may go well with you and that you may be in good health, as it goes well with your soul."

How did I spend my 15 minutes of "me" time today? _____

_____

How will I spend my 15 minutes of "me" time tomorrow? _____

_____

How did I show gratitude for the ability to move my body today? _____

_____

How will I move tomorrow? _____

_____

Growth:

1 Timothy 4:15 "Practice these things, immerse yourself in them, so that all may see your progress."

What steps did I take towards my goal today? _____

_____

What did today teach me that I will bring into tomorrow? _____

_____

Ephesians 2:10 "For we are his workmanship, created in Christ Jesus for good works, which God prepared beforehand, that we should walk in them."

This week it is tugging on my heart to remind you of these three simple words: YOU ARE ENOUGH. Let those words soak in and reflect. From reflection comes growth. Let this be all you need to hear this week.

Let this serve as a reminder to you this week:

He sees you.

He hears you.

He loves you.

<u>Weekly Challenge:</u>

It's time to reflect on your entries from last week. Pray. Meditate. Celebrate.

Date:_____

Reflection:

Jeremiah 29:11 "For I know the plans I have for you, declares the Lord, plans for welfare and not for evil, to give you a future and a hope."

What am I celebrating today? _____

_____

What am I grateful for today? _____

_____

What do I need to forgive myself for today? _____

_____

How did I use my gifts today?: _____

_____

Self-care:

3 John 1:2 "Beloved, I pray that all may go well with you and that you may be in good health, as it goes well with your soul."

How did I spend my 15 minutes of "me" time today? _____

_____

How will I spend my 15 minutes of "me" time tomorrow? _____

_____

How did I show gratitude for the ability to move my body today? _____

_____

How will I move tomorrow? _____

_____

Growth:

1 Timothy 4:15 "Practice these things, immerse yourself in them, so that all may see your progress."

What steps did I take towards my goal today? _____

_____

What did today teach me that I will bring into tomorrow? _____

_____

Date:_____

Reflection:

Jeremiah 29:11 "For I know the plans I have for you, declares the Lord, plans for welfare and not for evil, to give you a future and a hope."

What am I celebrating today? _____

_____

What am I grateful for today? _____

_____

What do I need to forgive myself for today? _____

_____

How did I use my gifts today?: _____

_____

Self-care:

3 John 1:2 "Beloved, I pray that all may go well with you and that you may be in good health, as it goes well with your soul."

How did I spend my 15 minutes of "me" time today? _____

_____

How will I spend my 15 minutes of "me" time tomorrow? _____

_____

How did I show gratitude for the ability to move my body today? _____

_____

How will I move tomorrow? _____

_____

Growth:

1 Timothy 4:15 "Practice these things, immerse yourself in them, so that all may see your progress."

What steps did I take towards my goal today? _____

_____

What did today teach me that I will bring into tomorrow? _____

_____

Date:_____

Reflection:

Jeremiah 29:11 "For I know the plans I have for you, declares the Lord, plans for welfare and not for evil, to give you a future and a hope."

What am I celebrating today? _____

_____

What am I grateful for today? _____

_____

What do I need to forgive myself for today? _____

_____

How did I use my gifts today?: _____

_____

Self-care:

3 John 1:2 "Beloved, I pray that all may go well with you and that you may be in good health, as it goes well with your soul."

How did I spend my 15 minutes of "me" time today? _____

_____

How will I spend my 15 minutes of "me" time tomorrow? _____

_____

How did I show gratitude for the ability to move my body today? _____

_____

How will I move tomorrow? _____

_____

Growth:

1 Timothy 4:15 "Practice these things, immerse yourself in them, so that all may see your progress."

What steps did I take towards my goal today? _____

_____

What did today teach me that I will bring into tomorrow? _____

_____

Reflection:

Jeremiah 29:11 "For I know the plans I have for you, declares the Lord, plans for welfare and not for evil, to give you a future and a hope."

What am I celebrating today? _____

_____

What am I grateful for today? _____

_____

What do I need to forgive myself for today? _____

_____

How did I use my gifts today?: _____

_____

Self-care:

3 John 1:2 "Beloved, I pray that all may go well with you and that you may be in good health, as it goes well with your soul."

How did I spend my 15 minutes of "me" time today? _____

_____

How will I spend my 15 minutes of "me" time tomorrow? _____

_____

How did I show gratitude for the ability to move my body today? _____

_____

How will I move tomorrow? _____

_____

Growth:

1 Timothy 4:15 "Practice these things, immerse yourself in them, so that all may see your progress."

What steps did I take towards my goal today? _____

_____

What did today teach me that I will bring into tomorrow? _____

_____

Date:_____

Reflection:

Jeremiah 29:11 "For I know the plans I have for you, declares the Lord, plans for welfare and not for evil, to give you a future and a hope."

What am I celebrating today? _____

_____

What am I grateful for today? _____

_____

What do I need to forgive myself for today? _____

_____

How did I use my gifts today?: _____

_____

Self-care:

3 John 1:2 "Beloved, I pray that all may go well with you and that you may be in good health, as it goes well with your soul."

How did I spend my 15 minutes of "me" time today? _____

_____

How will I spend my 15 minutes of "me" time tomorrow? _____

_____

How did I show gratitude for the ability to move my body today? _____

_____

How will I move tomorrow? _____

_____

Growth:

1 Timothy 4:15 "Practice these things, immerse yourself in them, so that all may see your progress."

What steps did I take towards my goal today? _____

_____

What did today teach me that I will bring into tomorrow? _____

_____

Date:_____

Reflection:

Jeremiah 29:11 "For I know the plans I have for you, declares the Lord, plans for welfare and not for evil, to give you a future and a hope."

What am I celebrating today? _____

_____

What am I grateful for today? _____

_____

What do I need to forgive myself for today? _____

_____

How did I use my gifts today?: _____

_____

Self-care:

3 John 1:2 "Beloved, I pray that all may go well with you and that you may be in good health, as it goes well with your soul."

How did I spend my 15 minutes of "me" time today? _____

_____

How will I spend my 15 minutes of "me" time tomorrow? _____

_____

How did I show gratitude for the ability to move my body today? _____

_____

How will I move tomorrow? _____

_____

Growth:

1 Timothy 4:15 "Practice these things, immerse yourself in them, so that all may see your progress."

What steps did I take towards my goal today? _____

_____

What did today teach me that I will bring into tomorrow? _____

_____

Date:_____

Reflection:

Jeremiah 29:11 "For I know the plans I have for you, declares the Lord, plans for welfare and not for evil, to give you a future and a hope."

What am I celebrating today? _____

_____

What am I grateful for today? _____

_____

What do I need to forgive myself for today? _____

_____

How did I use my gifts today?: _____

_____

Self-care:

3 John 1:2 "Beloved, I pray that all may go well with you and that you may be in good health, as it goes well with your soul."

How did I spend my 15 minutes of "me" time today? _____

_____

How will I spend my 15 minutes of "me" time tomorrow? _____

_____

How did I show gratitude for the ability to move my body today? _____

_____

How will I move tomorrow? _____

_____

Growth:

1 Timothy 4:15 "Practice these things, immerse yourself in them, so that all may see your progress."

What steps did I take towards my goal today? _____

_____

What did today teach me that I will bring into tomorrow? _____

_____

Isaiah 40:29 "He gives power to the faint, and to him who has no might he increases strength."

Sometimes us moms forget how strong we are. We are so used to giving every bit of ourselves to caring for others, that we lose us at times. We all need something that brings us back to that place where we felt that strength. For me, I reflect on the birth of my two boys. I felt the strength of the Lord in both those moments. Think back at a time where you felt strong. That could be a time you felt physical strength or a time you felt mental strength. Reflect on that time when you feel weakness creeping in. Never forget "where we are weak, He is strong."

Let this serve as a reminder to you this week:

He sees you.

He hears you.

He loves you.

Weekly Challenge:

It's time to reflect on your entries from last week. Pray. Meditate. Celebrate.

Date:_____

Reflection:

Jeremiah 29:11 "For I know the plans I have for you, declares the Lord, plans for welfare and not for evil, to give you a future and a hope."

What am I celebrating today? _____

_____

What am I grateful for today? _____

_____

What do I need to forgive myself for today? _____

_____

How did I use my gifts today?: _____

_____

Self-care:

3 John 1:2 "Beloved, I pray that all may go well with you and that you may be in good health, as it goes well with your soul."

How did I spend my 15 minutes of "me" time today? _____

_____

How will I spend my 15 minutes of "me" time tomorrow? _____

_____

How did I show gratitude for the ability to move my body today? _____

_____

How will I move tomorrow? _____

_____

Growth:

1 Timothy 4:15 "Practice these things, immerse yourself in them, so that all may see your progress."

What steps did I take towards my goal today? _____

_____

What did today teach me that I will bring into tomorrow? _____

_____

Date:_____

Reflection:

Jeremiah 29:11 "For I know the plans I have for you, declares the Lord, plans for welfare and not for evil, to give you a future and a hope."

What am I celebrating today? _____

_____

What am I grateful for today? _____

_____

What do I need to forgive myself for today? _____

_____

How did I use my gifts today?: _____

_____

Self-care:

3 John 1:2 "Beloved, I pray that all may go well with you and that you may be in good health, as it goes well with your soul."

How did I spend my 15 minutes of "me" time today? _____

_____

How will I spend my 15 minutes of "me" time tomorrow? _____

_____

How did I show gratitude for the ability to move my body today? _____

_____

How will I move tomorrow? _____

_____

Growth:

1 Timothy 4:15 "Practice these things, immerse yourself in them, so that all may see your progress."

What steps did I take towards my goal today? _____

_____

What did today teach me that I will bring into tomorrow? _____

_____

Date:_____

Reflection:

Jeremiah 29:11 "For I know the plans I have for you, declares the Lord, plans for welfare and not for evil, to give you a future and a hope."

What am I celebrating today? _____

_____

What am I grateful for today? _____

_____

What do I need to forgive myself for today? _____

_____

How did I use my gifts today?: _____

_____

Self-care:

3 John 1:2 "Beloved, I pray that all may go well with you and that you may be in good health, as it goes well with your soul."

How did I spend my 15 minutes of "me" time today? _____

_____

How will I spend my 15 minutes of "me" time tomorrow? _____

_____

How did I show gratitude for the ability to move my body today? _____

_____

How will I move tomorrow? _____

_____

Growth:

1 Timothy 4:15 "Practice these things, immerse yourself in them, so that all may see your progress."

What steps did I take towards my goal today? _____

_____

What did today teach me that I will bring into tomorrow? _____

_____

Date:_____

Reflection:

Jeremiah 29:11 "For I know the plans I have for you, declares the Lord, plans for welfare and not for evil, to give you a future and a hope."

What am I celebrating today? _____

_____

What am I grateful for today? _____

_____

What do I need to forgive myself for today? _____

_____

How did I use my gifts today?: _____

_____

Self-care:

3 John 1:2 "Beloved, I pray that all may go well with you and that you may be in good health, as it goes well with your soul."

How did I spend my 15 minutes of "me" time today? _____

_____

How will I spend my 15 minutes of "me" time tomorrow? _____

_____

How did I show gratitude for the ability to move my body today? _____

_____

How will I move tomorrow? _____

_____

Growth:

1 Timothy 4:15 "Practice these things, immerse yourself in them, so that all may see your progress."

What steps did I take towards my goal today? _____

_____

What did today teach me that I will bring into tomorrow? _____

_____

Reflection:

Jeremiah 29:11 "For I know the plans I have for you, declares the Lord, plans for welfare and not for evil, to give you a future and a hope."

What am I celebrating today? _____

_____

What am I grateful for today? _____

_____

What do I need to forgive myself for today? _____

_____

How did I use my gifts today?: _____

_____

Self-care:

3 John 1:2 "Beloved, I pray that all may go well with you and that you may be in good health, as it goes well with your soul."

How did I spend my 15 minutes of "me" time today? _____

_____

How will I spend my 15 minutes of "me" time tomorrow? _____

_____

How did I show gratitude for the ability to move my body today? _____

_____

How will I move tomorrow? _____

_____

Growth:

1 Timothy 4:15 "Practice these things, immerse yourself in them, so that all may see your progress."

What steps did I take towards my goal today? _____

_____

What did today teach me that I will bring into tomorrow? _____

_____

Date:_____

Reflection:

Jeremiah 29:11 "For I know the plans I have for you, declares the Lord, plans for welfare and not for evil, to give you a future and a hope."

What am I celebrating today? _____
_____

What am I grateful for today? _____
_____

What do I need to forgive myself for today? _____
_____

How did I use my gifts today?: _____
_____

Self-care:

3 John 1:2 "Beloved, I pray that all may go well with you and that you may be in good health, as it goes well with your soul."

How did I spend my 15 minutes of "me" time today? _____
_____

How will I spend my 15 minutes of "me" time tomorrow? _____
_____

How did I show gratitude for the ability to move my body today? _____
_____

How will I move tomorrow? _____
_____

Growth:

1 Timothy 4:15 "Practice these things, immerse yourself in them, so that all may see your progress."

What steps did I take towards my goal today? _____
_____

What did today teach me that I will bring into tomorrow? _____
_____

Date:_____

Reflection:

Jeremiah 29:11 "For I know the plans I have for you, declares the Lord, plans for welfare and not for evil, to give you a future and a hope."

What am I celebrating today? _____

_____

What am I grateful for today? _____

_____

What do I need to forgive myself for today? _____

_____

How did I use my gifts today?: _____

_____

Self-care:

3 John 1:2 "Beloved, I pray that all may go well with you and that you may be in good health, as it goes well with your soul."

How did I spend my 15 minutes of "me" time today? _____

_____

How will I spend my 15 minutes of "me" time tomorrow? _____

_____

How did I show gratitude for the ability to move my body today? _____

_____

How will I move tomorrow? _____

_____

Growth:

1 Timothy 4:15 "Practice these things, immerse yourself in them, so that all may see your progress."

What steps did I take towards my goal today? _____

_____

What did today teach me that I will bring into tomorrow? _____

_____

Psalms 73:26 "My flesh and my heart may fail, but God is the strength of my heart and my portion forever."

Words I hope to leave my children with one day: The thing you are most afraid to step out of your comfort zone to do…DO IT! Fear should never hold you back. If there is a fire in your heart, God put it there for a reason.

I have always been a "yes" person. I have said "yes" to things that I have felt a strong "no" on. There were times I had put aside my desires and dreams to help others build theirs. Now, there is nothing wrong with helping others build, however, after a while that little voice that urges you to complete what you have started in your heart will become louder and louder. Once you begin to say "yes" to that fire God has put in your heart, abundance begins! No idea is too small!! No task is too big!! If you lean on the Lord to give you the courage to begin, He will see you all the way through. If I hadn't leaned on the Lord for courage and strength to write this planner, you would not be reading MY stories in hopes to guide you along your own personal journey. Think big, mom. He has you all the way through.

Let this serve as a reminder to you this week:

He sees you.

He hears you.

He loves you.

Weekly Challenge:

It's time to reflect on your entries from last week. Pray. Meditate. Celebrate.

Date:_____

Reflection:

Jeremiah 29:11 "For I know the plans I have for you, declares the Lord, plans for welfare and not for evil, to give you a future and a hope."

What am I celebrating today? _____

_____

What am I grateful for today? _____

_____

What do I need to forgive myself for today? _____

_____

How did I use my gifts today?: _____

_____

Self-care:

3 John 1:2 "Beloved, I pray that all may go well with you and that you may be in good health, as it goes well with your soul."

How did I spend my 15 minutes of "me" time today? _____

_____

How will I spend my 15 minutes of "me" time tomorrow? _____

_____

How did I show gratitude for the ability to move my body today? _____

_____

How will I move tomorrow? _____

_____

Growth:

1 Timothy 4:15 "Practice these things, immerse yourself in them, so that all may see your progress."

What steps did I take towards my goal today? _____

_____

What did today teach me that I will bring into tomorrow? _____

_____

Date:_____

Reflection:

Jeremiah 29:11 "For I know the plans I have for you, declares the Lord, plans for welfare and not for evil, to give you a future and a hope."

What am I celebrating today? _____

_____

What am I grateful for today? _____

_____

What do I need to forgive myself for today? _____

_____

How did I use my gifts today?: _____

_____

Self-care:

3 John 1:2 "Beloved, I pray that all may go well with you and that you may be in good health, as it goes well with your soul."

How did I spend my 15 minutes of "me" time today? _____

_____

How will I spend my 15 minutes of "me" time tomorrow? _____

_____

How did I show gratitude for the ability to move my body today? _____

_____

How will I move tomorrow? _____

_____

Growth:

1 Timothy 4:15 "Practice these things, immerse yourself in them, so that all may see your progress."

What steps did I take towards my goal today? _____

_____

What did today teach me that I will bring into tomorrow? _____

_____

Date:_____

Reflection:

Jeremiah 29:11 "For I know the plans I have for you, declares the Lord, plans for welfare and not for evil, to give you a future and a hope."

What am I celebrating today? _____

_____

What am I grateful for today? _____

_____

What do I need to forgive myself for today? _____

_____

How did I use my gifts today?: _____

_____

Self-care:

3 John 1:2 "Beloved, I pray that all may go well with you and that you may be in good health, as it goes well with your soul."

How did I spend my 15 minutes of "me" time today? _____

_____

How will I spend my 15 minutes of "me" time tomorrow? _____

_____

How did I show gratitude for the ability to move my body today? _____

_____

How will I move tomorrow? _____

_____

Growth:

1 Timothy 4:15 "Practice these things, immerse yourself in them, so that all may see your progress."

What steps did I take towards my goal today? _____

_____

What did today teach me that I will bring into tomorrow? _____

_____

Date:_____

Reflection:

Jeremiah 29:11 "For I know the plans I have for you, declares the Lord, plans for welfare and not for evil, to give you a future and a hope."

What am I celebrating today? _____

_____

What am I grateful for today? _____

_____

What do I need to forgive myself for today? _____

_____

How did I use my gifts today?: _____

_____

Self-care:

3 John 1:2 "Beloved, I pray that all may go well with you and that you may be in good health, as it goes well with your soul."

How did I spend my 15 minutes of "me" time today? _____

_____

How will I spend my 15 minutes of "me" time tomorrow? _____

_____

How did I show gratitude for the ability to move my body today? _____

_____

How will I move tomorrow? _____

_____

Growth:

1 Timothy 4:15 "Practice these things, immerse yourself in them, so that all may see your progress."

What steps did I take towards my goal today? _____

_____

What did today teach me that I will bring into tomorrow? _____

_____

Date:_____

Reflection:

Jeremiah 29:11 "For I know the plans I have for you, declares the Lord, plans for welfare and not for evil, to give you a future and a hope."

What am I celebrating today? _____

_____

What am I grateful for today? _____

_____

What do I need to forgive myself for today? _____

_____

How did I use my gifts today?: _____

_____

Self-care:

3 John 1:2 "Beloved, I pray that all may go well with you and that you may be in good health, as it goes well with your soul."

How did I spend my 15 minutes of "me" time today? _____

_____

How will I spend my 15 minutes of "me" time tomorrow? _____

_____

How did I show gratitude for the ability to move my body today? _____

_____

How will I move tomorrow? _____

_____

Growth:

1 Timothy 4:15 "Practice these things, immerse yourself in them, so that all may see your progress."

What steps did I take towards my goal today? _____

_____

What did today teach me that I will bring into tomorrow? _____

_____

Date:_____

Reflection:

Jeremiah 29:11 "For I know the plans I have for you, declares the Lord, plans for welfare and not for evil, to give you a future and a hope."

What am I celebrating today? _____

_____

What am I grateful for today? _____

_____

What do I need to forgive myself for today? _____

_____

How did I use my gifts today?: _____

_____

Self-care:

3 John 1:2 "Beloved, I pray that all may go well with you and that you may be in good health, as it goes well with your soul."

How did I spend my 15 minutes of "me" time today? _____

_____

How will I spend my 15 minutes of "me" time tomorrow? _____

_____

How did I show gratitude for the ability to move my body today? _____

_____

How will I move tomorrow? _____

_____

Growth:

1 Timothy 4:15 "Practice these things, immerse yourself in them, so that all may see your progress."

What steps did I take towards my goal today? _____

_____

What did today teach me that I will bring into tomorrow? _____

_____

Date:_____

Reflection:

Jeremiah 29:11 "For I know the plans I have for you, declares the Lord, plans for welfare and not for evil, to give you a future and a hope."

What am I celebrating today? _____

_____

What am I grateful for today? _____

_____

What do I need to forgive myself for today? _____

_____

How did I use my gifts today?: _____

_____

Self-care:

3 John 1:2 "Beloved, I pray that all may go well with you and that you may be in good health, as it goes well with your soul."

How did I spend my 15 minutes of "me" time today? _____

_____

How will I spend my 15 minutes of "me" time tomorrow? _____

_____

How did I show gratitude for the ability to move my body today? _____

_____

How will I move tomorrow? _____

_____

Growth:

1 Timothy 4:15 "Practice these things, immerse yourself in them, so that all may see your progress."

What steps did I take towards my goal today? _____

_____

What did today teach me that I will bring into tomorrow? _____

_____

Psalms 139:13-14 "For you formed my inward parts; you knitted me together in my mother's womb. I praise you, for I am fearfully and wonderfully made. Wonderful are your works; my soul knows it very well."

Mom, I was wanting to take this opportunity to acknowledge how amazing you are. Whether you feel like you have it all together or completely falling apart. Either way, that is ok! I will share a little secret with you. Some days it takes me HOURS to get it together. Some days it takes me over 4 hours just to get some makeup on, do my hair, all to go to work for an evening shift. There are days start getting ready at 11:30am and I walk around with only one eye of makeup done for over 2 hours until I can put the baby down and finish with the other eye. Does this sound familiar? As stressed as I am in those moments, it always works out ok. You may feel nothing but chaos in that moment. Wait for that moment to pass and I promise if you rest in the Lord and find peace in Him, as difficult as it may be in that exact moment, it will all be ok.

Let this serve as a reminder to you this week:

He sees you.

He hears you.

He loves you.

Weekly Challenge:

It's time to reflect on your entries from last week. Pray. Meditate. Celebrate.

Date:_____

Reflection:

Jeremiah 29:11 "For I know the plans I have for you, declares the Lord, plans for welfare and not for evil, to give you a future and a hope."

What am I celebrating today? _____

_____

What am I grateful for today? _____

_____

What do I need to forgive myself for today? _____

_____

How did I use my gifts today?: _____

_____

Self-care:

3 John 1:2 "Beloved, I pray that all may go well with you and that you may be in good health, as it goes well with your soul."

How did I spend my 15 minutes of "me" time today? _____

_____

How will I spend my 15 minutes of "me" time tomorrow? _____

_____

How did I show gratitude for the ability to move my body today? _____

_____

How will I move tomorrow? _____

_____

Growth:

1 Timothy 4:15 "Practice these things, immerse yourself in them, so that all may see your progress."

What steps did I take towards my goal today? _____

_____

What did today teach me that I will bring into tomorrow? _____

_____

Date:_____

Reflection:

Jeremiah 29:11 "For I know the plans I have for you, declares the Lord, plans for welfare and not for evil, to give you a future and a hope."

What am I celebrating today? _____

_____

What am I grateful for today? _____

_____

What do I need to forgive myself for today? _____

_____

How did I use my gifts today?: _____

_____

Self-care:

3 John 1:2 "Beloved, I pray that all may go well with you and that you may be in good health, as it goes well with your soul."

How did I spend my 15 minutes of "me" time today? _____

_____

How will I spend my 15 minutes of "me" time tomorrow? _____

_____

How did I show gratitude for the ability to move my body today? _____

_____

How will I move tomorrow? _____

_____

Growth:

1 Timothy 4:15 "Practice these things, immerse yourself in them, so that all may see your progress."

What steps did I take towards my goal today? _____

_____

What did today teach me that I will bring into tomorrow? _____

_____

Date:_____

Reflection:

Jeremiah 29:11 "For I know the plans I have for you, declares the Lord, plans for welfare and not for evil, to give you a future and a hope."

What am I celebrating today? _____

_____

What am I grateful for today? _____

_____

What do I need to forgive myself for today? _____

_____

How did I use my gifts today?: _____

_____

Self-care:

3 John 1:2 "Beloved, I pray that all may go well with you and that you may be in good health, as it goes well with your soul."

How did I spend my 15 minutes of "me" time today? _____

_____

How will I spend my 15 minutes of "me" time tomorrow? _____

_____

How did I show gratitude for the ability to move my body today? _____

_____

How will I move tomorrow? _____

_____

Growth:

1 Timothy 4:15 "Practice these things, immerse yourself in them, so that all may see your progress."

What steps did I take towards my goal today? _____

_____

What did today teach me that I will bring into tomorrow? _____

_____

Date:_____

Reflection:

Jeremiah 29:11 "For I know the plans I have for you, declares the Lord, plans for welfare and not for evil, to give you a future and a hope."

What am I celebrating today? _____

_____

What am I grateful for today? _____

_____

What do I need to forgive myself for today? _____

_____

How did I use my gifts today?: _____

_____

Self-care:

3 John 1:2 "Beloved, I pray that all may go well with you and that you may be in good health, as it goes well with your soul."

How did I spend my 15 minutes of "me" time today? _____

_____

How will I spend my 15 minutes of "me" time tomorrow? _____

_____

How did I show gratitude for the ability to move my body today? _____

_____

How will I move tomorrow? _____

_____

Growth:

1 Timothy 4:15 "Practice these things, immerse yourself in them, so that all may see your progress."

What steps did I take towards my goal today? _____

_____

What did today teach me that I will bring into tomorrow? _____

_____

Date:_____

Reflection:

Jeremiah 29:11 "For I know the plans I have for you, declares the Lord, plans for welfare and not for evil, to give you a future and a hope."

What am I celebrating today? _____

_____

What am I grateful for today? _____

_____

What do I need to forgive myself for today? _____

_____

How did I use my gifts today?: _____

_____

Self-care:

3 John 1:2 "Beloved, I pray that all may go well with you and that you may be in good health, as it goes well with your soul."

How did I spend my 15 minutes of "me" time today? _____

_____

How will I spend my 15 minutes of "me" time tomorrow? _____

_____

How did I show gratitude for the ability to move my body today? _____

_____

How will I move tomorrow? _____

_____

Growth:

1 Timothy 4:15 "Practice these things, immerse yourself in them, so that all may see your progress."

What steps did I take towards my goal today? _____

_____

What did today teach me that I will bring into tomorrow? _____

_____

Date:_____

Reflection:

Jeremiah 29:11 "For I know the plans I have for you, declares the Lord, plans for welfare and not for evil, to give you a future and a hope."

What am I celebrating today? _____
_____

What am I grateful for today? _____
_____

What do I need to forgive myself for today? _____
_____

How did I use my gifts today?: _____
_____

Self-care:

3 John 1:2 "Beloved, I pray that all may go well with you and that you may be in good health, as it goes well with your soul."

How did I spend my 15 minutes of "me" time today? _____
_____

How will I spend my 15 minutes of "me" time tomorrow? _____
_____

How did I show gratitude for the ability to move my body today? _____
_____

How will I move tomorrow? _____
_____

Growth:

1 Timothy 4:15 "Practice these things, immerse yourself in them, so that all may see your progress."

What steps did I take towards my goal today? _____
_____

What did today teach me that I will bring into tomorrow? _____
_____

Reflection:

Jeremiah 29:11 "For I know the plans I have for you, declares the Lord, plans for welfare and not for evil, to give you a future and a hope."

What am I celebrating today? _____

What am I grateful for today? _____

What do I need to forgive myself for today? _____

How did I use my gifts today?: _____

Self-care:

3 John 1:2 "Beloved, I pray that all may go well with you and that you may be in good health, as it goes well with your soul."

How did I spend my 15 minutes of "me" time today? _____

How will I spend my 15 minutes of "me" time tomorrow? _____

How did I show gratitude for the ability to move my body today? _____

How will I move tomorrow? _____

Growth:

1 Timothy 4:15 "Practice these things, immerse yourself in them, so that all may see your progress."

What steps did I take towards my goal today? _____

What did today teach me that I will bring into tomorrow? _____

Matthew 11:28-30 "Come to me, all who labor and are heavy laden, and I will give you rest. Take my yoke upon you, and learn from me, for I am gentle and lowly in heart, and you will find rest for your souls. For my yoke is easy, and my burden is light."

I am sure you have heard the saying "keep going because your children are always watching." This is true, they are always watching. This is one reason why we need to be shining examples to them of how to walk in His will. However, mom, please remember if you cannot keep going, it is OK to rest. This journey is about progress and not about perfection. You cannot forget to pour into yourself. It is difficult to be the best mom you can be if you are running on empty. Just because someone may say "they are always watching," remember that they are also watching what you are doing for YOU. They are watching when you are allowing your needs to be met mentally, spiritually, and physically. Do not forget that the Lord put you on this journey because He knew only YOU could be the best mother to the children you have. Rest in Him and your children will follow your example.

Let this serve as a reminder to you this week:

He sees you.

He hears you.

He loves you.

Weekly Challenge:

It's time to reflect on your entries from last week. Pray. Meditate. Celebrate.

Date:_____

Reflection:

Jeremiah 29:11 "For I know the plans I have for you, declares the Lord, plans for welfare and not for evil, to give you a future and a hope."

What am I celebrating today? _____

_____

What am I grateful for today? _____

_____

What do I need to forgive myself for today? _____

_____

How did I use my gifts today?: _____

_____

Self-care:

3 John 1:2 "Beloved, I pray that all may go well with you and that you may be in good health, as it goes well with your soul."

How did I spend my 15 minutes of "me" time today? _____

_____

How will I spend my 15 minutes of "me" time tomorrow? _____

_____

How did I show gratitude for the ability to move my body today? _____

_____

How will I move tomorrow? _____

_____

Growth:

1 Timothy 4:15 "Practice these things, immerse yourself in them, so that all may see your progress."

What steps did I take towards my goal today? _____

_____

What did today teach me that I will bring into tomorrow? _____

_____

Date:_____

Reflection:

Jeremiah 29:11 "For I know the plans I have for you, declares the Lord, plans for welfare and not for evil, to give you a future and a hope."

What am I celebrating today? _____

_____

What am I grateful for today? _____

_____

What do I need to forgive myself for today? _____

_____

How did I use my gifts today?: _____

_____

Self-care:

3 John 1:2 "Beloved, I pray that all may go well with you and that you may be in good health, as it goes well with your soul."

How did I spend my 15 minutes of "me" time today? _____

_____

How will I spend my 15 minutes of "me" time tomorrow? _____

_____

How did I show gratitude for the ability to move my body today? _____

_____

How will I move tomorrow? _____

_____

Growth:

1 Timothy 4:15 "Practice these things, immerse yourself in them, so that all may see your progress."

What steps did I take towards my goal today? _____

_____

What did today teach me that I will bring into tomorrow? _____

_____

Date:_____

Reflection:

Jeremiah 29:11 "For I know the plans I have for you, declares the Lord, plans for welfare and not for evil, to give you a future and a hope."

What am I celebrating today? _____

_____

What am I grateful for today? _____

_____

What do I need to forgive myself for today? _____

_____

How did I use my gifts today?: _____

_____

Self-care:

3 John 1:2 "Beloved, I pray that all may go well with you and that you may be in good health, as it goes well with your soul."

How did I spend my 15 minutes of "me" time today? _____

_____

How will I spend my 15 minutes of "me" time tomorrow? _____

_____

How did I show gratitude for the ability to move my body today? _____

_____

How will I move tomorrow? _____

_____

Growth:

1 Timothy 4:15 "Practice these things, immerse yourself in them, so that all may see your progress."

What steps did I take towards my goal today? _____

_____

What did today teach me that I will bring into tomorrow? _____

_____

Date:_____

Reflection:

Jeremiah 29:11 "For I know the plans I have for you, declares the Lord, plans for welfare and not for evil, to give you a future and a hope."

What am I celebrating today? _____

What am I grateful for today? _____

What do I need to forgive myself for today? _____

How did I use my gifts today?: _____

Self-care:

3 John 1:2 "Beloved, I pray that all may go well with you and that you may be in good health, as it goes well with your soul."

How did I spend my 15 minutes of "me" time today? _____

How will I spend my 15 minutes of "me" time tomorrow? _____

How did I show gratitude for the ability to move my body today? _____

How will I move tomorrow? _____

Growth:

1 Timothy 4:15 "Practice these things, immerse yourself in them, so that all may see your progress."

What steps did I take towards my goal today? _____

What did today teach me that I will bring into tomorrow? _____

Date:_____

Reflection:

Jeremiah 29:11 "For I know the plans I have for you, declares the Lord, plans for welfare and not for evil, to give you a future and a hope."

What am I celebrating today? _____

_____

What am I grateful for today? _____

_____

What do I need to forgive myself for today? _____

_____

How did I use my gifts today?: _____

_____

Self-care:

3 John 1:2 "Beloved, I pray that all may go well with you and that you may be in good health, as it goes well with your soul."

How did I spend my 15 minutes of "me" time today? _____

_____

How will I spend my 15 minutes of "me" time tomorrow? _____

_____

How did I show gratitude for the ability to move my body today? _____

_____

How will I move tomorrow? _____

_____

Growth:

1 Timothy 4:15 "Practice these things, immerse yourself in them, so that all may see your progress."

What steps did I take towards my goal today? _____

_____

What did today teach me that I will bring into tomorrow? _____

_____

Date:_____

Reflection:

Jeremiah 29:11 "For I know the plans I have for you, declares the Lord, plans for welfare and not for evil, to give you a future and a hope."

What am I celebrating today? _____

_____

What am I grateful for today? _____

_____

What do I need to forgive myself for today? _____

_____

How did I use my gifts today?: _____

_____

Self-care:

3 John 1:2 "Beloved, I pray that all may go well with you and that you may be in good health, as it goes well with your soul."

How did I spend my 15 minutes of "me" time today? _____

_____

How will I spend my 15 minutes of "me" time tomorrow? _____

_____

How did I show gratitude for the ability to move my body today? _____

_____

How will I move tomorrow? _____

_____

Growth:

1 Timothy 4:15 "Practice these things, immerse yourself in them, so that all may see your progress."

What steps did I take towards my goal today? _____

_____

What did today teach me that I will bring into tomorrow? _____

_____

Date:_____

Reflection:

Jeremiah 29:11 "For I know the plans I have for you, declares the Lord, plans for welfare and not for evil, to give you a future and a hope."

What am I celebrating today? _____

_____

What am I grateful for today? _____

_____

What do I need to forgive myself for today? _____

_____

How did I use my gifts today?: _____

_____

Self-care:

3 John 1:2 "Beloved, I pray that all may go well with you and that you may be in good health, as it goes well with your soul."

How did I spend my 15 minutes of "me" time today? _____

_____

How will I spend my 15 minutes of "me" time tomorrow? _____

_____

How did I show gratitude for the ability to move my body today? _____

_____

How will I move tomorrow? _____

_____

Growth:

1 Timothy 4:15 "Practice these things, immerse yourself in them, so that all may see your progress."

What steps did I take towards my goal today? _____

_____

What did today teach me that I will bring into tomorrow? _____

_____

2 Timothy 4:7 "I have fought the good fight, I have finished the race, I have kept the faith."

Empowerment. What does that mean to you? As a mom, how important is it to feel empowered? To me and my journey, this is something I needed to feel many times. Now, let us think about how you are empowering OTHER moms. Are you empowering others by giving them words of encouragement and telling them "you can do it! You'll get through this!" To me, to empower a mom or anyone else, means to give them the tools they may need to succeed. When you see a mom, or anyone at that, who may need help just to get through the day, it may be more helpful to not just stop to let them know it gets easier or that they can do it. Let us make a commitment, as a community of moms and sisters, to help guide them through the tough time. Let us begin to mentor other mothers on the strengths we may have. Let us take that mom under our wing and be there when they may need a hand to hold. That is what the Lord does for us each day. As we strive to be more like Him, it a good reminder to guide other moms along this journey. We are not called to compete with one another. We are called to encourage and empower one another in every way we can. Pour into another mom today. I encourage you to not look at any other mother as "less than." Make her feel "greater" than!

Let this serve as a reminder to you this week:

He sees you.

He hears you.

He loves you.

Weekly Challenge:

It's time to reflect on your entries from last week. Pray. Meditate. Celebrate.

Date:_____

Reflection:

Jeremiah 29:11 "For I know the plans I have for you, declares the Lord, plans for welfare and not for evil, to give you a future and a hope."

What am I celebrating today? _____
_____

What am I grateful for today? _____
_____

What do I need to forgive myself for today? _____
_____

How did I use my gifts today?: _____
_____

Self-care:

3 John 1:2 "Beloved, I pray that all may go well with you and that you may be in good health, as it goes well with your soul."

How did I spend my 15 minutes of "me" time today? _____
_____

How will I spend my 15 minutes of "me" time tomorrow? _____
_____

How did I show gratitude for the ability to move my body today? _____
_____

How will I move tomorrow? _____
_____

Growth:

1 Timothy 4:15 "Practice these things, immerse yourself in them, so that all may see your progress."

What steps did I take towards my goal today? _____
_____

What did today teach me that I will bring into tomorrow? _____
_____

Date:_____

Reflection:

Jeremiah 29:11 "For I know the plans I have for you, declares the Lord, plans for welfare and not for evil, to give you a future and a hope."

What am I celebrating today? _____
_____

What am I grateful for today? _____
_____

What do I need to forgive myself for today? _____
_____

How did I use my gifts today?: _____
_____

Self-care:

3 John 1:2 "Beloved, I pray that all may go well with you and that you may be in good health, as it goes well with your soul."

How did I spend my 15 minutes of "me" time today? _____
_____

How will I spend my 15 minutes of "me" time tomorrow? _____
_____

How did I show gratitude for the ability to move my body today? _____
_____

How will I move tomorrow? _____
_____

Growth:

1 Timothy 4:15 "Practice these things, immerse yourself in them, so that all may see your progress."

What steps did I take towards my goal today? _____
_____

What did today teach me that I will bring into tomorrow? _____
_____

Date:_____

Reflection:

Jeremiah 29:11 "For I know the plans I have for you, declares the Lord, plans for welfare and not for evil, to give you a future and a hope."

What am I celebrating today? _____

_____

What am I grateful for today? _____

_____

What do I need to forgive myself for today? _____

_____

How did I use my gifts today?: _____

_____

Self-care:

3 John 1:2 "Beloved, I pray that all may go well with you and that you may be in good health, as it goes well with your soul."

How did I spend my 15 minutes of "me" time today? _____

_____

How will I spend my 15 minutes of "me" time tomorrow? _____

_____

How did I show gratitude for the ability to move my body today? _____

_____

How will I move tomorrow? _____

_____

Growth:

1 Timothy 4:15 "Practice these things, immerse yourself in them, so that all may see your progress."

What steps did I take towards my goal today? _____

_____

What did today teach me that I will bring into tomorrow? _____

_____

Date:_____

Reflection:

Jeremiah 29:11 "For I know the plans I have for you, declares the Lord, plans for welfare and not for evil, to give you a future and a hope."

What am I celebrating today? _____

_____

What am I grateful for today? _____

_____

What do I need to forgive myself for today? _____

_____

How did I use my gifts today?: _____

_____

Self-care:

3 John 1:2 "Beloved, I pray that all may go well with you and that you may be in good health, as it goes well with your soul."

How did I spend my 15 minutes of "me" time today? _____

_____

How will I spend my 15 minutes of "me" time tomorrow? _____

_____

How did I show gratitude for the ability to move my body today? _____

_____

How will I move tomorrow? _____

_____

Growth:

1 Timothy 4:15 "Practice these things, immerse yourself in them, so that all may see your progress."

What steps did I take towards my goal today? _____

_____

What did today teach me that I will bring into tomorrow? _____

_____

Reflection:

Jeremiah 29:11 "For I know the plans I have for you, declares the Lord, plans for welfare and not for evil, to give you a future and a hope."

What am I celebrating today? _____

_____

What am I grateful for today? _____

_____

What do I need to forgive myself for today? _____

_____

How did I use my gifts today?: _____

_____

Self-care:

3 John 1:2 "Beloved, I pray that all may go well with you and that you may be in good health, as it goes well with your soul."

How did I spend my 15 minutes of "me" time today? _____

_____

How will I spend my 15 minutes of "me" time tomorrow? _____

_____

How did I show gratitude for the ability to move my body today? _____

_____

How will I move tomorrow? _____

_____

Growth:

1 Timothy 4:15 "Practice these things, immerse yourself in them, so that all may see your progress."

What steps did I take towards my goal today? _____

_____

What did today teach me that I will bring into tomorrow? _____

_____

Date:_____

Reflection:

Jeremiah 29:11 "For I know the plans I have for you, declares the Lord, plans for welfare and not for evil, to give you a future and a hope."

What am I celebrating today? _____

_____

What am I grateful for today? _____

_____

What do I need to forgive myself for today? _____

_____

How did I use my gifts today?: _____

_____

Self-care:

3 John 1:2 "Beloved, I pray that all may go well with you and that you may be in good health, as it goes well with your soul."

How did I spend my 15 minutes of "me" time today? _____

_____

How will I spend my 15 minutes of "me" time tomorrow? _____

_____

How did I show gratitude for the ability to move my body today? ____

_____

How will I move tomorrow? _____

_____

Growth:

1 Timothy 4:15 "Practice these things, immerse yourself in them, so that all may see your progress."

What steps did I take towards my goal today? _____

_____

What did today teach me that I will bring into tomorrow? _____

_____

Date:_____

Reflection:

Jeremiah 29:11 "For I know the plans I have for you, declares the Lord, plans for welfare and not for evil, to give you a future and a hope."

What am I celebrating today? _____

_____

What am I grateful for today? _____

_____

What do I need to forgive myself for today? _____

_____

How did I use my gifts today?: _____

_____

Self-care:

3 John 1:2 "Beloved, I pray that all may go well with you and that you may be in good health, as it goes well with your soul."

How did I spend my 15 minutes of "me" time today? _____

_____

How will I spend my 15 minutes of "me" time tomorrow? _____

_____

How did I show gratitude for the ability to move my body today? _____

_____

How will I move tomorrow? _____

_____

Growth:

1 Timothy 4:15 "Practice these things, immerse yourself in them, so that all may see your progress."

What steps did I take towards my goal today? _____

_____

What did today teach me that I will bring into tomorrow? _____

_____

Psalms 46:1-3 "God is our refuge and strength, a very present help in trouble. Therefore, we will not fear thought the Earth gives way, though the mountains be moved into the heart of the sea, though its waters roar and foam, though the mountains tremble at its swelling."

Some days in motherhood are quite character building. One thing about me is you will never hear me say is "I am having a bad day." No days are bad in my book. They are all a gift from God. However, some days help build character a little more than others. Here is an example of one of my "character building" days I recently experienced through my journey of motherhood: My poor oldest boy had woken up at 3:30am with the stomach flu and was sick throughout the entire day. The baby only let me get about 1 hour of sleep the night before. Everything I had planned for that day was put on hold for my little loves. Now, that is pretty much what being a mom is all about, right?

Here is the positive in that situation: Since it was a late start to the day, I was able to find time in the morning, amongst the chaos, to sit down and get my devotions done. Originally, I had on my agenda to get a workout in at the gym. That plan had to change due to a child with the stomach bug. Instead I made it a point to complete mommy and me workout video with the baby, which ended up being great quality time with him that I cherished. You see, all I had to do was adjust my day. It was not a "bad day." Instead it built character. If I had labeled it a "bad day" from the get-go, the negativity in those words probably would have directed my day in a different direction.

Words are powerful, and so is the love God shows us each day.

Let this serve as a reminder to you this week:

He sees you.

He hears you.

He loves you.

<u>Weekly Challenge:</u>

It's time to reflect on your entries from last week. Pray. Meditate. Celebrate.

Date:_____

Reflection:

Jeremiah 29:11 "For I know the plans I have for you, declares the Lord, plans for welfare and not for evil, to give you a future and a hope."

What am I celebrating today? _____

_____

What am I grateful for today? _____

_____

What do I need to forgive myself for today? _____

_____

How did I use my gifts today?: _____

_____

Self-care:

3 John 1:2 "Beloved, I pray that all may go well with you and that you may be in good health, as it goes well with your soul."

How did I spend my 15 minutes of "me" time today? _____

_____

How will I spend my 15 minutes of "me" time tomorrow? _____

_____

How did I show gratitude for the ability to move my body today? _____

_____

How will I move tomorrow? _____

_____

Growth:

1 Timothy 4:15 "Practice these things, immerse yourself in them, so that all may see your progress."

What steps did I take towards my goal today? _____

_____

What did today teach me that I will bring into tomorrow? _____

_____

Date:_____

Reflection:

Jeremiah 29:11 "For I know the plans I have for you, declares the Lord, plans for welfare and not for evil, to give you a future and a hope."

What am I celebrating today? _____

_____

What am I grateful for today? _____

_____

What do I need to forgive myself for today? _____

_____

How did I use my gifts today?: _____

_____

Self-care:

3 John 1:2 "Beloved, I pray that all may go well with you and that you may be in good health, as it goes well with your soul."

How did I spend my 15 minutes of "me" time today? _____

_____

How will I spend my 15 minutes of "me" time tomorrow? _____

_____

How did I show gratitude for the ability to move my body today? _____

_____

How will I move tomorrow? _____

_____

Growth:

1 Timothy 4:15 "Practice these things, immerse yourself in them, so that all may see your progress."

What steps did I take towards my goal today? _____

_____

What did today teach me that I will bring into tomorrow? _____

_____

Date:_____

Reflection:

Jeremiah 29:11 "For I know the plans I have for you, declares the Lord, plans for welfare and not for evil, to give you a future and a hope."

What am I celebrating today? _____
_____

What am I grateful for today? _____
_____

What do I need to forgive myself for today? _____
_____

How did I use my gifts today?: _____
_____

Self-care:

3 John 1:2 "Beloved, I pray that all may go well with you and that you may be in good health, as it goes well with your soul."

How did I spend my 15 minutes of "me" time today? _____
_____

How will I spend my 15 minutes of "me" time tomorrow? _____
_____

How did I show gratitude for the ability to move my body today? _____
_____

How will I move tomorrow? _____
_____

Growth:

1 Timothy 4:15 "Practice these things, immerse yourself in them, so that all may see your progress."

What steps did I take towards my goal today? _____
_____

What did today teach me that I will bring into tomorrow? _____
_____

Date:_____

Reflection:

Jeremiah 29:11 "For I know the plans I have for you, declares the Lord, plans for welfare and not for evil, to give you a future and a hope."

What am I celebrating today? _____

_____

What am I grateful for today? _____

_____

What do I need to forgive myself for today? _____

_____

How did I use my gifts today?: _____

_____

Self-care:

3 John 1:2 "Beloved, I pray that all may go well with you and that you may be in good health, as it goes well with your soul."

How did I spend my 15 minutes of "me" time today? _____

_____

How will I spend my 15 minutes of "me" time tomorrow? _____

_____

How did I show gratitude for the ability to move my body today? _____

_____

How will I move tomorrow? _____

_____

Growth:

1 Timothy 4:15 "Practice these things, immerse yourself in them, so that all may see your progress."

What steps did I take towards my goal today? _____

_____

What did today teach me that I will bring into tomorrow? _____

_____

Date:_____

Reflection:

Jeremiah 29:11 "For I know the plans I have for you, declares the Lord, plans for welfare and not for evil, to give you a future and a hope."

What am I celebrating today? _____

_____

What am I grateful for today? _____

_____

What do I need to forgive myself for today? _____

_____

How did I use my gifts today?: _____

_____

Self-care:

3 John 1:2 "Beloved, I pray that all may go well with you and that you may be in good health, as it goes well with your soul."

How did I spend my 15 minutes of "me" time today? _____

_____

How will I spend my 15 minutes of "me" time tomorrow? _____

_____

How did I show gratitude for the ability to move my body today? _____

_____

How will I move tomorrow? _____

_____

Growth:

1 Timothy 4:15 "Practice these things, immerse yourself in them, so that all may see your progress."

What steps did I take towards my goal today? _____

_____

What did today teach me that I will bring into tomorrow? _____

_____

Date:_____

Reflection:

Jeremiah 29:11 "For I know the plans I have for you, declares the Lord, plans for welfare and not for evil, to give you a future and a hope."

What am I celebrating today? _____

_____

What am I grateful for today? _____

_____

What do I need to forgive myself for today? _____

_____

How did I use my gifts today?: _____

_____

Self-care:

3 John 1:2 "Beloved, I pray that all may go well with you and that you may be in good health, as it goes well with your soul."

How did I spend my 15 minutes of "me" time today? _____

_____

How will I spend my 15 minutes of "me" time tomorrow? _____

_____

How did I show gratitude for the ability to move my body today? _____

_____

How will I move tomorrow? _____

_____

Growth:

1 Timothy 4:15 "Practice these things, immerse yourself in them, so that all may see your progress."

What steps did I take towards my goal today? _____

_____

What did today teach me that I will bring into tomorrow? _____

_____

Date:_____

Reflection:

Jeremiah 29:11 "For I know the plans I have for you, declares the Lord, plans for welfare and not for evil, to give you a future and a hope."

What am I celebrating today? _____

_____

What am I grateful for today? _____

_____

What do I need to forgive myself for today? _____

_____

How did I use my gifts today?: _____

_____

Self-care:

3 John 1:2 "Beloved, I pray that all may go well with you and that you may be in good health, as it goes well with your soul."

How did I spend my 15 minutes of "me" time today? _____

_____

How will I spend my 15 minutes of "me" time tomorrow? _____

_____

How did I show gratitude for the ability to move my body today? _____

_____

How will I move tomorrow? _____

_____

Growth:

1 Timothy 4:15 "Practice these things, immerse yourself in them, so that all may see your progress."

What steps did I take towards my goal today? _____

_____

What did today teach me that I will bring into tomorrow? _____

_____

***Psalms 16:11 "You make known to me the path
of lie; in your presence there if fullness of joy; at
your right hand are pleasures forevermore."***

I vividly remember a day when I was 3 ½ weeks postpartum with my
youngest son. The night before this day I had plans to get up a little
early and get so much done during the day. I was completely sleep
deprived with my newborn son awake all hours of the night, however, I
promised myself I would shower, put makeup on, get the laundry done,
give the baby a bath, prep dinner for the evening, all before picking my
oldest son up from school in the afternoon. This day was a reminder to
me that life has a way of saying "not today, mom, not today." During
that time, I had been having to trouble shoot with some medical issues
my newborn was dealing with. That meant mommy and baby did not
get sleep the night prior to. If my little man was comfortable (even if
that meant having to lay in an awkward position in bed just so he could
sleep on my cheek), then I had to be ok with sacrificing my luxury
shower so he could be comfortable. My newborn did not care if I did
the laundry or put makeup on all before 2:30pm. He just needed me
to be there for him. That was my number one job. Here is my message
to you, mom: Stop beating yourself up because your "list" may not be
done. Maybe go grab a coffee today WITHOUT your makeup on. Also,
let us try to remember not to judge another mom who may not look
exactly presentable at the coffee shop. You may never know the energy
it may have taken her to get herself that delicious hot cup of energy.

Let this serve as a reminder to you this week:

He sees you.

He hears you.

He loves you.

<u>Weekly Challenge:</u>

It's time to reflect on your entries from last week. Pray. Meditate. Celebrate.

Date:_____

Reflection:

Jeremiah 29:11 "For I know the plans I have for you, declares the Lord, plans for welfare and not for evil, to give you a future and a hope."

What am I celebrating today? _____
_____

What am I grateful for today? _____
_____

What do I need to forgive myself for today? _____
_____

How did I use my gifts today?: _____
_____

Self-care:

3 John 1:2 "Beloved, I pray that all may go well with you and that you may be in good health, as it goes well with your soul."

How did I spend my 15 minutes of "me" time today? _____
_____

How will I spend my 15 minutes of "me" time tomorrow? _____
_____

How did I show gratitude for the ability to move my body today? _____
_____

How will I move tomorrow? _____
_____

Growth:

1 Timothy 4:15 "Practice these things, immerse yourself in them, so that all may see your progress."

What steps did I take towards my goal today? _____
_____

What did today teach me that I will bring into tomorrow? _____
_____

Date:_____

Reflection:

Jeremiah 29:11 "For I know the plans I have for you, declares the Lord, plans for welfare and not for evil, to give you a future and a hope."

What am I celebrating today? _____
_____

What am I grateful for today? _____
_____

What do I need to forgive myself for today? _____
_____

How did I use my gifts today?: _____
_____

Self-care:

3 John 1:2 "Beloved, I pray that all may go well with you and that you may be in good health, as it goes well with your soul."

How did I spend my 15 minutes of "me" time today? _____
_____

How will I spend my 15 minutes of "me" time tomorrow? _____
_____

How did I show gratitude for the ability to move my body today? _____
_____

How will I move tomorrow? _____
_____

Growth:

1 Timothy 4:15 "Practice these things, immerse yourself in them, so that all may see your progress."

What steps did I take towards my goal today? _____
_____

What did today teach me that I will bring into tomorrow? _____
_____

Date:_____

Reflection:

Jeremiah 29:11 "For I know the plans I have for you, declares the Lord, plans for welfare and not for evil, to give you a future and a hope."

What am I celebrating today? _____

_____

What am I grateful for today? _____

_____

What do I need to forgive myself for today? _____

_____

How did I use my gifts today?: _____

_____

Self-care:

3 John 1:2 "Beloved, I pray that all may go well with you and that you may be in good health, as it goes well with your soul."

How did I spend my 15 minutes of "me" time today? _____

_____

How will I spend my 15 minutes of "me" time tomorrow? _____

_____

How did I show gratitude for the ability to move my body today? _____

_____

How will I move tomorrow? _____

_____

Growth:

1 Timothy 4:15 "Practice these things, immerse yourself in them, so that all may see your progress."

What steps did I take towards my goal today? _____

_____

What did today teach me that I will bring into tomorrow? _____

_____

Date:_____

Reflection:

Jeremiah 29:11 "For I know the plans I have for you, declares the Lord, plans for welfare and not for evil, to give you a future and a hope."

What am I celebrating today? _____

_____

What am I grateful for today? _____

_____

What do I need to forgive myself for today? _____

_____

How did I use my gifts today?: _____

_____

Self-care:

3 John 1:2 "Beloved, I pray that all may go well with you and that you may be in good health, as it goes well with your soul."

How did I spend my 15 minutes of "me" time today? _____

_____

How will I spend my 15 minutes of "me" time tomorrow? _____

_____

How did I show gratitude for the ability to move my body today? _____

_____

How will I move tomorrow? _____

_____

Growth:

1 Timothy 4:15 "Practice these things, immerse yourself in them, so that all may see your progress."

What steps did I take towards my goal today? _____

_____

What did today teach me that I will bring into tomorrow? _____

_____

Date:_____

Reflection:

Jeremiah 29:11 "For I know the plans I have for you, declares the Lord, plans for welfare and not for evil, to give you a future and a hope."

What am I celebrating today? _____

_____

What am I grateful for today? _____

_____

What do I need to forgive myself for today? _____

_____

How did I use my gifts today?: _____

_____

Self-care:

3 John 1:2 "Beloved, I pray that all may go well with you and that you may be in good health, as it goes well with your soul."

How did I spend my 15 minutes of "me" time today? _____

_____

How will I spend my 15 minutes of "me" time tomorrow? _____

_____

How did I show gratitude for the ability to move my body today? _____

_____

How will I move tomorrow? _____

_____

Growth:

1 Timothy 4:15 "Practice these things, immerse yourself in them, so that all may see your progress."

What steps did I take towards my goal today? _____

_____

What did today teach me that I will bring into tomorrow? _____

_____

Reflection:

Jeremiah 29:11 "For I know the plans I have for you, declares the Lord, plans for welfare and not for evil, to give you a future and a hope."

What am I celebrating today? _____

_____

What am I grateful for today? _____

_____

What do I need to forgive myself for today? _____

_____

How did I use my gifts today?: _____

_____

Self-care:

3 John 1:2 "Beloved, I pray that all may go well with you and that you may be in good health, as it goes well with your soul."

How did I spend my 15 minutes of "me" time today? _____

_____

How will I spend my 15 minutes of "me" time tomorrow? _____

_____

How did I show gratitude for the ability to move my body today? _____

_____

How will I move tomorrow? _____

_____

Growth:

1 Timothy 4:15 "Practice these things, immerse yourself in them, so that all may see your progress."

What steps did I take towards my goal today? _____

_____

What did today teach me that I will bring into tomorrow? _____

_____

Date:_____

Reflection:

Jeremiah 29:11 "For I know the plans I have for you, declares the Lord, plans for welfare and not for evil, to give you a future and a hope."

What am I celebrating today? _____

_____

What am I grateful for today? _____

_____

What do I need to forgive myself for today? _____

_____

How did I use my gifts today?: _____

_____

Self-care:

3 John 1:2 "Beloved, I pray that all may go well with you and that you may be in good health, as it goes well with your soul."

How did I spend my 15 minutes of "me" time today? _____

_____

How will I spend my 15 minutes of "me" time tomorrow? _____

_____

How did I show gratitude for the ability to move my body today? _____

_____

How will I move tomorrow? _____

_____

Growth:

1 Timothy 4:15 "Practice these things, immerse yourself in them, so that all may see your progress."

What steps did I take towards my goal today? _____

_____

What did today teach me that I will bring into tomorrow? _____

_____

Hebrews 10:23 "Let us hold fast the confession of our hope without wavering, for he who promised is faithful."

Mom, did you know God has made a special promise just for you? The Lord is our Shepherd. The role of a shepherd is to watch over the flock. WE are His flock. He is not only our Father, but our watchman and our protector. Those nights where you have not had a wink of sleep due to a cranky baby, or those mornings where it seems impossible to get your child out the door and, on his way to school…the Lord is there. You may not feel His presence in that exact moment. Why is that? This is because it is human nature to get consumed with being in the moment. Take a moment to pray, ask God for peace. He has been guiding us all along. However, as sheep, we may get distracted and stray along the way or in that "moment." He has promised to never leave us nor forsake us. Mom, you are not alone. You are never alone. Sometimes you may just need that reminder, and here it is.

Let this serve as a reminder to you this week:

He sees you.

He hears you.

He loves you.

Weekly Challenge:

It's time to reflect on your entries from last week. Pray. Meditate. Celebrate.

Date:_____

Reflection:

Jeremiah 29:11 "For I know the plans I have for you, declares the Lord, plans for welfare and not for evil, to give you a future and a hope."

What am I celebrating today? _____

_____

What am I grateful for today? _____

_____

What do I need to forgive myself for today? _____

_____

How did I use my gifts today?: _____

_____

Self-care:

3 John 1:2 "Beloved, I pray that all may go well with you and that you may be in good health, as it goes well with your soul."

How did I spend my 15 minutes of "me" time today? _____

_____

How will I spend my 15 minutes of "me" time tomorrow? _____

_____

How did I show gratitude for the ability to move my body today? _____

_____

How will I move tomorrow? _____

_____

Growth:

1 Timothy 4:15 "Practice these things, immerse yourself in them, so that all may see your progress."

What steps did I take towards my goal today? _____

_____

What did today teach me that I will bring into tomorrow? _____

_____

Reflection:

Jeremiah 29:11 "For I know the plans I have for you, declares the Lord, plans for welfare and not for evil, to give you a future and a hope."

What am I celebrating today? _____

_____

What am I grateful for today? _____

_____

What do I need to forgive myself for today? _____

_____

How did I use my gifts today?: _____

_____

Self-care:

3 John 1:2 "Beloved, I pray that all may go well with you and that you may be in good health, as it goes well with your soul."

How did I spend my 15 minutes of "me" time today? _____

_____

How will I spend my 15 minutes of "me" time tomorrow? _____

_____

How did I show gratitude for the ability to move my body today? _____

_____

How will I move tomorrow? _____

_____

Growth:

1 Timothy 4:15 "Practice these things, immerse yourself in them, so that all may see your progress."

What steps did I take towards my goal today? _____

_____

What did today teach me that I will bring into tomorrow? _____

_____

Date:_____

Reflection:

Jeremiah 29:11 "For I know the plans I have for you, declares the Lord, plans for welfare and not for evil, to give you a future and a hope."

What am I celebrating today? _____

_____

What am I grateful for today? _____

_____

What do I need to forgive myself for today? _____

_____

How did I use my gifts today?: _____

_____

Self-care:

3 John 1:2 "Beloved, I pray that all may go well with you and that you may be in good health, as it goes well with your soul."

How did I spend my 15 minutes of "me" time today? _____

_____

How will I spend my 15 minutes of "me" time tomorrow? ___

_____

How did I show gratitude for the ability to move my body today? _____

_____

How will I move tomorrow? _____

_____

Growth:

1 Timothy 4:15 "Practice these things, immerse yourself in them, so that all may see your progress."

What steps did I take towards my goal today? _____

_____

What did today teach me that I will bring into tomorrow? ___

_____

Date:_____

Reflection:

Jeremiah 29:11 "For I know the plans I have for you, declares the Lord, plans for welfare and not for evil, to give you a future and a hope."

What am I celebrating today? _____
_____

What am I grateful for today? _____
_____

What do I need to forgive myself for today? _____
_____

How did I use my gifts today?: _____
_____

Self-care:

3 John 1:2 "Beloved, I pray that all may go well with you and that you may be in good health, as it goes well with your soul."

How did I spend my 15 minutes of "me" time today? _____
_____

How will I spend my 15 minutes of "me" time tomorrow? _____
_____

How did I show gratitude for the ability to move my body today? _____
_____

How will I move tomorrow? _____
_____

Growth:

1 Timothy 4:15 "Practice these things, immerse yourself in them, so that all may see your progress."

What steps did I take towards my goal today? _____
_____

What did today teach me that I will bring into tomorrow? _____
_____

Date:_____

Reflection:

Jeremiah 29:11 "For I know the plans I have for you, declares the Lord, plans for welfare and not for evil, to give you a future and a hope."

What am I celebrating today? _____
_____

What am I grateful for today? _____
_____

What do I need to forgive myself for today? _____
_____

How did I use my gifts today?: _____
_____

Self-care:

3 John 1:2 "Beloved, I pray that all may go well with you and that you may be in good health, as it goes well with your soul."

How did I spend my 15 minutes of "me" time today? _____
_____

How will I spend my 15 minutes of "me" time tomorrow? _____
_____

How did I show gratitude for the ability to move my body today? _____
_____

How will I move tomorrow? _____
_____

Growth:

1 Timothy 4:15 "Practice these things, immerse yourself in them, so that all may see your progress."

What steps did I take towards my goal today? _____
_____

What did today teach me that I will bring into tomorrow? _____
_____

Date:_____

Reflection:

Jeremiah 29:11 "For I know the plans I have for you, declares the Lord, plans for welfare and not for evil, to give you a future and a hope."

What am I celebrating today? _____
_____

What am I grateful for today? _____
_____

What do I need to forgive myself for today? _____
_____

How did I use my gifts today?: _____
_____

Self-care:

3 John 1:2 "Beloved, I pray that all may go well with you and that you may be in good health, as it goes well with your soul."

How did I spend my 15 minutes of "me" time today? _____
_____

How will I spend my 15 minutes of "me" time tomorrow? _____
_____

How did I show gratitude for the ability to move my body today? _____
_____

How will I move tomorrow? _____
_____

Growth:

1 Timothy 4:15 "Practice these things, immerse yourself in them, so that all may see your progress."

What steps did I take towards my goal today? _____
_____

What did today teach me that I will bring into tomorrow? _____
_____

Date:_____

Reflection:

Jeremiah 29:11 "For I know the plans I have for you, declares the Lord, plans for welfare and not for evil, to give you a future and a hope."

What am I celebrating today? _____

_____

What am I grateful for today? _____

_____

What do I need to forgive myself for today? _____

_____

How did I use my gifts today?: _____

_____

Self-care:

3 John 1:2 "Beloved, I pray that all may go well with you and that you may be in good health, as it goes well with your soul."

How did I spend my 15 minutes of "me" time today? _____

_____

How will I spend my 15 minutes of "me" time tomorrow? _____

_____

How did I show gratitude for the ability to move my body today? _____

_____

How will I move tomorrow? _____

_____

Growth:

1 Timothy 4:15 "Practice these things, immerse yourself in them, so that all may see your progress."

What steps did I take towards my goal today? _____

_____

What did today teach me that I will bring into tomorrow? _____

_____

Ecclesiastes 3:4 "A time to weep, and a time to laugh; a time to mourn, and a time to dance;"

How amazing is it that God gave us the ability for laughter?! This may be an ability we take for granted at times. I like to think He gave this to us as a medicine for our souls. I also like to think He gave this to us to join communities together. It is a healing agent.

When my oldest son turned two, I began writing down funny things he would say as well as funny situations he put us in. Once he began to really speak, I realized I had brought a very funny boy into this world! That book is something we now bring out at family gathering. It brings laughter to the room. That book is also something I reference at times I may need a pick-me-up. If you need some laughter, I encourage you to look to your children. I challenge you to create a "book of laughter" in your own home that you may reference in troubling times. God has giving us the best medicine.

Let this serve as a reminder to you this week:

He sees you.

He hears you.

He loves you.

Weekly Challenge:

It's time to reflect on your entries from last week. Pray. Meditate. Celebrate.

Reflection:

Jeremiah 29:11 "For I know the plans I have for you, declares the Lord, plans for welfare and not for evil, to give you a future and a hope."

What am I celebrating today? _____

_____

What am I grateful for today? _____

_____

What do I need to forgive myself for today? _____

_____

How did I use my gifts today?: _____

_____

Self-care:

3 John 1:2 "Beloved, I pray that all may go well with you and that you may be in good health, as it goes well with your soul."

How did I spend my 15 minutes of "me" time today? _____

_____

How will I spend my 15 minutes of "me" time tomorrow? _____

_____

How did I show gratitude for the ability to move my body today? _____

_____

How will I move tomorrow? _____

_____

Growth:

1 Timothy 4:15 "Practice these things, immerse yourself in them, so that all may see your progress."

What steps did I take towards my goal today? _____

_____

What did today teach me that I will bring into tomorrow? _____

_____

Date:_____

Reflection:

Jeremiah 29:11 "For I know the plans I have for you, declares the Lord, plans for welfare and not for evil, to give you a future and a hope."

What am I celebrating today? _____

_____

What am I grateful for today? _____

_____

What do I need to forgive myself for today? _____

_____

How did I use my gifts today?: _____

_____

Self-care:

3 John 1:2 "Beloved, I pray that all may go well with you and that you may be in good health, as it goes well with your soul."

How did I spend my 15 minutes of "me" time today? _____

_____

How will I spend my 15 minutes of "me" time tomorrow? _____

_____

How did I show gratitude for the ability to move my body today? _____

_____

How will I move tomorrow? _____

_____

Growth:

1 Timothy 4:15 "Practice these things, immerse yourself in them, so that all may see your progress."

What steps did I take towards my goal today? _____

_____

What did today teach me that I will bring into tomorrow? _____

_____

Reflection:

Jeremiah 29:11 "For I know the plans I have for you, declares the Lord, plans for welfare and not for evil, to give you a future and a hope."

What am I celebrating today? _____

_____

What am I grateful for today? _____

_____

What do I need to forgive myself for today? _____

_____

How did I use my gifts today?: _____

_____

Self-care:

3 John 1:2 "Beloved, I pray that all may go well with you and that you may be in good health, as it goes well with your soul."

How did I spend my 15 minutes of "me" time today? _____

_____

How will I spend my 15 minutes of "me" time tomorrow? _____

_____

How did I show gratitude for the ability to move my body today? _____

_____

How will I move tomorrow? _____

_____

Growth:

1 Timothy 4:15 "Practice these things, immerse yourself in them, so that all may see your progress."

What steps did I take towards my goal today? _____

_____

What did today teach me that I will bring into tomorrow? _____

_____

Reflection:

Jeremiah 29:11 "For I know the plans I have for you, declares the Lord, plans for welfare and not for evil, to give you a future and a hope."

What am I celebrating today? _____

_____

What am I grateful for today? _____

_____

What do I need to forgive myself for today? _____

_____

How did I use my gifts today?: _____

_____

Self-care:

3 John 1:2 "Beloved, I pray that all may go well with you and that you may be in good health, as it goes well with your soul."

How did I spend my 15 minutes of "me" time today? _____

_____

How will I spend my 15 minutes of "me" time tomorrow? _____

_____

How did I show gratitude for the ability to move my body today? _____

_____

How will I move tomorrow? _____

_____

Growth:

1 Timothy 4:15 "Practice these things, immerse yourself in them, so that all may see your progress."

What steps did I take towards my goal today? _____

_____

What did today teach me that I will bring into tomorrow? _____

_____

Reflection:

Jeremiah 29:11 "For I know the plans I have for you, declares the Lord, plans for welfare and not for evil, to give you a future and a hope."

What am I celebrating today? _____

_____

What am I grateful for today? _____

_____

What do I need to forgive myself for today? _____

_____

How did I use my gifts today?: _____

_____

Self-care:

3 John 1:2 "Beloved, I pray that all may go well with you and that you may be in good health, as it goes well with your soul."

How did I spend my 15 minutes of "me" time today? _____

_____

How will I spend my 15 minutes of "me" time tomorrow? _____

_____

How did I show gratitude for the ability to move my body today? _____

_____

How will I move tomorrow? _____

_____

Growth:

1 Timothy 4:15 "Practice these things, immerse yourself in them, so that all may see your progress."

What steps did I take towards my goal today? _____

_____

What did today teach me that I will bring into tomorrow? _____

_____

Reflection:

Jeremiah 29:11 "For I know the plans I have for you, declares the Lord, plans for welfare and not for evil, to give you a future and a hope."

What am I celebrating today? _____
_____

What am I grateful for today? _____
_____

What do I need to forgive myself for today? _____
_____

How did I use my gifts today?: _____
_____

Self-care:

3 John 1:2 "Beloved, I pray that all may go well with you and that you may be in good health, as it goes well with your soul."

How did I spend my 15 minutes of "me" time today? _____
_____

How will I spend my 15 minutes of "me" time tomorrow? _____
_____

How did I show gratitude for the ability to move my body today? _____
_____

How will I move tomorrow? _____
_____

Growth:

1 Timothy 4:15 "Practice these things, immerse yourself in them, so that all may see your progress."

What steps did I take towards my goal today? _____
_____

What did today teach me that I will bring into tomorrow? _____
_____

Reflection:

Jeremiah 29:11 "For I know the plans I have for you, declares the Lord, plans for welfare and not for evil, to give you a future and a hope."

What am I celebrating today? _____

_____

What am I grateful for today? _____

_____

What do I need to forgive myself for today? _____

_____

How did I use my gifts today?: _____

_____

Self-care:

3 John 1:2 "Beloved, I pray that all may go well with you and that you may be in good health, as it goes well with your soul."

How did I spend my 15 minutes of "me" time today? _____

_____

How will I spend my 15 minutes of "me" time tomorrow? _____

_____

How did I show gratitude for the ability to move my body today? ____

_____

How will I move tomorrow? _____

_____

Growth:

1 Timothy 4:15 "Practice these things, immerse yourself in them, so that all may see your progress."

What steps did I take towards my goal today? _____

_____

What did today teach me that I will bring into tomorrow? _____

_____

Romans 8:18 "For I consider that the sufferings of this present time are not worth comparing with the glory that is to be revealed to us."

We all have good days in motherhood, and we have bad days, or as I like to say "character building" days. For me, the worst day of parenthood was the day I became a single mother. The plans I had for my life did not include caring for a 2-year-old on my own. It did not include coming home to an empty house some evenings. It certainly did not include a failed marriage. That was the day I looked at MYSELF as a failure. Then God rescued my thoughts. I may have viewed that time as the "worst day of my life," but God was taking me into something greater. I had not grown my relationship with the Lord during the time with my eldest's father. In fact, I turned away for the Lord. The amazing thing is this: when I became a single mother, I never became angry with God. I took it as an opportunity to run right back into His arms. God had a different plan for my life. He set me apart for greatness. I was not able to grow where I was at. At times, the messiness you are experiencing may be the Lord taking you out of a season, and into your greatness. I can look back at that time now and give thanks. Since becoming a single mother, God has placed an amazing husband in my life. We have a beautiful new family. We have taken steps into ministry together. Whatever your storm may be in this moment, God is taking you into a new season. You may have to let go of the old, to take hold of the abundance He will provide for you. For me, I had to let go of the idea I had for my perfect life. His map for my life is far greater than anything I could have imagined.

Let this serve as a reminder to you this week:

He sees you.

He hears you.

He loves you.

<u>Weekly Challenge:</u>

It's time to reflect on your entries from last week. Pray. Meditate. Cele

Date:_____

Reflection:

Jeremiah 29:11 "For I know the plans I have for you, declares the Lord, plans for welfare and not for evil, to give you a future and a hope."

What am I celebrating today? _____
_____

What am I grateful for today? _____
_____

What do I need to forgive myself for today? _____
_____

How did I use my gifts today?: _____
_____

Self-care:

3 John 1:2 "Beloved, I pray that all may go well with you and that you may be in good health, as it goes well with your soul."

How did I spend my 15 minutes of "me" time today? _____
_____

How will I spend my 15 minutes of "me" time tomorrow? _____
_____

How did I show gratitude for the ability to move my body today? _____
_____

How will I move tomorrow? _____
_____

Growth:

1 Timothy 4:15 "Practice these things, immerse yourself in them, so that all may see your progress."

What steps did I take towards my goal today? _____
_____

What did today teach me that I will bring into tomorrow? _____
_____

Date:_____

Reflection:

Jeremiah 29:11 "For I know the plans I have for you, declares the Lord, plans for welfare and not for evil, to give you a future and a hope."

What am I celebrating today? _____

_____

What am I grateful for today? _____

_____

What do I need to forgive myself for today? _____

_____

How did I use my gifts today?: _____

_____

Self-care:

3 John 1:2 "Beloved, I pray that all may go well with you and that you may be in good health, as it goes well with your soul."

How did I spend my 15 minutes of "me" time today? _____

_____

How will I spend my 15 minutes of "me" time tomorrow? _____

_____

How did I show gratitude for the ability to move my body today? _____

_____

How will I move tomorrow? _____

_____

Growth:

1 Timothy 4:15 "Practice these things, immerse yourself in them, so that all may see your progress."

What steps did I take towards my goal today? _____

_____

What did today teach me that I will bring into tomorrow? _____

_____

Date:_____

Reflection:

Jeremiah 29:11 "For I know the plans I have for you, declares the Lord, plans for welfare and not for evil, to give you a future and a hope."

What am I celebrating today? _____

_____

What am I grateful for today? _____

_____

What do I need to forgive myself for today? _____

_____

How did I use my gifts today?: _____

_____

Self-care:

3 John 1:2 "Beloved, I pray that all may go well with you and that you may be in good health, as it goes well with your soul."

How did I spend my 15 minutes of "me" time today? _____

_____

How will I spend my 15 minutes of "me" time tomorrow? _____

_____

How did I show gratitude for the ability to move my body today? _____

_____

How will I move tomorrow? _____

_____

Growth:

1 Timothy 4:15 "Practice these things, immerse yourself in them, so that all may see your progress."

What steps did I take towards my goal today? _____

_____

What did today teach me that I will bring into tomorrow? _____

_____

Date:_____

Reflection:

Jeremiah 29:11 "For I know the plans I have for you, declares the Lord, plans for welfare and not for evil, to give you a future and a hope."

What am I celebrating today? _____

_____

What am I grateful for today? _____

_____

What do I need to forgive myself for today? _____

_____

How did I use my gifts today?: _____

_____

Self-care:

3 John 1:2 "Beloved, I pray that all may go well with you and that you may be in good health, as it goes well with your soul."

How did I spend my 15 minutes of "me" time today? _____

_____

How will I spend my 15 minutes of "me" time tomorrow? _____

_____

How did I show gratitude for the ability to move my body today? _____

_____

How will I move tomorrow? _____

_____

Growth:

1 Timothy 4:15 "Practice these things, immerse yourself in them, so that all may see your progress."

What steps did I take towards my goal today? _____

_____

What did today teach me that I will bring into tomorrow? _____

_____

Date:_____

Reflection:

Jeremiah 29:11 "For I know the plans I have for you, declares the Lord, plans for welfare and not for evil, to give you a future and a hope."

What am I celebrating today? _____

_____

What am I grateful for today? _____

_____

What do I need to forgive myself for today? _____

_____

How did I use my gifts today?: _____

_____

Self-care:

3 John 1:2 "Beloved, I pray that all may go well with you and that you may be in good health, as it goes well with your soul."

How did I spend my 15 minutes of "me" time today? _____

_____

How will I spend my 15 minutes of "me" time tomorrow? _____

_____

How did I show gratitude for the ability to move my body today? _____

_____

How will I move tomorrow? _____

_____

Growth:

1 Timothy 4:15 "Practice these things, immerse yourself in them, so that all may see your progress."

What steps did I take towards my goal today? _____

_____

What did today teach me that I will bring into tomorrow? _____

_____

Date:_____

Reflection:

Jeremiah 29:11 "For I know the plans I have for you, declares the Lord, plans for welfare and not for evil, to give you a future and a hope."

What am I celebrating today? _____

_____

What am I grateful for today? _____

_____

What do I need to forgive myself for today? _____

_____

How did I use my gifts today?: _____

_____

Self-care:

3 John 1:2 "Beloved, I pray that all may go well with you and that you may be in good health, as it goes well with your soul."

How did I spend my 15 minutes of "me" time today? _____

_____

How will I spend my 15 minutes of "me" time tomorrow? _____

_____

How did I show gratitude for the ability to move my body today? _____

_____

How will I move tomorrow? _____

_____

Growth:

1 Timothy 4:15 "Practice these things, immerse yourself in them, so that all may see your progress."

What steps did I take towards my goal today? _____

_____

What did today teach me that I will bring into tomorrow? _____

_____

Date:_____

Reflection:

Jeremiah 29:11 "For I know the plans I have for you, declares the Lord, plans for welfare and not for evil, to give you a future and a hope."

What am I celebrating today? _____

_____

What am I grateful for today? _____

_____

What do I need to forgive myself for today? _____

_____

How did I use my gifts today?: _____

_____

Self-care:

3 John 1:2 "Beloved, I pray that all may go well with you and that you may be in good health, as it goes well with your soul."

How did I spend my 15 minutes of "me" time today? _____

_____

How will I spend my 15 minutes of "me" time tomorrow? _____

_____

How did I show gratitude for the ability to move my body today? _____

_____

How will I move tomorrow? _____

_____

Growth:

1 Timothy 4:15 "Practice these things, immerse yourself in them, so that all may see your progress."

What steps did I take towards my goal today? _____

_____

What did today teach me that I will bring into tomorrow? _____

_____

1 John 1:9 "If we confess our sins, he is faithful and just to forgive us our sins and to cleanse us from all unrighteousness."

I am sure us moms have at least one thing in common. If I had to guess what it was, I would guess that ability to confess to our little ones when we were wrong. That is such a difficult one!! How many times have we yelled at out child for not getting on the school bus fast enough? How many times have we lashed out at our little one for putting their shoes in the wrong place because we tripped on them? Now, how many times have you felt awful for making your child upset after you may have lashed out on him? I am going to share a story in hopes it resonates with you. I was running late taking my son to the bus stop one morning. He was taking his time getting dressed, eating breakfast, as well as brushing his teeth. It felt as though my child had turned into a sloth at this point. I was sleep deprived from being up with the baby the night before, and my husband had to leave for work before the sun came up, which left me alone with the children in the morning. I will admit, that frustrated me. After raising my voice at my son numerous times, I finally got him on the bus. However, instead of letting out a sigh of relief, I felt awful inside. I left my child for the day after making HIM feel terrible. Later that afternoon, I picked him up from the bus stop. Before driving away, I looked at him with tears in my eyes. I confessed to him that I was so wrong. I should have never allowed myself to get that upset over something so small. He forgave me! He cried. I cried. We both learned something that day. I learned that as a mom, I am the greatest example my son has when it comes to becoming a parent himself one day. He learned that I am not always right, and when I am wrong, I am humble enough to admit that to him, even if he was only six years old. Teaching our children to confess our sins when we are wrong is a difficult one to teach. Showing by example can humble us and bring us to tears. Our children will love us regardless. Let us try to be an example of what 1 John 1:9 tells us to do.

Let this serve as a reminder to you this week:

He sees you.

He hears you.

He loves you.

<u>Weekly Challenge:</u>

It's time to reflect on your entries from last week. Pray. Meditate. Celebrate.

Reflection:

Jeremiah 29:11 "For I know the plans I have for you, declares the Lord, plans for welfare and not for evil, to give you a future and a hope."

What am I celebrating today? _____
_____

What am I grateful for today? _____
_____

What do I need to forgive myself for today? _____
_____

How did I use my gifts today?: _____
_____

Self-care:

3 John 1:2 "Beloved, I pray that all may go well with you and that you may be in good health, as it goes well with your soul."

How did I spend my 15 minutes of "me" time today? _____
_____

How will I spend my 15 minutes of "me" time tomorrow? _____
_____

How did I show gratitude for the ability to move my body today? _____
_____

How will I move tomorrow? _____
_____

Growth:

1 Timothy 4:15 "Practice these things, immerse yourself in them, so that all may see your progress."

What steps did I take towards my goal today? _____
_____

What did today teach me that I will bring into tomorrow? _____
_____

Date:_____

Reflection:

Jeremiah 29:11 "For I know the plans I have for you, declares the Lord, plans for welfare and not for evil, to give you a future and a hope."

What am I celebrating today? _____

_____

What am I grateful for today? _____

_____

What do I need to forgive myself for today? _____

_____

How did I use my gifts today?: _____

_____

Self-care:

3 John 1:2 "Beloved, I pray that all may go well with you and that you may be in good health, as it goes well with your soul."

How did I spend my 15 minutes of "me" time today? _____

_____

How will I spend my 15 minutes of "me" time tomorrow? _____

_____

How did I show gratitude for the ability to move my body today? _____

_____

How will I move tomorrow? _____

_____

Growth:

1 Timothy 4:15 "Practice these things, immerse yourself in them, so that all may see your progress."

What steps did I take towards my goal today? _____

_____

What did today teach me that I will bring into tomorrow? _____

_____

Date:_____

Reflection:

Jeremiah 29:11 "For I know the plans I have for you, declares the Lord, plans for welfare and not for evil, to give you a future and a hope."

What am I celebrating today? _____

_____

What am I grateful for today? _____

_____

What do I need to forgive myself for today? _____

_____

How did I use my gifts today?: _____

_____

Self-care:

3 John 1:2 "Beloved, I pray that all may go well with you and that you may be in good health, as it goes well with your soul."

How did I spend my 15 minutes of "me" time today? _____

_____

How will I spend my 15 minutes of "me" time tomorrow? _____

_____

How did I show gratitude for the ability to move my body today? _____

_____

How will I move tomorrow? _____

_____

Growth:

1 Timothy 4:15 "Practice these things, immerse yourself in them, so that all may see your progress."

What steps did I take towards my goal today? _____

_____

What did today teach me that I will bring into tomorrow? _____

_____

Date:_____

Reflection:

Jeremiah 29:11 "For I know the plans I have for you, declares the Lord, plans for welfare and not for evil, to give you a future and a hope."

What am I celebrating today? _____
_____

What am I grateful for today? _____
_____

What do I need to forgive myself for today? _____
_____

How did I use my gifts today?: _____
_____

Self-care:

3 John 1:2 "Beloved, I pray that all may go well with you and that you may be in good health, as it goes well with your soul."

How did I spend my 15 minutes of "me" time today? _____
_____

How will I spend my 15 minutes of "me" time tomorrow? _____
_____

How did I show gratitude for the ability to move my body today? _____
_____

How will I move tomorrow? _____
_____

Growth:

1 Timothy 4:15 "Practice these things, immerse yourself in them, so that all may see your progress."

What steps did I take towards my goal today? _____
_____

What did today teach me that I will bring into tomorrow? _____
_____

Date:_____

Reflection:

Jeremiah 29:11 "For I know the plans I have for you, declares the Lord, plans for welfare and not for evil, to give you a future and a hope."

What am I celebrating today? _____

_____

What am I grateful for today? _____

_____

What do I need to forgive myself for today? _____

_____

How did I use my gifts today?: _____

_____

Self-care:

3 John 1:2 "Beloved, I pray that all may go well with you and that you may be in good health, as it goes well with your soul."

How did I spend my 15 minutes of "me" time today? _____

_____

How will I spend my 15 minutes of "me" time tomorrow? ____

_____

How did I show gratitude for the ability to move my body today? _____

_____

How will I move tomorrow? _____

_____

Growth:

1 Timothy 4:15 "Practice these things, immerse yourself in them, so that all may see your progress."

What steps did I take towards my goal today? _____

_____

What did today teach me that I will bring into tomorrow? ____

_____

Date:_____

Reflection:

Jeremiah 29:11 "For I know the plans I have for you, declares the Lord, plans for welfare and not for evil, to give you a future and a hope."

What am I celebrating today? _____

_____

What am I grateful for today? _____

_____

What do I need to forgive myself for today? _____

_____

How did I use my gifts today?: _____

_____

Self-care:

3 John 1:2 "Beloved, I pray that all may go well with you and that you may be in good health, as it goes well with your soul."

How did I spend my 15 minutes of "me" time today? _____

_____

How will I spend my 15 minutes of "me" time tomorrow? _____

_____

How did I show gratitude for the ability to move my body today? _____

_____

How will I move tomorrow? _____

_____

Growth:

1 Timothy 4:15 "Practice these things, immerse yourself in them, so that all may see your progress."

What steps did I take towards my goal today? _____

_____

What did today teach me that I will bring into tomorrow? _____

_____

Date:_____

Reflection:

Jeremiah 29:11 "For I know the plans I have for you, declares the Lord, plans for welfare and not for evil, to give you a future and a hope."

What am I celebrating today? _____

_____

What am I grateful for today? _____

_____

What do I need to forgive myself for today? _____

_____

How did I use my gifts today?: _____

_____

Self-care:

3 John 1:2 "Beloved, I pray that all may go well with you and that you may be in good health, as it goes well with your soul."

How did I spend my 15 minutes of "me" time today? _____

_____

How will I spend my 15 minutes of "me" time tomorrow? _____

_____

How did I show gratitude for the ability to move my body today? _____

_____

How will I move tomorrow? _____

_____

Growth:

1 Timothy 4:15 "Practice these things, immerse yourself in them, so that all may see your progress."

What steps did I take towards my goal today? _____

_____

What did today teach me that I will bring into tomorrow? _____

_____

1 Corinthians 6:19-20 "Or do you not know that your body is a temple of the Holy Spirit within you, whom you have from God? You are not your own, for you were bought with a price. So glorify God in your body"

Why is it so important to move your body daily? I will give you a few reasons. First, moving your body with exercise gives glory to the Lord. It means we are caring for His temple the way he entrusted us to. It means we are giving Him thanks for the ABILITY to move, which some may not have. Second, exercise lowers your risk for disease. Third, exercise relieves stress and puts you in a better mood. There are countless benefits to exercise. Therefore, I encourage all you moms to move daily.

On the other side of this, I understand why it can be so hard to get moving for yourself. Mom, you oversee a lot of things! Human beings, households, cooking, making lunches, homework, working… the list feels endless. All the reasons I listed previously are the reasons I encourage you all to find a rhythm. Start slow and work your way up from there. Your children need you healthy just as much as you do. Do it fore YOU! This is YOUR time, Mom. Congratulations for moving your body all week. Keep up the good work.

Let this serve as a reminder to you this week:

He sees you.

He hears you.

He loves you.

<u>Weekly Challenge:</u>

It's time to reflect on your entries from last week. Pray. Meditate. Celebrate.

Date:_____

Reflection:

Jeremiah 29:11 "For I know the plans I have for you, declares the Lord, plans for welfare and not for evil, to give you a future and a hope."

What am I celebrating today? _____
_____

What am I grateful for today? _____
_____

What do I need to forgive myself for today? _____
_____

How did I use my gifts today?: _____
_____

Self-care:

3 John 1:2 "Beloved, I pray that all may go well with you and that you may be in good health, as it goes well with your soul."

How did I spend my 15 minutes of "me" time today? _____
_____

How will I spend my 15 minutes of "me" time tomorrow? _____
_____

How did I show gratitude for the ability to move my body today? _____
_____

How will I move tomorrow? _____
_____

Growth:

1 Timothy 4:15 "Practice these things, immerse yourself in them, so that all may see your progress."

What steps did I take towards my goal today? _____
_____

What did today teach me that I will bring into tomorrow? _____
_____

Date:_____

Reflection:

Jeremiah 29:11 "For I know the plans I have for you, declares the Lord, plans for welfare and not for evil, to give you a future and a hope."

What am I celebrating today? _____

_____

What am I grateful for today? _____

_____

What do I need to forgive myself for today? _____

_____

How did I use my gifts today?: _____

_____

Self-care:

3 John 1:2 "Beloved, I pray that all may go well with you and that you may be in good health, as it goes well with your soul."

How did I spend my 15 minutes of "me" time today? _____

_____

How will I spend my 15 minutes of "me" time tomorrow? _____

_____

How did I show gratitude for the ability to move my body today? _____

_____

How will I move tomorrow? _____

_____

Growth:

1 Timothy 4:15 "Practice these things, immerse yourself in them, so that all may see your progress."

What steps did I take towards my goal today? _____

_____

What did today teach me that I will bring into tomorrow? _____

_____

Date:_____

Reflection:

Jeremiah 29:11 "For I know the plans I have for you, declares the Lord, plans for welfare and not for evil, to give you a future and a hope."

What am I celebrating today? _____

_____

What am I grateful for today? _____

_____

What do I need to forgive myself for today? _____

_____

How did I use my gifts today?: _____

_____

Self-care:

3 John 1:2 "Beloved, I pray that all may go well with you and that you may be in good health, as it goes well with your soul."

How did I spend my 15 minutes of "me" time today? _____

_____

How will I spend my 15 minutes of "me" time tomorrow? _____

_____

How did I show gratitude for the ability to move my body today? _____

_____

How will I move tomorrow? _____

_____

Growth:

1 Timothy 4:15 "Practice these things, immerse yourself in them, so that all may see your progress."

What steps did I take towards my goal today? _____

_____

What did today teach me that I will bring into tomorrow? _____

_____

Date:_____

Reflection:

Jeremiah 29:11 "For I know the plans I have for you, declares the Lord, plans for welfare and not for evil, to give you a future and a hope."

What am I celebrating today? _____

_____

What am I grateful for today? _____

_____

What do I need to forgive myself for today? _____

_____

How did I use my gifts today?: _____

_____

Self-care:

3 John 1:2 "Beloved, I pray that all may go well with you and that you may be in good health, as it goes well with your soul."

How did I spend my 15 minutes of "me" time today? _____

_____

How will I spend my 15 minutes of "me" time tomorrow? _____

_____

How did I show gratitude for the ability to move my body today? _____

_____

How will I move tomorrow? _____

_____

Growth:

1 Timothy 4:15 "Practice these things, immerse yourself in them, so that all may see your progress."

What steps did I take towards my goal today? _____

_____

What did today teach me that I will bring into tomorrow? _____

_____

Date:_____

Reflection:

Jeremiah 29:11 "For I know the plans I have for you, declares the Lord, plans for welfare and not for evil, to give you a future and a hope."

What am I celebrating today? _____
_____

What am I grateful for today? _____
_____

What do I need to forgive myself for today? _____
_____

How did I use my gifts today?: _____
_____

Self-care:

3 John 1:2 "Beloved, I pray that all may go well with you and that you may be in good health, as it goes well with your soul."

How did I spend my 15 minutes of "me" time today? _____
_____

How will I spend my 15 minutes of "me" time tomorrow? _____
_____

How did I show gratitude for the ability to move my body today? _____
_____

How will I move tomorrow? _____
_____

Growth:

1 Timothy 4:15 "Practice these things, immerse yourself in them, so that all may see your progress."

What steps did I take towards my goal today? _____
_____

What did today teach me that I will bring into tomorrow? _____
_____

Date:_____

Reflection:

Jeremiah 29:11 "For I know the plans I have for you, declares the Lord, plans for welfare and not for evil, to give you a future and a hope."

What am I celebrating today? _____

_____

What am I grateful for today? _____

_____

What do I need to forgive myself for today? _____

_____

How did I use my gifts today?: _____

_____

Self-care:

3 John 1:2 "Beloved, I pray that all may go well with you and that you may be in good health, as it goes well with your soul."

How did I spend my 15 minutes of "me" time today? _____

_____

How will I spend my 15 minutes of "me" time tomorrow? _____

_____

How did I show gratitude for the ability to move my body today? _____

_____

How will I move tomorrow? _____

_____

Growth:

1 Timothy 4:15 "Practice these things, immerse yourself in them, so that all may see your progress."

What steps did I take towards my goal today? _____

_____

What did today teach me that I will bring into tomorrow? _____

_____

Date:_____

Reflection:

Jeremiah 29:11 "For I know the plans I have for you, declares the Lord, plans for welfare and not for evil, to give you a future and a hope."

What am I celebrating today? _____

_____

What am I grateful for today? _____

_____

What do I need to forgive myself for today? _____

_____

How did I use my gifts today?: _____

_____

Self-care:

3 John 1:2 "Beloved, I pray that all may go well with you and that you may be in good health, as it goes well with your soul."

How did I spend my 15 minutes of "me" time today? _____

_____

How will I spend my 15 minutes of "me" time tomorrow? _____

_____

How did I show gratitude for the ability to move my body today? _____

_____

How will I move tomorrow? _____

_____

Growth:

1 Timothy 4:15 "Practice these things, immerse yourself in them, so that all may see your progress."

What steps did I take towards my goal today? _____

_____

What did today teach me that I will bring into tomorrow? _____

_____

Philippians 4:8 "Finally, brothers, whatever is true, whatever is honorable, whatever is just, whatever is pure, whatever is lovely, whatever is commendable, if there is any excellence, if there is anything worthy of praise, think about these things."

This week I was to keep this insert short. Whatever it is that you have been keeping heavy on your heart, I ask you to meditate on it today. Whatever it is that has been keeping you awake at night, mom, He hears you and sees you. Take time now to pray on this thing. Take time now to ask the Lord to reveal His will in your life. Ask the Lord now to make new the areas that have turned old. Mom, you carry the weight of the world on your shoulders. It is no wonder you are tired. Praise Him in this moment, wherever you are at. This is my prayer for you.

Let this serve as a reminder to you this week:

He sees you.

He hears you.

He loves you.

Weekly Challenge:

It's time to reflect on your entries from last week. Pray. Meditate. Celebrate.

Date:_____

Reflection:

Jeremiah 29:11 "For I know the plans I have for you, declares the Lord, plans for welfare and not for evil, to give you a future and a hope."

What am I celebrating today? _____

_____

What am I grateful for today? _____

_____

What do I need to forgive myself for today? _____

_____

How did I use my gifts today?: _____

_____

Self-care:

3 John 1:2 "Beloved, I pray that all may go well with you and that you may be in good health, as it goes well with your soul."

How did I spend my 15 minutes of "me" time today? _____

_____

How will I spend my 15 minutes of "me" time tomorrow? _____

_____

How did I show gratitude for the ability to move my body today? ____

_____

How will I move tomorrow? _____

_____

Growth:

1 Timothy 4:15 "Practice these things, immerse yourself in them, so that all may see your progress."

What steps did I take towards my goal today? _____

_____

What did today teach me that I will bring into tomorrow? _____

_____

Date:_____

Reflection:

Jeremiah 29:11 "For I know the plans I have for you, declares the Lord, plans for welfare and not for evil, to give you a future and a hope."

What am I celebrating today? _____
_____

What am I grateful for today? _____
_____

What do I need to forgive myself for today? _____
_____

How did I use my gifts today?: _____
_____

Self-care:

3 John 1:2 "Beloved, I pray that all may go well with you and that you may be in good health, as it goes well with your soul."

How did I spend my 15 minutes of "me" time today? _____
_____

How will I spend my 15 minutes of "me" time tomorrow? _____
_____

How did I show gratitude for the ability to move my body today? _____
_____

How will I move tomorrow? _____
_____

Growth:

1 Timothy 4:15 "Practice these things, immerse yourself in them, so that all may see your progress."

What steps did I take towards my goal today? _____
_____

What did today teach me that I will bring into tomorrow? _____
_____

Reflection:

Jeremiah 29:11 "For I know the plans I have for you, declares the Lord, plans for welfare and not for evil, to give you a future and a hope."

What am I celebrating today? _____

_____

What am I grateful for today? _____

_____

What do I need to forgive myself for today? _____

_____

How did I use my gifts today?: _____

_____

Self-care:

3 John 1:2 "Beloved, I pray that all may go well with you and that you may be in good health, as it goes well with your soul."

How did I spend my 15 minutes of "me" time today? _____

_____

How will I spend my 15 minutes of "me" time tomorrow? _____

_____

How did I show gratitude for the ability to move my body today? _____

_____

How will I move tomorrow? _____

_____

Growth:

1 Timothy 4:15 "Practice these things, immerse yourself in them, so that all may see your progress."

What steps did I take towards my goal today? _____

_____

What did today teach me that I will bring into tomorrow? _____

_____

Date:_____

Reflection:

Jeremiah 29:11 "For I know the plans I have for you, declares the Lord, plans for welfare and not for evil, to give you a future and a hope."

What am I celebrating today? _____

_____

What am I grateful for today? _____

_____

What do I need to forgive myself for today? _____

_____

How did I use my gifts today?: _____

_____

Self-care:

3 John 1:2 "Beloved, I pray that all may go well with you and that you may be in good health, as it goes well with your soul."

How did I spend my 15 minutes of "me" time today? _____

_____

How will I spend my 15 minutes of "me" time tomorrow? _____

_____

How did I show gratitude for the ability to move my body today? _____

_____

How will I move tomorrow? _____

_____

Growth:

1 Timothy 4:15 "Practice these things, immerse yourself in them, so that all may see your progress."

What steps did I take towards my goal today? _____

_____

What did today teach me that I will bring into tomorrow? _____

_____

Reflection:

Jeremiah 29:11 "For I know the plans I have for you, declares the Lord, plans for welfare and not for evil, to give you a future and a hope."

What am I celebrating today? _____

_____

What am I grateful for today? _____

_____

What do I need to forgive myself for today? _____

_____

How did I use my gifts today?: _____

_____

Self-care:

3 John 1:2 "Beloved, I pray that all may go well with you and that you may be in good health, as it goes well with your soul."

How did I spend my 15 minutes of "me" time today? _____

_____

How will I spend my 15 minutes of "me" time tomorrow? _____

_____

How did I show gratitude for the ability to move my body today? _____

_____

How will I move tomorrow? _____

_____

Growth:

1 Timothy 4:15 "Practice these things, immerse yourself in them, so that all may see your progress."

What steps did I take towards my goal today? _____

_____

What did today teach me that I will bring into tomorrow? _____

_____

Date:_____

Reflection:

Jeremiah 29:11 "For I know the plans I have for you, declares the Lord, plans for welfare and not for evil, to give you a future and a hope."

What am I celebrating today? _____

_____

What am I grateful for today? _____

_____

What do I need to forgive myself for today? _____

_____

How did I use my gifts today?: _____

_____

Self-care:

3 John 1:2 "Beloved, I pray that all may go well with you and that you may be in good health, as it goes well with your soul."

How did I spend my 15 minutes of "me" time today? _____

_____

How will I spend my 15 minutes of "me" time tomorrow? _____

_____

How did I show gratitude for the ability to move my body today? _____

_____

How will I move tomorrow? _____

_____

Growth:

1 Timothy 4:15 "Practice these things, immerse yourself in them, so that all may see your progress."

What steps did I take towards my goal today? _____

_____

What did today teach me that I will bring into tomorrow? _____

_____

Date:_____

Reflection:

Jeremiah 29:11 "For I know the plans I have for you, declares the Lord, plans for welfare and not for evil, to give you a future and a hope."

What am I celebrating today? _____

_____

What am I grateful for today? _____

_____

What do I need to forgive myself for today? _____

_____

How did I use my gifts today?: _____

_____

Self-care:

3 John 1:2 "Beloved, I pray that all may go well with you and that you may be in good health, as it goes well with your soul."

How did I spend my 15 minutes of "me" time today? _____

_____

How will I spend my 15 minutes of "me" time tomorrow? _____

_____

How did I show gratitude for the ability to move my body today? _____

_____

How will I move tomorrow? _____

_____

Growth:

1 Timothy 4:15 "Practice these things, immerse yourself in them, so that all may see your progress."

What steps did I take towards my goal today? _____

_____

What did today teach me that I will bring into tomorrow? _____

_____

Proverbs 3:5-6 "Trust in the Lord with all you heart, and do not lean on your own understanding. In all your ways acknowledge him, and he will make straight your paths."

Mom, I know you must struggle with guilt at times. Guilt that you may not have the right decision. There are so many decisions to make as a mom! Breastfed or bottle fed? Day care or stay at home mom? School bus or drive to school? I believe a lot of this guilt has to do with something I call "mom-petition." It is defined as moms non intentionally competing over what is best for children. We let what we see in movies, tv, and social media paint a picture in our mind of what motherhood must look like. It is hypnotizing. It is these "influential" mothers that are playing a huge role in setting these unrealistic goals that us moms need to reach each day. If something works for one mom, it may not work for the next. I will share a little story with you. When I gave birth to my first son, he was born with his tongue almost stuck to the roof of his mouth. I intended on breastfeeding; however, he just would not latch. Each day I was in the hospital after giving birth, the lactation specialists would come in the room and try and try again. Nothing would work. Eventually the specialists found a way to spoon feed him the breastmilk, while forcing his tongue downward with a plastic spoon. This devastated me. To me, breastfeeding was not supposed to be like this. Once I was sent home with my little one, he was continuing to have trouble latching. He was up all hours of the night crying and I just could not help him. I would try and feed him, then put him to sleep. That was not working. The lactation specialist came to visit my home. I explained the situation and she began to weigh him. She asked me to feed him, then she weighed him again. He was not gaining any weight!! That is when we found out the issue from his tongue was still preventing him from latching, therefore, all the crying he was doing was due to him starving! She told me to get formula and begin to feed him immediately. For a lactation specialist to tell a mother to start formula, you know it had to have been a serious situation. In that moment, I felt like a failure. I felt I was not doing it right! The specialist saw how defeated I felt. She left me with words I will never forget. She told me that the only thing that matters is that my son eats, and it truly does not matter how. Since that day, I have passed those words on to countless mothers dealing with the same situation. Mom guilt can weigh heavy. Just remember you are doing the absolute best you can, and THAT is what matters. God sees you and has not left you. You are never alone.

Let this serve as a reminder to you this week:

He sees you.

He hears you.

He loves you.

Weekly Challenge:

It's time to reflect on your entries from last week. Pray. Meditate. Celebrate.

Date:_____

Reflection:

Jeremiah 29:11 "For I know the plans I have for you, declares the Lord, plans for welfare and not for evil, to give you a future and a hope."

What am I celebrating today? _____

_____

What am I grateful for today? _____

_____

What do I need to forgive myself for today? _____

_____

How did I use my gifts today?: _____

_____

Self-care:

3 John 1:2 "Beloved, I pray that all may go well with you and that you may be in good health, as it goes well with your soul."

How did I spend my 15 minutes of "me" time today? _____

_____

How will I spend my 15 minutes of "me" time tomorrow? _____

_____

How did I show gratitude for the ability to move my body today? _____

_____

How will I move tomorrow? _____

_____

Growth:

1 Timothy 4:15 "Practice these things, immerse yourself in them, so that all may see your progress."

What steps did I take towards my goal today? _____

_____

What did today teach me that I will bring into tomorrow? _____

_____

Date:_____

Reflection:

Jeremiah 29:11 "For I know the plans I have for you, declares the Lord, plans for welfare and not for evil, to give you a future and a hope."

What am I celebrating today? _____
_____

What am I grateful for today? _____
_____

What do I need to forgive myself for today? _____
_____

How did I use my gifts today?: _____
_____

Self-care:

3 John 1:2 "Beloved, I pray that all may go well with you and that you may be in good health, as it goes well with your soul."

How did I spend my 15 minutes of "me" time today? _____
_____

How will I spend my 15 minutes of "me" time tomorrow? _____
_____

How did I show gratitude for the ability to move my body today? _____
_____

How will I move tomorrow? _____
_____

Growth:

1 Timothy 4:15 "Practice these things, immerse yourself in them, so that all may see your progress."

What steps did I take towards my goal today? _____
_____

What did today teach me that I will bring into tomorrow? _____
_____

Date:_____

Reflection:

Jeremiah 29:11 "For I know the plans I have for you, declares the Lord, plans for welfare and not for evil, to give you a future and a hope."

What am I celebrating today? _____

_____

What am I grateful for today? _____

_____

What do I need to forgive myself for today? _____

_____

How did I use my gifts today?: _____

_____

Self-care:

3 John 1:2 "Beloved, I pray that all may go well with you and that you may be in good health, as it goes well with your soul."

How did I spend my 15 minutes of "me" time today? _____

_____

How will I spend my 15 minutes of "me" time tomorrow? _____

_____

How did I show gratitude for the ability to move my body today? _____

_____

How will I move tomorrow? _____

_____

Growth:

1 Timothy 4:15 "Practice these things, immerse yourself in them, so that all may see your progress."

What steps did I take towards my goal today? _____

_____

What did today teach me that I will bring into tomorrow? _____

_____

Date:_____

Reflection:

Jeremiah 29:11 "For I know the plans I have for you, declares the Lord, plans for welfare and not for evil, to give you a future and a hope."

What am I celebrating today? _____
_____

What am I grateful for today? _____
_____

What do I need to forgive myself for today? _____
_____

How did I use my gifts today?: _____
_____

Self-care:

3 John 1:2 "Beloved, I pray that all may go well with you and that you may be in good health, as it goes well with your soul."

How did I spend my 15 minutes of "me" time today? _____
_____

How will I spend my 15 minutes of "me" time tomorrow? _____
_____

How did I show gratitude for the ability to move my body today? _____
_____

How will I move tomorrow? _____
_____

Growth:

1 Timothy 4:15 "Practice these things, immerse yourself in them, so that all may see your progress."

What steps did I take towards my goal today? _____
_____

What did today teach me that I will bring into tomorrow? _____
_____

Date:_____

Reflection:

Jeremiah 29:11 "For I know the plans I have for you, declares the Lord, plans for welfare and not for evil, to give you a future and a hope."

What am I celebrating today? _____

_____

What am I grateful for today? _____

_____

What do I need to forgive myself for today? _____

_____

How did I use my gifts today?: _____

_____

Self-care:

3 John 1:2 "Beloved, I pray that all may go well with you and that you may be in good health, as it goes well with your soul."

How did I spend my 15 minutes of "me" time today? _____

_____

How will I spend my 15 minutes of "me" time tomorrow? _____

_____

How did I show gratitude for the ability to move my body today? _____

_____

How will I move tomorrow? _____

_____

Growth:

1 Timothy 4:15 "Practice these things, immerse yourself in them, so that all may see your progress."

What steps did I take towards my goal today? _____

_____

What did today teach me that I will bring into tomorrow? _____

_____

Date:_____

Reflection:

Jeremiah 29:11 "For I know the plans I have for you, declares the Lord, plans for welfare and not for evil, to give you a future and a hope."

What am I celebrating today? _____

_____

What am I grateful for today? _____

_____

What do I need to forgive myself for today? _____

_____

How did I use my gifts today?: _____

_____

Self-care:

3 John 1:2 "Beloved, I pray that all may go well with you and that you may be in good health, as it goes well with your soul."

How did I spend my 15 minutes of "me" time today? _____

_____

How will I spend my 15 minutes of "me" time tomorrow? _____

_____

How did I show gratitude for the ability to move my body today? _____

_____

How will I move tomorrow? _____

_____

Growth:

1 Timothy 4:15 "Practice these things, immerse yourself in them, so that all may see your progress."

What steps did I take towards my goal today? _____

_____

What did today teach me that I will bring into tomorrow? _____

_____

Date:_____

Reflection:

Jeremiah 29:11 "For I know the plans I have for you, declares the Lord, plans for welfare and not for evil, to give you a future and a hope."

What am I celebrating today? _____

_____

What am I grateful for today? _____

_____

What do I need to forgive myself for today? _____

_____

How did I use my gifts today?: _____

_____

Self-care:

3 John 1:2 "Beloved, I pray that all may go well with you and that you may be in good health, as it goes well with your soul."

How did I spend my 15 minutes of "me" time today? _____

_____

How will I spend my 15 minutes of "me" time tomorrow? _____

_____

How did I show gratitude for the ability to move my body today? _____

_____

How will I move tomorrow? _____

_____

Growth:

1 Timothy 4:15 "Practice these things, immerse yourself in them, so that all may see your progress."

What steps did I take towards my goal today? _____

_____

What did today teach me that I will bring into tomorrow? _____

_____

Matthew 10:31 "Fear not, therefore; you are of more value than many sparrows."

Mom, you give so much of yourself to your family. You care for them. You tirelessly put a smile on your face on days you just want to cry. There are days you hold the weight of the world on your shoulders. Let's face it, our job as a mother can be a thankless job. I would be lying if I said that did not weigh heavy on my heart some days. How many nights have you laid awake in bed and longed for someone to say, "I am proud of you?" Chances are those words have left your lips countless times throughout the day when speaking to your children. But why aren't those words spoken to you just as often? I mean, you are pouring your heart and soul into this job called motherhood! Mom, I get it! I see you and I hear you. Better yet, GOD hears you and GOD sees you. Your reward is waiting for you. When you meet the Lord face to face one day, how good will it be to hear those words you have longed to hear, "well done my good and faithful servant." God gave you this job title "mom" because He knew that no one could do a better job with our child(ren) that you. Some days on Earth may feel like no one sees the work you are putting in to raising those precious little ones, but I pray you find comfort knowing that your work does not go unnoticed. In those moments where you feel the need to hear those words, "I am proud of you," I urge you to cry out to Him. No matter where you are in that moment, cry out to Him. He hears you. Remember, you are NEVER alone, mom.

Let this serve as a reminder to you this week:

He sees you.

He hears you.

He loves you.

Weekly Challenge:

It's time to reflect on your entries from last week. Pray. Meditate. Celebrate.

Date:_____

Reflection:

Jeremiah 29:11 "For I know the plans I have for you, declares the Lord, plans for welfare and not for evil, to give you a future and a hope."

What am I celebrating today? _____
_____

What am I grateful for today? _____
_____

What do I need to forgive myself for today? _____
_____

How did I use my gifts today?: _____
_____

Self-care:

3 John 1:2 "Beloved, I pray that all may go well with you and that you may be in good health, as it goes well with your soul."

How did I spend my 15 minutes of "me" time today? _____
_____

How will I spend my 15 minutes of "me" time tomorrow? _____
_____

How did I show gratitude for the ability to move my body today? _____
_____

How will I move tomorrow? _____
_____

Growth:

1 Timothy 4:15 "Practice these things, immerse yourself in them, so that all may see your progress."

What steps did I take towards my goal today? _____
_____

What did today teach me that I will bring into tomorrow? _____
_____

Date:_____

Reflection:

Jeremiah 29:11 "For I know the plans I have for you, declares the Lord, plans for welfare and not for evil, to give you a future and a hope."

What am I celebrating today? _____

_____

What am I grateful for today? _____

_____

What do I need to forgive myself for today? _____

_____

How did I use my gifts today?: _____

_____

Self-care:

3 John 1:2 "Beloved, I pray that all may go well with you and that you may be in good health, as it goes well with your soul."

How did I spend my 15 minutes of "me" time today? _____

_____

How will I spend my 15 minutes of "me" time tomorrow? _____

_____

How did I show gratitude for the ability to move my body today? _____

_____

How will I move tomorrow? _____

_____

Growth:

1 Timothy 4:15 "Practice these things, immerse yourself in them, so that all may see your progress."

What steps did I take towards my goal today? _____

_____

What did today teach me that I will bring into tomorrow? _____

_____

Date:_____

Reflection:

Jeremiah 29:11 "For I know the plans I have for you, declares the Lord, plans for welfare and not for evil, to give you a future and a hope."

What am I celebrating today? _____

_____

What am I grateful for today? _____

_____

What do I need to forgive myself for today? _____

_____

How did I use my gifts today?: _____

_____

Self-care:

3 John 1:2 "Beloved, I pray that all may go well with you and that you may be in good health, as it goes well with your soul."

How did I spend my 15 minutes of "me" time today? _____

_____

How will I spend my 15 minutes of "me" time tomorrow? _____

_____

How did I show gratitude for the ability to move my body today? _____

_____

How will I move tomorrow? _____

_____

Growth:

1 Timothy 4:15 "Practice these things, immerse yourself in them, so that all may see your progress."

What steps did I take towards my goal today? _____

_____

What did today teach me that I will bring into tomorrow? _____

_____

Date:_____

Reflection:

Jeremiah 29:11 "For I know the plans I have for you, declares the Lord, plans for welfare and not for evil, to give you a future and a hope."

What am I celebrating today? _____

_____

What am I grateful for today? _____

_____

What do I need to forgive myself for today? _____

_____

How did I use my gifts today?: _____

_____

Self-care:

3 John 1:2 "Beloved, I pray that all may go well with you and that you may be in good health, as it goes well with your soul."

How did I spend my 15 minutes of "me" time today? _____

_____

How will I spend my 15 minutes of "me" time tomorrow? _____

_____

How did I show gratitude for the ability to move my body today? _____

_____

How will I move tomorrow? _____

_____

Growth:

1 Timothy 4:15 "Practice these things, immerse yourself in them, so that all may see your progress."

What steps did I take towards my goal today? _____

_____

What did today teach me that I will bring into tomorrow? _____

_____

Date:_____

Reflection:

Jeremiah 29:11 "For I know the plans I have for you, declares the Lord, plans for welfare and not for evil, to give you a future and a hope."

What am I celebrating today? _____

_____

What am I grateful for today? _____

_____

What do I need to forgive myself for today? _____

_____

How did I use my gifts today?: _____

_____

Self-care:

3 John 1:2 "Beloved, I pray that all may go well with you and that you may be in good health, as it goes well with your soul."

How did I spend my 15 minutes of "me" time today? _____

_____

How will I spend my 15 minutes of "me" time tomorrow? _____

_____

How did I show gratitude for the ability to move my body today? _____

_____

How will I move tomorrow? _____

_____

Growth:

1 Timothy 4:15 "Practice these things, immerse yourself in them, so that all may see your progress."

What steps did I take towards my goal today? _____

_____

What did today teach me that I will bring into tomorrow? _____

_____

Reflection:

Jeremiah 29:11 "For I know the plans I have for you, declares the Lord, plans for welfare and not for evil, to give you a future and a hope."

What am I celebrating today? _____
_____

What am I grateful for today? _____
_____

What do I need to forgive myself for today? _____
_____

How did I use my gifts today?: _____
_____

Self-care:

3 John 1:2 "Beloved, I pray that all may go well with you and that you may be in good health, as it goes well with your soul."

How did I spend my 15 minutes of "me" time today? _____
_____

How will I spend my 15 minutes of "me" time tomorrow? _____
_____

How did I show gratitude for the ability to move my body today? _____
_____

How will I move tomorrow? _____
_____

Growth:

1 Timothy 4:15 "Practice these things, immerse yourself in them, so that all may see your progress."

What steps did I take towards my goal today? _____
_____

What did today teach me that I will bring into tomorrow? _____
_____

Date:_____

Reflection:

Jeremiah 29:11 "For I know the plans I have for you, declares the Lord, plans for welfare and not for evil, to give you a future and a hope."

What am I celebrating today? _____
_____

What am I grateful for today? _____
_____

What do I need to forgive myself for today? _____
_____

How did I use my gifts today?: _____
_____

Self-care:

3 John 1:2 "Beloved, I pray that all may go well with you and that you may be in good health, as it goes well with your soul."

How did I spend my 15 minutes of "me" time today? _____
_____

How will I spend my 15 minutes of "me" time tomorrow? _____
_____

How did I show gratitude for the ability to move my body today? _____
_____

How will I move tomorrow? _____
_____

Growth:

1 Timothy 4:15 "Practice these things, immerse yourself in them, so that all may see your progress."

What steps did I take towards my goal today? _____
_____

What did today teach me that I will bring into tomorrow? _____
_____

***John 10:10** "The thief comes only to steal and kill and destroy. I came that they may have life and have it abundantly."*

Words are so powerful. Words can tear a person down. Words can build a person up. In Hebrews 4:12 God says "For the word of God is living and active, sharper than any two-edged sword, piercing to the division of soul and of spirit, of joints and of marrow, and discerning the thoughts and intentions of the heart." This goes for the words you speak into your own life. I will give you an example. Through the years, I have shared my personal story of growing up, getting married, and having children with several people. I have always finished my story with saying the phrase, "I am going to write a book one day". I would close that statement with giving a little giggle. I never actually had ANY intentions to write a book. In fact, growing up I would despise reading so why would I ever intend to write a book?! Well, those words that I spoke into my life repeatedly, came to pass. Here you are reading the book I wrote. I spoke those words into my life, and God heard them. He made a way to use those words to give Him glory. When we get discouraged in our journey of parenthood, we tend to speak negativity in our lives without the intent of those words taking over that specific area. In my personal journey of motherhood, I have spoken words that I immediately regretted. There were times I said, "I am too exhausted, and I just can't do anything right from this sleep deprivation." What I SHOULD have said was "I am so exhausted and sleep deprived. Now is when I really need to lean of the Lord to be my strength because I can do all things through HIM." (Do not forget that it is ok to reach out for help from other in moments such as this as well). This is one reason I ask you to write down a victory for the day. This is also why I ask you to forgive yourself for something daily. I could have said "how did you mess up" …but how would that benefit your mind and soul? It is about wording it in a way that you recognize you would do something differently, however, you are not focusing on the negative. Instead, you are recognizing it, forgiving yourself, and moving forward. Speak life into every area of your journey. Mom, you got this! God is by your side.

Let this serve as a reminder to you this week:

He sees you.

He hears you.

He loves you.

Weekly Challenge:

It's time to reflect on your entries from last week. Pray. Meditate. Celebrate.

Date:_____

Reflection:

Jeremiah 29:11 "For I know the plans I have for you, declares the Lord, plans for welfare and not for evil, to give you a future and a hope."

What am I celebrating today? _____

_____

What am I grateful for today? _____

_____

What do I need to forgive myself for today? _____

_____

How did I use my gifts today?: _____

_____

Self-care:

3 John 1:2 "Beloved, I pray that all may go well with you and that you may be in good health, as it goes well with your soul."

How did I spend my 15 minutes of "me" time today? _____

_____

How will I spend my 15 minutes of "me" time tomorrow? _____

_____

How did I show gratitude for the ability to move my body today? ____

_____

How will I move tomorrow? _____

_____

Growth:

1 Timothy 4:15 "Practice these things, immerse yourself in them, so that all may see your progress."

What steps did I take towards my goal today? _____

_____

What did today teach me that I will bring into tomorrow? _____

_____

Date:_____

Reflection:

Jeremiah 29:11 "For I know the plans I have for you, declares the Lord, plans for welfare and not for evil, to give you a future and a hope."

What am I celebrating today? _____
_____

What am I grateful for today? _____
_____

What do I need to forgive myself for today? _____
_____

How did I use my gifts today?: _____
_____

Self-care:

3 John 1:2 "Beloved, I pray that all may go well with you and that you may be in good health, as it goes well with your soul."

How did I spend my 15 minutes of "me" time today? _____
_____

How will I spend my 15 minutes of "me" time tomorrow? _____
_____

How did I show gratitude for the ability to move my body today? _____
_____

How will I move tomorrow? _____
_____

Growth:

1 Timothy 4:15 "Practice these things, immerse yourself in them, so that all may see your progress."

What steps did I take towards my goal today? _____
_____

What did today teach me that I will bring into tomorrow? _____
_____

Date:_____

Reflection:

Jeremiah 29:11 "For I know the plans I have for you, declares the Lord, plans for welfare and not for evil, to give you a future and a hope."

What am I celebrating today? _____
_____

What am I grateful for today? _____
_____

What do I need to forgive myself for today? _____
_____

How did I use my gifts today?: _____
_____

Self-care:

3 John 1:2 "Beloved, I pray that all may go well with you and that you may be in good health, as it goes well with your soul."

How did I spend my 15 minutes of "me" time today? _____
_____

How will I spend my 15 minutes of "me" time tomorrow? _____
_____

How did I show gratitude for the ability to move my body today? ____
_____

How will I move tomorrow? _____
_____

Growth:

1 Timothy 4:15 "Practice these things, immerse yourself in them, so that all may see your progress."

What steps did I take towards my goal today? _____
_____

What did today teach me that I will bring into tomorrow? _____
_____

Date:_____

Reflection:

Jeremiah 29:11 "For I know the plans I have for you, declares the Lord, plans for welfare and not for evil, to give you a future and a hope."

What am I celebrating today? _____

_____

What am I grateful for today? _____

_____

What do I need to forgive myself for today? _____

_____

How did I use my gifts today?: _____

_____

Self-care:

3 John 1:2 "Beloved, I pray that all may go well with you and that you may be in good health, as it goes well with your soul."

How did I spend my 15 minutes of "me" time today? _____

_____

How will I spend my 15 minutes of "me" time tomorrow? _____

_____

How did I show gratitude for the ability to move my body today? _____

_____

How will I move tomorrow? _____

_____

Growth:

1 Timothy 4:15 "Practice these things, immerse yourself in them, so that all may see your progress."

What steps did I take towards my goal today? _____

_____

What did today teach me that I will bring into tomorrow? _____

_____

Date:_____

Reflection:

Jeremiah 29:11 "For I know the plans I have for you, declares the Lord, plans for welfare and not for evil, to give you a future and a hope."

What am I celebrating today? _____
_____

What am I grateful for today? _____
_____

What do I need to forgive myself for today? _____
_____

How did I use my gifts today?: _____
_____

Self-care:

3 John 1:2 "Beloved, I pray that all may go well with you and that you may be in good health, as it goes well with your soul."

How did I spend my 15 minutes of "me" time today? _____
_____

How will I spend my 15 minutes of "me" time tomorrow? _____
_____

How did I show gratitude for the ability to move my body today? _____
_____

How will I move tomorrow? _____
_____

Growth:

1 Timothy 4:15 "Practice these things, immerse yourself in them, so that all may see your progress."

What steps did I take towards my goal today? _____
_____

What did today teach me that I will bring into tomorrow? _____
_____

Date:_____

Reflection:

Jeremiah 29:11 "For I know the plans I have for you, declares the Lord, plans for welfare and not for evil, to give you a future and a hope."

What am I celebrating today? _____
_____

What am I grateful for today? _____
_____

What do I need to forgive myself for today? _____
_____

How did I use my gifts today?: _____
_____

Self-care:

3 John 1:2 "Beloved, I pray that all may go well with you and that you may be in good health, as it goes well with your soul."

How did I spend my 15 minutes of "me" time today? _____
_____

How will I spend my 15 minutes of "me" time tomorrow? _____
_____

How did I show gratitude for the ability to move my body today? _____
_____

How will I move tomorrow? _____
_____

Growth:

1 Timothy 4:15 "Practice these things, immerse yourself in them, so that all may see your progress."

What steps did I take towards my goal today? _____
_____

What did today teach me that I will bring into tomorrow? _____
_____

Reflection:

Jeremiah 29:11 "For I know the plans I have for you, declares the Lord, plans for welfare and not for evil, to give you a future and a hope."

What am I celebrating today? _____

_____

What am I grateful for today? _____

_____

What do I need to forgive myself for today? _____

_____

How did I use my gifts today?: _____

_____

Self-care:

3 John 1:2 "Beloved, I pray that all may go well with you and that you may be in good health, as it goes well with your soul."

How did I spend my 15 minutes of "me" time today? _____

_____

How will I spend my 15 minutes of "me" time tomorrow? _____

_____

How did I show gratitude for the ability to move my body today? _____

_____

How will I move tomorrow? _____

_____

Growth:

1 Timothy 4:15 "Practice these things, immerse yourself in them, so that all may see your progress."

What steps did I take towards my goal today? _____

_____

What did today teach me that I will bring into tomorrow? _____

_____

1 Peter 4:10 "As each has received a gift, use it to serve one another, as good stewards of God's varied grace."

We have all been given a gift or multiple gifts. It may be hard to see that gift when you are giving your all to others day in and day out. Mothers tend to push aside our dreams or our gifts in order to support our significant others, or in order to dedicate your days to your children and their needs. This is the time where you are called to tune in to that gift and use it. Why is this so important? God has placed a gift inside all of us on Earth. When we begin to use that gift, we are serving others, in turn that serves Him. If you are struggling with figuring out what your gift is, maybe it is because you have given yourself to motherhood for so long that you forgot who you are as an individual; now is the time to search deep inside yourself to discover your talents and gift. You have been asked daily in write down a way you have used your gift today. Writing this down each day, you may discover a new talent or gift you possess. I am applauding you for doing this for YOU, which in return will serve others around you. You may find something that brings a new type of happiness in your life. That happiness will pour out into your children. It will pour out into your home. It causes a ripple effect. You are talented. You are chosen by God to use that gift. You are a shining example to your children for them to follow their own dreams. Mom, I am so proud of you.

Let this serve as a reminder to you this week:

He sees you.

He hears you.

He loves you.

Weekly Challenge:

It's time to reflect on your entries from last week. Pray. Meditate. Celebrate.

Date:_____

Reflection:

Jeremiah 29:11 "For I know the plans I have for you, declares the Lord, plans for welfare and not for evil, to give you a future and a hope."

What am I celebrating today? _____

_____

What am I grateful for today? _____

_____

What do I need to forgive myself for today? _____

_____

How did I use my gifts today?: _____

_____

Self-care:

3 John 1:2 "Beloved, I pray that all may go well with you and that you may be in good health, as it goes well with your soul."

How did I spend my 15 minutes of "me" time today? _____

_____

How will I spend my 15 minutes of "me" time tomorrow? _____

_____

How did I show gratitude for the ability to move my body today? _____

_____

How will I move tomorrow? _____

_____

Growth:

1 Timothy 4:15 "Practice these things, immerse yourself in them, so that all may see your progress."

What steps did I take towards my goal today? _____

_____

What did today teach me that I will bring into tomorrow? _____

_____

Date:_____

Reflection:

Jeremiah 29:11 "For I know the plans I have for you, declares the Lord, plans for welfare and not for evil, to give you a future and a hope."

What am I celebrating today? _____

_____

What am I grateful for today? _____

_____

What do I need to forgive myself for today? _____

_____

How did I use my gifts today?: _____

_____

Self-care:

3 John 1:2 "Beloved, I pray that all may go well with you and that you may be in good health, as it goes well with your soul."

How did I spend my 15 minutes of "me" time today? _____

_____

How will I spend my 15 minutes of "me" time tomorrow? _____

_____

How did I show gratitude for the ability to move my body today? _____

_____

How will I move tomorrow? _____

_____

Growth:

1 Timothy 4:15 "Practice these things, immerse yourself in them, so that all may see your progress."

What steps did I take towards my goal today? _____

_____

What did today teach me that I will bring into tomorrow? _____

_____

Date:_____

Reflection:

Jeremiah 29:11 "For I know the plans I have for you, declares the Lord, plans for welfare and not for evil, to give you a future and a hope."

What am I celebrating today? _____

_____

What am I grateful for today? _____

_____

What do I need to forgive myself for today? _____

_____

How did I use my gifts today?: _____

_____

Self-care:

3 John 1:2 "Beloved, I pray that all may go well with you and that you may be in good health, as it goes well with your soul."

How did I spend my 15 minutes of "me" time today? _____

_____

How will I spend my 15 minutes of "me" time tomorrow? _____

_____

How did I show gratitude for the ability to move my body today? _____

_____

How will I move tomorrow? _____

_____

Growth:

1 Timothy 4:15 "Practice these things, immerse yourself in them, so that all may see your progress."

What steps did I take towards my goal today? _____

_____

What did today teach me that I will bring into tomorrow? _____

_____

Date:_____

Reflection:

Jeremiah 29:11 "For I know the plans I have for you, declares the Lord, plans for welfare and not for evil, to give you a future and a hope."

What am I celebrating today? _____

_____

What am I grateful for today? _____

_____

What do I need to forgive myself for today? _____

_____

How did I use my gifts today?: _____

_____

Self-care:

3 John 1:2 "Beloved, I pray that all may go well with you and that you may be in good health, as it goes well with your soul."

How did I spend my 15 minutes of "me" time today? _____

_____

How will I spend my 15 minutes of "me" time tomorrow? _____

_____

How did I show gratitude for the ability to move my body today? _____

_____

How will I move tomorrow? _____

_____

Growth:

1 Timothy 4:15 "Practice these things, immerse yourself in them, so that all may see your progress."

What steps did I take towards my goal today? _____

_____

What did today teach me that I will bring into tomorrow? _____

_____

Date:_____

Reflection:

Jeremiah 29:11 "For I know the plans I have for you, declares the Lord, plans for welfare and not for evil, to give you a future and a hope."

What am I celebrating today? _____
_____

What am I grateful for today? _____
_____

What do I need to forgive myself for today? _____
_____

How did I use my gifts today?: _____
_____

Self-care:

3 John 1:2 "Beloved, I pray that all may go well with you and that you may be in good health, as it goes well with your soul."

How did I spend my 15 minutes of "me" time today? _____
_____

How will I spend my 15 minutes of "me" time tomorrow? _____
_____

How did I show gratitude for the ability to move my body today? _____
_____

How will I move tomorrow? _____
_____

Growth:

1 Timothy 4:15 "Practice these things, immerse yourself in them, so that all may see your progress."

What steps did I take towards my goal today? _____
_____

What did today teach me that I will bring into tomorrow? _____
_____

Date:_____

Reflection:

Jeremiah 29:11 "For I know the plans I have for you, declares the Lord, plans for welfare and not for evil, to give you a future and a hope."

What am I celebrating today? _____
_____

What am I grateful for today? _____
_____

What do I need to forgive myself for today? _____
_____

How did I use my gifts today?: _____
_____

Self-care:

3 John 1:2 "Beloved, I pray that all may go well with you and that you may be in good health, as it goes well with your soul."

How did I spend my 15 minutes of "me" time today? _____
_____

How will I spend my 15 minutes of "me" time tomorrow? _____
_____

How did I show gratitude for the ability to move my body today? _____
_____

How will I move tomorrow? _____
_____

Growth:

1 Timothy 4:15 "Practice these things, immerse yourself in them, so that all may see your progress."

What steps did I take towards my goal today? _____
_____

What did today teach me that I will bring into tomorrow? _____
_____

Date:_____

Reflection:

Jeremiah 29:11 "For I know the plans I have for you, declares the Lord, plans for welfare and not for evil, to give you a future and a hope."

What am I celebrating today? _____

_____

What am I grateful for today? _____

_____

What do I need to forgive myself for today? _____

_____

How did I use my gifts today?: _____

_____

Self-care:

3 John 1:2 "Beloved, I pray that all may go well with you and that you may be in good health, as it goes well with your soul."

How did I spend my 15 minutes of "me" time today? _____

_____

How will I spend my 15 minutes of "me" time tomorrow? _____

_____

How did I show gratitude for the ability to move my body today? _____

_____

How will I move tomorrow? _____

_____

Growth:

1 Timothy 4:15 "Practice these things, immerse yourself in them, so that all may see your progress."

What steps did I take towards my goal today? _____

_____

What did today teach me that I will bring into tomorrow? _____

_____

John 14:27 "Peace I leave with you; my peace I give to you. Not as the world gives do I give to you. Let not your heart be troubled, neither let them be afraid."

I am just going to be blunt and come right out and say: Mom, get out of your own head! I apologize if that came out rough. Not my intentions. However, these are the words I needed to hear in order to do something about the fact I was absorbed with the battle in my own head. In many cases, getting stuck in your own head could be the effect of a trauma we have experienced in our life. That is not your fault. This may be a cycle you experience such as anger, fear, or depression. The list could go on and on. Once we finally give that over to God, the healing can take over. We get so stuck on words that may have been told to us our entire lives. We may get stuck on feelings such as worthlessness, hopeless, or shameful. Let me remind you that God does NOT view you as any of those. What do we do when our own child gets bullies? We tell him/her repeatedly how untrue those words are that were spoken into his life. We assure our child how loved he/she is. We speak life into our little one. Yet, we struggle to do this when it comes to our own selves. If you struggle with this, look yourself in the mirror today and tell yourself one thing the Lord values about you. Do this every day until these words become a part of who you are instead of just "words." Mom, you are valued. You are loved. You are precious in HIS sight.

Let this serve as a reminder to you this week:

He sees you.

He hears you.

He loves you.

Weekly Challenge:

It's time to reflect on your entries from last week. Pray. Meditate. Celebrate.

Date:_____

Reflection:

Jeremiah 29:11 "For I know the plans I have for you, declares the Lord, plans for welfare and not for evil, to give you a future and a hope."

What am I celebrating today? _____

_____

What am I grateful for today? _____

_____

What do I need to forgive myself for today? _____

_____

How did I use my gifts today?: _____

_____

Self-care:

3 John 1:2 "Beloved, I pray that all may go well with you and that you may be in good health, as it goes well with your soul."

How did I spend my 15 minutes of "me" time today? _____

_____

How will I spend my 15 minutes of "me" time tomorrow? _____

_____

How did I show gratitude for the ability to move my body today? _____

_____

How will I move tomorrow? _____

_____

Growth:

1 Timothy 4:15 "Practice these things, immerse yourself in them, so that all may see your progress."

What steps did I take towards my goal today? _____

_____

What did today teach me that I will bring into tomorrow? _____

_____

Date:_____

Reflection:

Jeremiah 29:11 "For I know the plans I have for you, declares the Lord, plans for welfare and not for evil, to give you a future and a hope."

What am I celebrating today? _____

_____

What am I grateful for today? _____

_____

What do I need to forgive myself for today? _____

_____

How did I use my gifts today?: _____

_____

Self-care:

3 John 1:2 "Beloved, I pray that all may go well with you and that you may be in good health, as it goes well with your soul."

How did I spend my 15 minutes of "me" time today? _____

_____

How will I spend my 15 minutes of "me" time tomorrow? _____

_____

How did I show gratitude for the ability to move my body today? _____

_____

How will I move tomorrow? _____

_____

Growth:

1 Timothy 4:15 "Practice these things, immerse yourself in them, so that all may see your progress."

What steps did I take towards my goal today? _____

_____

What did today teach me that I will bring into tomorrow? _____

_____

Date:_____

Reflection:

Jeremiah 29:11 "For I know the plans I have for you, declares the Lord, plans for welfare and not for evil, to give you a future and a hope."

What am I celebrating today? _____

_____

What am I grateful for today? _____

_____

What do I need to forgive myself for today? _____

_____

How did I use my gifts today?: _____

_____

Self-care:

3 John 1:2 "Beloved, I pray that all may go well with you and that you may be in good health, as it goes well with your soul."

How did I spend my 15 minutes of "me" time today? _____

_____

How will I spend my 15 minutes of "me" time tomorrow? _____

_____

How did I show gratitude for the ability to move my body today? _____

_____

How will I move tomorrow? _____

_____

Growth:

1 Timothy 4:15 "Practice these things, immerse yourself in them, so that all may see your progress."

What steps did I take towards my goal today? _____

_____

What did today teach me that I will bring into tomorrow? _____

_____

Date:_____

Reflection:

Jeremiah 29:11 "For I know the plans I have for you, declares the Lord, plans for welfare and not for evil, to give you a future and a hope."

What am I celebrating today? _____

_____

What am I grateful for today? _____

_____

What do I need to forgive myself for today? _____

_____

How did I use my gifts today?: _____

_____

Self-care:

3 John 1:2 "Beloved, I pray that all may go well with you and that you may be in good health, as it goes well with your soul."

How did I spend my 15 minutes of "me" time today? _____

_____

How will I spend my 15 minutes of "me" time tomorrow? _____

_____

How did I show gratitude for the ability to move my body today? _____

_____

How will I move tomorrow? _____

_____

Growth:

1 Timothy 4:15 "Practice these things, immerse yourself in them, so that all may see your progress."

What steps did I take towards my goal today? _____

_____

What did today teach me that I will bring into tomorrow? _____

_____

Date:_____

Reflection:

Jeremiah 29:11 "For I know the plans I have for you, declares the Lord, plans for welfare and not for evil, to give you a future and a hope."

What am I celebrating today? _____

_____

What am I grateful for today? _____

_____

What do I need to forgive myself for today? _____

_____

How did I use my gifts today?: _____

_____

Self-care:

3 John 1:2 "Beloved, I pray that all may go well with you and that you may be in good health, as it goes well with your soul."

How did I spend my 15 minutes of "me" time today? _____

_____

How will I spend my 15 minutes of "me" time tomorrow? _____

_____

How did I show gratitude for the ability to move my body today? _____

_____

How will I move tomorrow? _____

_____

Growth:

1 Timothy 4:15 "Practice these things, immerse yourself in them, so that all may see your progress."

What steps did I take towards my goal today? _____

_____

What did today teach me that I will bring into tomorrow? _____

_____

Date:_____

Reflection:

Jeremiah 29:11 "For I know the plans I have for you, declares the Lord, plans for welfare and not for evil, to give you a future and a hope."

What am I celebrating today? _____

_____

What am I grateful for today? _____

_____

What do I need to forgive myself for today? _____

_____

How did I use my gifts today?: _____

_____

Self-care:

3 John 1:2 "Beloved, I pray that all may go well with you and that you may be in good health, as it goes well with your soul."

How did I spend my 15 minutes of "me" time today? _____

_____

How will I spend my 15 minutes of "me" time tomorrow? _____

_____

How did I show gratitude for the ability to move my body today? _____

_____

How will I move tomorrow? _____

_____

Growth:

1 Timothy 4:15 "Practice these things, immerse yourself in them, so that all may see your progress."

What steps did I take towards my goal today? _____

_____

What did today teach me that I will bring into tomorrow? _____

_____

Reflection:

Jeremiah 29:11 "For I know the plans I have for you, declares the Lord, plans for welfare and not for evil, to give you a future and a hope."

What am I celebrating today? _____

_____

What am I grateful for today? _____

_____

What do I need to forgive myself for today? _____

_____

How did I use my gifts today?: _____

_____

Self-care:

3 John 1:2 "Beloved, I pray that all may go well with you and that you may be in good health, as it goes well with your soul."

How did I spend my 15 minutes of "me" time today? _____

_____

How will I spend my 15 minutes of "me" time tomorrow? _____

_____

How did I show gratitude for the ability to move my body today? _____

_____

How will I move tomorrow? _____

_____

Growth:

1 Timothy 4:15 "Practice these things, immerse yourself in them, so that all may see your progress."

What steps did I take towards my goal today? _____

_____

What did today teach me that I will bring into tomorrow? _____

_____

*1 John 4:7 "Beloved, let us love one another,
for love is from God, and whoever loves has
been born of God and knows God."*

Mom, have you had days where you find yourself apologizing repeatedly
for your child's behavior? I do not mean if your child is purposely
harming someone or something. I am speaking about those days you
may take your child to the grocery store. You know you only have
limited amount of time before your precious little one turns rears his
ugly head. Those days where out of the blue your child has decided to
throw a monstrous temper tantrum in the middle of grocery shopping.
You have no idea where it came from, but there is not going back from
here. Maybe your child is tired, hungry, or just simply does not want
to be there. Do you find yourself apologizing to everyone who walks
by you? You are completely horrified by the reaction on the faces of
complete strangers who are shopping as well. If you are anything like
me, you may apologize profusely, make your way to the car, and let out a
cry in the parking lot before you even begin to drive away. That felt good
to cry, didn't it? This would happen often to me with my youngest. With
him, I knew I had a limited window of opportunity to do just about
anything that did not cater to his needs (no wonder they diagnosed me
with postpartum depression). There were days I wanted to snap at the
other patrons in that grocery store and shout, "what are you looking at?!
Can't you see I can not control his crying right now?!" After a few weeks
past, I began turning that anger and sadness over the God. I would pray
for peace BEFORE we even left the house. Walking through the store,
if my child were having a moment, I would just look at other moms and
say, "you just can't win every day." That made other moms smile and say,
"you're right. I get it." PHEW! The stares and judgment started to turn
into compassion and understanding. When we begin to soften our hearts
in moments such as this, our hearts are open for peace! I never have
been one to judge another mom who seems to be struggling. Instead I
have always offered help. That softens the hearts of those around you as
well. Showing the LOVE of Christ, even in stressful situations, is what

God has asked us to do. I began to realize that the prayer for peace I was praying before I would leave my house, was not a prayer for my child, but it turns out I was the one who needed the peace. I continue to do this still, every day before I leave my house. I encourage you to pray this as well. God may show you areas of your life where you needed the peace and not your children. Mom, I will be praying for you as well.

Let this serve as a reminder to you this week:

He sees you.

He hears you.

He loves you.

Weekly Challenge:

It's time to reflect on your entries from last week. Pray. Meditate. Celebrate.

Date:_____

Reflection:

Jeremiah 29:11 "For I know the plans I have for you, declares the Lord, plans for welfare and not for evil, to give you a future and a hope."

What am I celebrating today? _____
_____

What am I grateful for today? _____
_____

What do I need to forgive myself for today? _____
_____

How did I use my gifts today?: _____
_____

Self-care:

3 John 1:2 "Beloved, I pray that all may go well with you and that you may be in good health, as it goes well with your soul."

How did I spend my 15 minutes of "me" time today? _____
_____

How will I spend my 15 minutes of "me" time tomorrow? _____
_____

How did I show gratitude for the ability to move my body today? ____
_____

How will I move tomorrow? _____
_____

Growth:

1 Timothy 4:15 "Practice these things, immerse yourself in them, so that all may see your progress."

What steps did I take towards my goal today? _____
_____

What did today teach me that I will bring into tomorrow? _____
_____

Date:_____

Reflection:

Jeremiah 29:11 "For I know the plans I have for you, declares the Lord, plans for welfare and not for evil, to give you a future and a hope."

What am I celebrating today? _____
_____

What am I grateful for today? _____
_____

What do I need to forgive myself for today? _____
_____

How did I use my gifts today?: _____
_____

Self-care:

3 John 1:2 "Beloved, I pray that all may go well with you and that you may be in good health, as it goes well with your soul."

How did I spend my 15 minutes of "me" time today? _____
_____

How will I spend my 15 minutes of "me" time tomorrow? _____
_____

How did I show gratitude for the ability to move my body today? _____
_____

How will I move tomorrow? _____
_____

Growth:

1 Timothy 4:15 "Practice these things, immerse yourself in them, so that all may see your progress."

What steps did I take towards my goal today? _____
_____

What did today teach me that I will bring into tomorrow? _____
_____

Date:_____

Reflection:

Jeremiah 29:11 "For I know the plans I have for you, declares the Lord, plans for welfare and not for evil, to give you a future and a hope."

What am I celebrating today? _____

_____

What am I grateful for today? _____

_____

What do I need to forgive myself for today? _____

_____

How did I use my gifts today?: _____

_____

Self-care:

3 John 1:2 "Beloved, I pray that all may go well with you and that you may be in good health, as it goes well with your soul."

How did I spend my 15 minutes of "me" time today? _____

_____

How will I spend my 15 minutes of "me" time tomorrow? _____

_____

How did I show gratitude for the ability to move my body today? _____

_____

How will I move tomorrow? _____

_____

Growth:

1 Timothy 4:15 "Practice these things, immerse yourself in them, so that all may see your progress."

What steps did I take towards my goal today? _____

_____

What did today teach me that I will bring into tomorrow? _____

_____

Date:_____

Reflection:

Jeremiah 29:11 "For I know the plans I have for you, declares the Lord, plans for welfare and not for evil, to give you a future and a hope."

What am I celebrating today? _____

_____

What am I grateful for today? _____

_____

What do I need to forgive myself for today? _____

_____

How did I use my gifts today?: _____

_____

Self-care:

3 John 1:2 "Beloved, I pray that all may go well with you and that you may be in good health, as it goes well with your soul."

How did I spend my 15 minutes of "me" time today? _____

_____

How will I spend my 15 minutes of "me" time tomorrow? _____

_____

How did I show gratitude for the ability to move my body today? _____

_____

How will I move tomorrow? _____

_____

Growth:

1 Timothy 4:15 "Practice these things, immerse yourself in them, so that all may see your progress."

What steps did I take towards my goal today? _____

_____

What did today teach me that I will bring into tomorrow? _____

_____

Date:_____

Reflection:

Jeremiah 29:11 "For I know the plans I have for you, declares the Lord, plans for welfare and not for evil, to give you a future and a hope."

What am I celebrating today? _____

_____

What am I grateful for today? _____

_____

What do I need to forgive myself for today? _____

_____

How did I use my gifts today?: _____

_____

Self-care:

3 John 1:2 "Beloved, I pray that all may go well with you and that you may be in good health, as it goes well with your soul."

How did I spend my 15 minutes of "me" time today? _____

_____

How will I spend my 15 minutes of "me" time tomorrow? _____

_____

How did I show gratitude for the ability to move my body today? _____

_____

How will I move tomorrow? _____

_____

Growth:

1 Timothy 4:15 "Practice these things, immerse yourself in them, so that all may see your progress."

What steps did I take towards my goal today? _____

_____

What did today teach me that I will bring into tomorrow? _____

_____

Reflection:

Jeremiah 29:11 "For I know the plans I have for you, declares the Lord, plans for welfare and not for evil, to give you a future and a hope."

What am I celebrating today? _____

_____

What am I grateful for today? _____

_____

What do I need to forgive myself for today? _____

_____

How did I use my gifts today?: _____

_____

Self-care:

3 John 1:2 "Beloved, I pray that all may go well with you and that you may be in good health, as it goes well with your soul."

How did I spend my 15 minutes of "me" time today? _____

_____

How will I spend my 15 minutes of "me" time tomorrow? _____

_____

How did I show gratitude for the ability to move my body today? ____

_____

How will I move tomorrow? _____

_____

Growth:

1 Timothy 4:15 "Practice these things, immerse yourself in them, so that all may see your progress."

What steps did I take towards my goal today? _____

_____

What did today teach me that I will bring into tomorrow? _____

_____

Date:_____

Reflection:

Jeremiah 29:11 "For I know the plans I have for you, declares the Lord, plans for welfare and not for evil, to give you a future and a hope."

What am I celebrating today? _____

_____

What am I grateful for today? _____

_____

What do I need to forgive myself for today? _____

_____

How did I use my gifts today?: _____

_____

Self-care:

3 John 1:2 "Beloved, I pray that all may go well with you and that you may be in good health, as it goes well with your soul."

How did I spend my 15 minutes of "me" time today? _____

_____

How will I spend my 15 minutes of "me" time tomorrow? _____

_____

How did I show gratitude for the ability to move my body today? _____

_____

How will I move tomorrow? _____

_____

Growth:

1 Timothy 4:15 "Practice these things, immerse yourself in them, so that all may see your progress."

What steps did I take towards my goal today? _____

_____

What did today teach me that I will bring into tomorrow? _____

_____

Proverbs 13:22 "A good man leaves an inheritance to his children's children, but the sinner's wealth is laid up for the righteous."

Mom, I want you to think out what is one thing you want to leave your children with one day? I am not speaking about a material item. I am speaking about a value. I will share mine. I hope to teach my children the value of forgiving and forgetting. This is a tough one indeed! It can be easy for us to say we forgive a person; however, it is not that easy to forgive AND forget. We may have been taught to fight back when we get knocked down, so that is what we pass along to our own children.

However, the scripture says we are to FORGIVE and FORGET. In my lifetime, I have experienced some adult bullying. My oldest son is extremely protective over me and he unfortunately has been exposed to some of the bullying. His immediate response was, "mommy can I slap the person for treating you that way?" Of course, I explained to him why that is the wrong action to take. Instead, I invited him to sit with me while I prayed for that person's soul. He sat along with me as I prayed, "dear Lord, I forgive this person for what they have done to me. I pray he/she turns to you and accepts you into his/her heart. Let this person see my kindness as a reaction and that we are able to use that as a testimony as to how great you are, Lord." My son continues to pray for this person each day in his nighttime prays. If I can leave him with the lesson to forgive and forget, I can be confident in knowing I am doing my job pretty well. What is something you want to leave your child/children with and how can you begin that lesson this week?

Let this serve as a reminder to you this week:

He sees you.

He hears you.

He loves you.

<u>Weekly Challenge:</u>

It's time to reflect on your entries from last
week. Pray. Meditate. Celebrate.

Date:_____

Reflection:

Jeremiah 29:11 "For I know the plans I have for you, declares the Lord, plans for welfare and not for evil, to give you a future and a hope."

What am I celebrating today? _____
_____

What am I grateful for today? _____
_____

What do I need to forgive myself for today? _____
_____

How did I use my gifts today?: _____
_____

Self-care:

3 John 1:2 "Beloved, I pray that all may go well with you and that you may be in good health, as it goes well with your soul."

How did I spend my 15 minutes of "me" time today? _____
_____

How will I spend my 15 minutes of "me" time tomorrow? _____
_____

How did I show gratitude for the ability to move my body today? _____
_____

How will I move tomorrow? _____
_____

Growth:

1 Timothy 4:15 "Practice these things, immerse yourself in them, so that all may see your progress."

What steps did I take towards my goal today? _____
_____

What did today teach me that I will bring into tomorrow? _____
_____

Date:_____

Reflection:

Jeremiah 29:11 "For I know the plans I have for you, declares the Lord, plans for welfare and not for evil, to give you a future and a hope."

What am I celebrating today? _____

_____

What am I grateful for today? _____

_____

What do I need to forgive myself for today? _____

_____

How did I use my gifts today?: _____

_____

Self-care:

3 John 1:2 "Beloved, I pray that all may go well with you and that you may be in good health, as it goes well with your soul."

How did I spend my 15 minutes of "me" time today? _____

_____

How will I spend my 15 minutes of "me" time tomorrow? _____

_____

How did I show gratitude for the ability to move my body today? ____

_____

How will I move tomorrow? _____

_____

Growth:

1 Timothy 4:15 "Practice these things, immerse yourself in them, so that all may see your progress."

What steps did I take towards my goal today? _____

_____

What did today teach me that I will bring into tomorrow? _____

_____

Date:_____

Reflection:

Jeremiah 29:11 "For I know the plans I have for you, declares the Lord, plans for welfare and not for evil, to give you a future and a hope."

What am I celebrating today? _____
_____

What am I grateful for today? _____
_____

What do I need to forgive myself for today? _____
_____

How did I use my gifts today?: _____
_____

Self-care:

3 John 1:2 "Beloved, I pray that all may go well with you and that you may be in good health, as it goes well with your soul."

How did I spend my 15 minutes of "me" time today? _____
_____

How will I spend my 15 minutes of "me" time tomorrow? _____
_____

How did I show gratitude for the ability to move my body today? _____
_____

How will I move tomorrow? _____
_____

Growth:

1 Timothy 4:15 "Practice these things, immerse yourself in them, so that all may see your progress."

What steps did I take towards my goal today? _____
_____

What did today teach me that I will bring into tomorrow? _____
_____

Date:_____

Reflection:

Jeremiah 29:11 "For I know the plans I have for you, declares the Lord, plans for welfare and not for evil, to give you a future and a hope."

What am I celebrating today? _____

_____

What am I grateful for today? _____

_____

What do I need to forgive myself for today? _____

_____

How did I use my gifts today?: _____

_____

Self-care:

3 John 1:2 "Beloved, I pray that all may go well with you and that you may be in good health, as it goes well with your soul."

How did I spend my 15 minutes of "me" time today? _____

_____

How will I spend my 15 minutes of "me" time tomorrow? _____

_____

How did I show gratitude for the ability to move my body today? _____

_____

How will I move tomorrow? _____

_____

Growth:

1 Timothy 4:15 "Practice these things, immerse yourself in them, so that all may see your progress."

What steps did I take towards my goal today? _____

_____

What did today teach me that I will bring into tomorrow? _____

_____

Reflection:

Jeremiah 29:11 "For I know the plans I have for you, declares the Lord, plans for welfare and not for evil, to give you a future and a hope."

What am I celebrating today? _____

_____

What am I grateful for today? _____

_____

What do I need to forgive myself for today? _____

_____

How did I use my gifts today?: _____

_____

Self-care:

3 John 1:2 "Beloved, I pray that all may go well with you and that you may be in good health, as it goes well with your soul."

How did I spend my 15 minutes of "me" time today? _____

_____

How will I spend my 15 minutes of "me" time tomorrow? _____

_____

How did I show gratitude for the ability to move my body today? _____

_____

How will I move tomorrow? _____

_____

Growth:

1 Timothy 4:15 "Practice these things, immerse yourself in them, so that all may see your progress."

What steps did I take towards my goal today? _____

_____

What did today teach me that I will bring into tomorrow? _____

_____

Date:_____

Reflection:

Jeremiah 29:11 "For I know the plans I have for you, declares the Lord, plans for welfare and not for evil, to give you a future and a hope."

What am I celebrating today? _____

_____

What am I grateful for today? _____

_____

What do I need to forgive myself for today? _____

_____

How did I use my gifts today?: _____

_____

Self-care:

3 John 1:2 "Beloved, I pray that all may go well with you and that you may be in good health, as it goes well with your soul."

How did I spend my 15 minutes of "me" time today? _____

_____

How will I spend my 15 minutes of "me" time tomorrow? _____

_____

How did I show gratitude for the ability to move my body today? _____

_____

How will I move tomorrow? _____

_____

Growth:

1 Timothy 4:15 "Practice these things, immerse yourself in them, so that all may see your progress."

What steps did I take towards my goal today? _____

_____

What did today teach me that I will bring into tomorrow? _____

_____

Reflection:

Jeremiah 29:11 "For I know the plans I have for you, declares the Lord, plans for welfare and not for evil, to give you a future and a hope."

What am I celebrating today? _____

_____

What am I grateful for today? _____

_____

What do I need to forgive myself for today? _____

_____

How did I use my gifts today?: _____

_____

Self-care:

3 John 1:2 "Beloved, I pray that all may go well with you and that you may be in good health, as it goes well with your soul."

How did I spend my 15 minutes of "me" time today? _____

_____

How will I spend my 15 minutes of "me" time tomorrow? _____

_____

How did I show gratitude for the ability to move my body today? _____

_____

How will I move tomorrow? _____

_____

Growth:

1 Timothy 4:15 "Practice these things, immerse yourself in them, so that all may see your progress."

What steps did I take towards my goal today? _____

_____

What did today teach me that I will bring into tomorrow? _____

_____

Psalms 118:24 "This is the day that the Lord has made; let us rejoice and be glad in it."

I will tell you a story about how a new tradition came to be in our home. Each year when Mother's Day and Father's Day would roll around, my oldest son would always say, "why can't there be a kid's day?" At first, I would begin explaining how mommies and daddies do so much throughout the year that we needed a day to celebrate that. I explained that he has a celebration on his birthday each year so that was enough. He responded with, "you have a birthday too. That isn't fair." He had a point! One morning I decided to wake him up and surprise him with "Kid's Day." I fed him breakfast in bed. I did the chores. I took him to the zoo. I made the day fun for him as a special memory. He was so taken back with joy that he was filled with tears. Since then, each year, I have surprised him with "Kid's day" once a year. He never knows which day it will be, which makes it even more fun. This is a tradition we began in my home. It is something I am sure he will continue in his home when he has children. Traditions are special and sacred. If you do not carry on a tradition in your own home, I encourage you to create one for you and your children. Traditions bring families together in such a special way. Begin one today. Make sure you celebrate what you have created.

Let this serve as a reminder to you this week:

He sees you.

He hears you.

He loves you.

<u>Weekly Challenge:</u>

It's time to reflect on your entries from last week. Pray. Meditate. Celebrate.

Reflection:

Jeremiah 29:11 "For I know the plans I have for you, declares the Lord, plans for welfare and not for evil, to give you a future and a hope."

What am I celebrating today? _____

_____

What am I grateful for today? _____

_____

What do I need to forgive myself for today? _____

_____

How did I use my gifts today?: _____

_____

Self-care:

3 John 1:2 "Beloved, I pray that all may go well with you and that you may be in good health, as it goes well with your soul."

How did I spend my 15 minutes of "me" time today? _____

_____

How will I spend my 15 minutes of "me" time tomorrow? _____

_____

How did I show gratitude for the ability to move my body today? _____

_____

How will I move tomorrow? _____

_____

Growth:

1 Timothy 4:15 "Practice these things, immerse yourself in them, so that all may see your progress."

What steps did I take towards my goal today? _____

_____

What did today teach me that I will bring into tomorrow? _____

_____

Date:_____

Reflection:

Jeremiah 29:11 "For I know the plans I have for you, declares the Lord, plans for welfare and not for evil, to give you a future and a hope."

What am I celebrating today? _____

_____

What am I grateful for today? _____

_____

What do I need to forgive myself for today? _____

_____

How did I use my gifts today?: _____

_____

Self-care:

3 John 1:2 "Beloved, I pray that all may go well with you and that you may be in good health, as it goes well with your soul."

How did I spend my 15 minutes of "me" time today? _____

_____

How will I spend my 15 minutes of "me" time tomorrow? _____

_____

How did I show gratitude for the ability to move my body today? _____

_____

How will I move tomorrow? _____

_____

Growth:

1 Timothy 4:15 "Practice these things, immerse yourself in them, so that all may see your progress."

What steps did I take towards my goal today? _____

_____

What did today teach me that I will bring into tomorrow? _____

_____

Reflection:

Jeremiah 29:11 "For I know the plans I have for you, declares the Lord, plans for welfare and not for evil, to give you a future and a hope."

What am I celebrating today? _____

_____

What am I grateful for today? _____

_____

What do I need to forgive myself for today? _____

_____

How did I use my gifts today?: _____

_____

Self-care:

3 John 1:2 "Beloved, I pray that all may go well with you and that you may be in good health, as it goes well with your soul."

How did I spend my 15 minutes of "me" time today? _____

_____

How will I spend my 15 minutes of "me" time tomorrow? _____

_____

How did I show gratitude for the ability to move my body today? _____

_____

How will I move tomorrow? _____

_____

Growth:

1 Timothy 4:15 "Practice these things, immerse yourself in them, so that all may see your progress."

What steps did I take towards my goal today? _____

_____

What did today teach me that I will bring into tomorrow? _____

_____

Date:_____

Reflection:

Jeremiah 29:11 "For I know the plans I have for you, declares the Lord, plans for welfare and not for evil, to give you a future and a hope."

What am I celebrating today? _____

_____

What am I grateful for today? _____

_____

What do I need to forgive myself for today? _____

_____

How did I use my gifts today?: _____

_____

Self-care:

3 John 1:2 "Beloved, I pray that all may go well with you and that you may be in good health, as it goes well with your soul."

How did I spend my 15 minutes of "me" time today? _____

_____

How will I spend my 15 minutes of "me" time tomorrow? _____

_____

How did I show gratitude for the ability to move my body today? _____

_____

How will I move tomorrow? _____

_____

Growth:

1 Timothy 4:15 "Practice these things, immerse yourself in them, so that all may see your progress."

What steps did I take towards my goal today? _____

_____

What did today teach me that I will bring into tomorrow? _____

_____

Date:_____

Reflection:

Jeremiah 29:11 "For I know the plans I have for you, declares the Lord, plans for welfare and not for evil, to give you a future and a hope."

What am I celebrating today? _____

_____

What am I grateful for today? _____

_____

What do I need to forgive myself for today? _____

_____

How did I use my gifts today?: _____

_____

Self-care:

3 John 1:2 "Beloved, I pray that all may go well with you and that you may be in good health, as it goes well with your soul."

How did I spend my 15 minutes of "me" time today? _____

_____

How will I spend my 15 minutes of "me" time tomorrow? _____

_____

How did I show gratitude for the ability to move my body today? ____

_____

How will I move tomorrow? _____

_____

Growth:

1 Timothy 4:15 "Practice these things, immerse yourself in them, so that all may see your progress."

What steps did I take towards my goal today? _____

_____

What did today teach me that I will bring into tomorrow? _____

_____

Date:_____

Reflection:

Jeremiah 29:11 "For I know the plans I have for you, declares the Lord, plans for welfare and not for evil, to give you a future and a hope."

What am I celebrating today? _____

_____

What am I grateful for today? _____

_____

What do I need to forgive myself for today? _____

_____

How did I use my gifts today?: _____

_____

Self-care:

3 John 1:2 "Beloved, I pray that all may go well with you and that you may be in good health, as it goes well with your soul."

How did I spend my 15 minutes of "me" time today? _____

_____

How will I spend my 15 minutes of "me" time tomorrow? _____

_____

How did I show gratitude for the ability to move my body today? _____

_____

How will I move tomorrow? _____

_____

Growth:

1 Timothy 4:15 "Practice these things, immerse yourself in them, so that all may see your progress."

What steps did I take towards my goal today? _____

_____

What did today teach me that I will bring into tomorrow? _____

_____

Reflection:

Jeremiah 29:11 "For I know the plans I have for you, declares the Lord, plans for welfare and not for evil, to give you a future and a hope."

What am I celebrating today? _____

_____

What am I grateful for today? _____

_____

What do I need to forgive myself for today? _____

_____

How did I use my gifts today?: _____

_____

Self-care:

3 John 1:2 "Beloved, I pray that all may go well with you and that you may be in good health, as it goes well with your soul."

How did I spend my 15 minutes of "me" time today? _____

_____

How will I spend my 15 minutes of "me" time tomorrow? _____

_____

How did I show gratitude for the ability to move my body today? _____

_____

How will I move tomorrow? _____

_____

Growth:

1 Timothy 4:15 "Practice these things, immerse yourself in them, so that all may see your progress."

What steps did I take towards my goal today? _____

_____

What did today teach me that I will bring into tomorrow? _____

_____

2 Corinthians 12:9-10 "But he said to me, "My grace is sufficient for you, for my power is made perfect in weakness." Therefore I will boast all more gladly of my weakness, so that the power of Christ may rest upon me. For the sake of Christ, then, I am content with weaknesses, insults, hardships, persecutions, and calamities. For when I am weak, then I am strong."

I want to share a story with you, mom. I title this, "My Biggest Parenting Fail." My oldest was having a rough day. On days such as this one, I typically will pull him aside in a quiet room as ask him what is going through his mind and what is in his heart, hoping to get to the bottom of the source for his actions. I will never forget this day as long as I live. His response on this day made my feel as though I failed as a mom. All seven years of me being a mom, washed down the drain. When I presented him with my usual questioned, he came back with a question for me to answer. He said, "Mommy, can I ask you a question and will you promise to be honest with me?" Of course, I would never lie to him. He proceeded to explain what was on his heart. He asked, "do you feel that things would be easier if I just wasn't around? Would things be easier for you with my baby brother?" That is when my heart sank, and I could not hold in my tears. I hugged him tightly and cried, "of course I do not feel that way!! I love you and your brother with all my heart! I would be lost without you!" I did not even know how to answer that exactly. I tried the best I could, but the words just would not come out of my mouth. My heart was broken. I remember crying to my husband that evening. I said to him, "I failed as a mom! Why would my son think that? I am the worst mom alive!" He reassured me that I was doing everything correctly, however, my heart still hurt. The next day, I brought it up to my son again. He explained to me that he asked me that question because he saw how challenging his little brother was at times and it makes him sad that he does not help. That day, we came to an agreement. He offered to help feed the baby and read him books each day to help me, and I agreed to that. That day will forever stick with me. The memory is there, but with time my heart has healed from the pain. As a mom, there will come a time where you will have your own story about your "parenting fail," if you do not already have one. Try to give it to God and let it go. Mom, what you are doing is not easy!! The best part is you are not doing it alone. Lean on Him. He is with you. Cry to Him. He hears you. Mom, I am praying for you today.

Let this serve as a reminder to you this week:

He sees you.

He hears you.

He loves you.

Weekly Challenge:

It's time to reflect on your entries from last week. Pray. Meditate. Celebrate.

Date:_____

Reflection:

Jeremiah 29:11 "For I know the plans I have for you, declares the Lord, plans for welfare and not for evil, to give you a future and a hope."

What am I celebrating today? _____

_____

What am I grateful for today? _____

_____

What do I need to forgive myself for today? _____

_____

How did I use my gifts today?: _____

_____

Self-care:

3 John 1:2 "Beloved, I pray that all may go well with you and that you may be in good health, as it goes well with your soul."

How did I spend my 15 minutes of "me" time today? _____

_____

How will I spend my 15 minutes of "me" time tomorrow? _____

_____

How did I show gratitude for the ability to move my body today? _____

_____

How will I move tomorrow? _____

_____

Growth:

1 Timothy 4:15 "Practice these things, immerse yourself in them, so that all may see your progress."

What steps did I take towards my goal today? _____

_____

What did today teach me that I will bring into tomorrow? _____

_____

Date:_____

Reflection:

Jeremiah 29:11 "For I know the plans I have for you, declares the Lord, plans for welfare and not for evil, to give you a future and a hope."

What am I celebrating today? _____
_____

What am I grateful for today? _____
_____

What do I need to forgive myself for today? _____
_____

How did I use my gifts today?: _____
_____

Self-care:

3 John 1:2 "Beloved, I pray that all may go well with you and that you may be in good health, as it goes well with your soul."

How did I spend my 15 minutes of "me" time today? _____
_____

How will I spend my 15 minutes of "me" time tomorrow? _____
_____

How did I show gratitude for the ability to move my body today? _____
_____

How will I move tomorrow? _____
_____

Growth:

1 Timothy 4:15 "Practice these things, immerse yourself in them, so that all may see your progress."

What steps did I take towards my goal today? _____
_____

What did today teach me that I will bring into tomorrow? _____
_____

Date:_____

Reflection:

Jeremiah 29:11 "For I know the plans I have for you, declares the Lord, plans for welfare and not for evil, to give you a future and a hope."

What am I celebrating today? _____

_____

What am I grateful for today? _____

_____

What do I need to forgive myself for today? _____

_____

How did I use my gifts today?: _____

_____

Self-care:

3 John 1:2 "Beloved, I pray that all may go well with you and that you may be in good health, as it goes well with your soul."

How did I spend my 15 minutes of "me" time today? _____

_____

How will I spend my 15 minutes of "me" time tomorrow? _____

_____

How did I show gratitude for the ability to move my body today? _____

_____

How will I move tomorrow? _____

_____

Growth:

1 Timothy 4:15 "Practice these things, immerse yourself in them, so that all may see your progress."

What steps did I take towards my goal today? _____

_____

What did today teach me that I will bring into tomorrow? _____

_____

Reflection:

Jeremiah 29:11 "For I know the plans I have for you, declares the Lord, plans for welfare and not for evil, to give you a future and a hope."

What am I celebrating today? _____
_____

What am I grateful for today? _____
_____

What do I need to forgive myself for today? _____
_____

How did I use my gifts today?: _____
_____

Self-care:

3 John 1:2 "Beloved, I pray that all may go well with you and that you may be in good health, as it goes well with your soul."

How did I spend my 15 minutes of "me" time today? _____
_____

How will I spend my 15 minutes of "me" time tomorrow? _____
_____

How did I show gratitude for the ability to move my body today? _____
_____

How will I move tomorrow? _____
_____

Growth:

1 Timothy 4:15 "Practice these things, immerse yourself in them, so that all may see your progress."

What steps did I take towards my goal today? _____
_____

What did today teach me that I will bring into tomorrow? _____
_____

Date:_____

Reflection:

Jeremiah 29:11 "For I know the plans I have for you, declares the Lord, plans for welfare and not for evil, to give you a future and a hope."

What am I celebrating today? _____

_____

What am I grateful for today? _____

_____

What do I need to forgive myself for today? _____

_____

How did I use my gifts today?: _____

_____

Self-care:

3 John 1:2 "Beloved, I pray that all may go well with you and that you may be in good health, as it goes well with your soul."

How did I spend my 15 minutes of "me" time today? _____

_____

How will I spend my 15 minutes of "me" time tomorrow? _____

_____

How did I show gratitude for the ability to move my body today? _____

_____

How will I move tomorrow? _____

_____

Growth:

1 Timothy 4:15 "Practice these things, immerse yourself in them, so that all may see your progress."

What steps did I take towards my goal today? _____

_____

What did today teach me that I will bring into tomorrow? _____

_____

Date:_____

Reflection:

Jeremiah 29:11 "For I know the plans I have for you, declares the Lord, plans for welfare and not for evil, to give you a future and a hope."

What am I celebrating today? _____

_____

What am I grateful for today? _____

_____

What do I need to forgive myself for today? _____

_____

How did I use my gifts today?: _____

_____

Self-care:

3 John 1:2 "Beloved, I pray that all may go well with you and that you may be in good health, as it goes well with your soul."

How did I spend my 15 minutes of "me" time today? _____

_____

How will I spend my 15 minutes of "me" time tomorrow? _____

_____

How did I show gratitude for the ability to move my body today? _____

_____

How will I move tomorrow? _____

_____

Growth:

1 Timothy 4:15 "Practice these things, immerse yourself in them, so that all may see your progress."

What steps did I take towards my goal today? _____

_____

What did today teach me that I will bring into tomorrow? _____

_____

Date:_____

Reflection:

Jeremiah 29:11 "For I know the plans I have for you, declares the Lord, plans for welfare and not for evil, to give you a future and a hope."

What am I celebrating today? _____
_____

What am I grateful for today? _____
_____

What do I need to forgive myself for today? _____
_____

How did I use my gifts today?: _____
_____

Self-care:

3 John 1:2 "Beloved, I pray that all may go well with you and that you may be in good health, as it goes well with your soul."

How did I spend my 15 minutes of "me" time today? _____
_____

How will I spend my 15 minutes of "me" time tomorrow? _____
_____

How did I show gratitude for the ability to move my body today? _____
_____

How will I move tomorrow? _____
_____

Growth:

1 Timothy 4:15 "Practice these things, immerse yourself in them, so that all may see your progress."

What steps did I take towards my goal today? _____
_____

What did today teach me that I will bring into tomorrow? _____
_____

2 Chronicles 15:7 "But you, take courage! Do not let your hands be weak, for your work shall be rewarded."

Mom, what has been your goal with this planner? What will be your goal once the planner is complete? It is easy to get lost in the journey of motherhood. Do not let that defer what your own personal goals are. Is your goal to be able to organize your day more efficiently? Is your goal to love yourself more? Or is your goal to find happiness in this journey where you have felt so alone? Whatever you are feeling, and whatever your personal goal is, speak life and existence into that! This reflection time is meant for you to be real, raw, and honest with yourself. Do you need to find more balance in the day? Do you need to find more balance in your relationships? If you have not asked yourself these questions along this journey, stop what you are doing now, and reflect on them. Mom, this time is for YOU! Take that step towards a happier, healthier you. Let's celebrate how far you have come!! Give thanks for He is so so good!

Let this serve as a reminder to you this week:

He sees you.

He hears you.

He loves you.

Weekly Challenge:

It's time to reflect on your entries from last week. Pray. Meditate. Celebrate.

Date:_____

Reflection:

Jeremiah 29:11 "For I know the plans I have for you, declares the Lord, plans for welfare and not for evil, to give you a future and a hope."

What am I celebrating today? _____

_____

What am I grateful for today? _____

_____

What do I need to forgive myself for today? _____

_____

How did I use my gifts today?: _____

_____

Self-care:

3 John 1:2 "Beloved, I pray that all may go well with you and that you may be in good health, as it goes well with your soul."

How did I spend my 15 minutes of "me" time today? _____

_____

How will I spend my 15 minutes of "me" time tomorrow? _____

_____

How did I show gratitude for the ability to move my body today? _____

_____

How will I move tomorrow? _____

_____

Growth:

1 Timothy 4:15 "Practice these things, immerse yourself in them, so that all may see your progress."

What steps did I take towards my goal today? _____

_____

What did today teach me that I will bring into tomorrow? _____

_____

Reflection:

Jeremiah 29:11 "For I know the plans I have for you, declares the Lord, plans for welfare and not for evil, to give you a future and a hope."

What am I celebrating today? _____

_____

What am I grateful for today? _____

_____

What do I need to forgive myself for today? _____

_____

How did I use my gifts today?: _____

_____

Self-care:

3 John 1:2 "Beloved, I pray that all may go well with you and that you may be in good health, as it goes well with your soul."

How did I spend my 15 minutes of "me" time today? _____

_____

How will I spend my 15 minutes of "me" time tomorrow? _____

_____

How did I show gratitude for the ability to move my body today? _____

_____

How will I move tomorrow? _____

_____

Growth:

1 Timothy 4:15 "Practice these things, immerse yourself in them, so that all may see your progress."

What steps did I take towards my goal today? _____

_____

What did today teach me that I will bring into tomorrow? _____

_____

Date:_____

Reflection:

Jeremiah 29:11 "For I know the plans I have for you, declares the Lord, plans for welfare and not for evil, to give you a future and a hope."

What am I celebrating today? _____

_____

What am I grateful for today? _____

_____

What do I need to forgive myself for today? _____

_____

How did I use my gifts today?: _____

_____

Self-care:

3 John 1:2 "Beloved, I pray that all may go well with you and that you may be in good health, as it goes well with your soul."

How did I spend my 15 minutes of "me" time today? _____

_____

How will I spend my 15 minutes of "me" time tomorrow? _____

_____

How did I show gratitude for the ability to move my body today? _____

_____

How will I move tomorrow? _____

_____

Growth:

1 Timothy 4:15 "Practice these things, immerse yourself in them, so that all may see your progress."

What steps did I take towards my goal today? _____

_____

What did today teach me that I will bring into tomorrow? _____

_____

Reflection:

Jeremiah 29:11 "For I know the plans I have for you, declares the Lord, plans for welfare and not for evil, to give you a future and a hope."

What am I celebrating today? _____

_____

What am I grateful for today? _____

_____

What do I need to forgive myself for today? _____

_____

How did I use my gifts today?: _____

_____

Self-care:

3 John 1:2 "Beloved, I pray that all may go well with you and that you may be in good health, as it goes well with your soul."

How did I spend my 15 minutes of "me" time today? _____

_____

How will I spend my 15 minutes of "me" time tomorrow? _____

_____

How did I show gratitude for the ability to move my body today? _____

_____

How will I move tomorrow? _____

_____

Growth:

1 Timothy 4:15 "Practice these things, immerse yourself in them, so that all may see your progress."

What steps did I take towards my goal today? _____

_____

What did today teach me that I will bring into tomorrow? _____

_____

Date:_____

Reflection:

Jeremiah 29:11 "For I know the plans I have for you, declares the Lord, plans for welfare and not for evil, to give you a future and a hope."

What am I celebrating today? _____

_____

What am I grateful for today? _____

_____

What do I need to forgive myself for today? _____

_____

How did I use my gifts today?: _____

_____

Self-care:

3 John 1:2 "Beloved, I pray that all may go well with you and that you may be in good health, as it goes well with your soul."

How did I spend my 15 minutes of "me" time today? _____

_____

How will I spend my 15 minutes of "me" time tomorrow? _____

_____

How did I show gratitude for the ability to move my body today? _____

_____

How will I move tomorrow? _____

_____

Growth:

1 Timothy 4:15 "Practice these things, immerse yourself in them, so that all may see your progress."

What steps did I take towards my goal today? _____

_____

What did today teach me that I will bring into tomorrow? _____

_____

Reflection:

Jeremiah 29:11 "For I know the plans I have for you, declares the Lord, plans for welfare and not for evil, to give you a future and a hope."

What am I celebrating today? _____

_____

What am I grateful for today? _____

_____

What do I need to forgive myself for today? _____

_____

How did I use my gifts today?: _____

_____

Self-care:

3 John 1:2 "Beloved, I pray that all may go well with you and that you may be in good health, as it goes well with your soul."

How did I spend my 15 minutes of "me" time today? _____

_____

How will I spend my 15 minutes of "me" time tomorrow? _____

_____

How did I show gratitude for the ability to move my body today? _____

_____

How will I move tomorrow? _____

_____

Growth:

1 Timothy 4:15 "Practice these things, immerse yourself in them, so that all may see your progress."

What steps did I take towards my goal today? _____

_____

What did today teach me that I will bring into tomorrow? _____

_____

Date:_____

Reflection:

Jeremiah 29:11 "For I know the plans I have for you, declares the Lord, plans for welfare and not for evil, to give you a future and a hope."

What am I celebrating today? _____

_____

What am I grateful for today? _____

_____

What do I need to forgive myself for today? _____

_____

How did I use my gifts today?: _____

_____

Self-care:

3 John 1:2 "Beloved, I pray that all may go well with you and that you may be in good health, as it goes well with your soul."

How did I spend my 15 minutes of "me" time today? _____

_____

How will I spend my 15 minutes of "me" time tomorrow? _____

_____

How did I show gratitude for the ability to move my body today? _____

_____

How will I move tomorrow? _____

_____

Growth:

1 Timothy 4:15 "Practice these things, immerse yourself in them, so that all may see your progress."

What steps did I take towards my goal today? _____

_____

What did today teach me that I will bring into tomorrow? _____

_____

Ecclesiastes 3:11 "He has made everything beautiful in its time. Also, he has put eternity into man's heart, yet so that he cannot find out what God has done from the beginning to the end."

A common question I get asked time and time again is, "will you and your husband have more children?" I understand why we are asked that often. We have great relationships with our boys. We love being parents. I mean, I even started a business just for moms! It's my passion! I used to respond to this question with my map of how I wanted my life to be. I would answer with "yes" or "no," depending on my mood that day. My husband and I would change our answer on this topic often. Sometimes it became an argument in our home if we did not agree. One other factor in both of our minds was adoption. It was something we both had on our heart, yet we couldn't make a decision on it. After being on my knees in prayer on the topic of growing our family, the Lord spoke to me. He reminded me that His plans are far greater than my plans. He reminded me of a time in my early 20's when I had my whole life mapped out. I would tell everyone I would get married around 26, have my first child before 30, and have a total of 3 children. I wanted two boys and one girl. I explained how I would work and take care of the children. I even had a plan of where and when I would buy my first house. On my knees, God reminded me how terribly my own plans failed. He reminded me of how I felt when those plans failed. He also reminded me how he pulled me from my lowest point to remind me who I was in Him. From that moment forward, I changed my answer when I was presented with that question. My answer became, "we would love one more, whether birth or adoption. However, we would love His plan to come to pass." We have had peace since our answer changed. God has a plan for you. If you try to take control of that plan, God has a way of showing you how much you need Him to be the guide. Surrender your plan today. He has never left you and never will.

Let this serve as a reminder to you this week:

He sees you.

He hears you.

He loves you.

Weekly Challenge:

It's time to reflect on your entries from last week. Pray. Meditate. Celebrate.

Date:_____

Reflection:

Jeremiah 29:11 "For I know the plans I have for you, declares the Lord, plans for welfare and not for evil, to give you a future and a hope."

What am I celebrating today? _____

_____

What am I grateful for today? _____

_____

What do I need to forgive myself for today? _____

_____

How did I use my gifts today?: _____

_____

Self-care:

3 John 1:2 "Beloved, I pray that all may go well with you and that you may be in good health, as it goes well with your soul."

How did I spend my 15 minutes of "me" time today? _____

_____

How will I spend my 15 minutes of "me" time tomorrow? _____

_____

How did I show gratitude for the ability to move my body today? _____

_____

How will I move tomorrow? _____

_____

Growth:

1 Timothy 4:15 "Practice these things, immerse yourself in them, so that all may see your progress."

What steps did I take towards my goal today? _____

_____

What did today teach me that I will bring into tomorrow? _____

_____

Date:_____

Reflection:

Jeremiah 29:11 "For I know the plans I have for you, declares the Lord, plans for welfare and not for evil, to give you a future and a hope."

What am I celebrating today? _____

_____

What am I grateful for today? _____

_____

What do I need to forgive myself for today? _____

_____

How did I use my gifts today?: _____

_____

Self-care:

3 John 1:2 "Beloved, I pray that all may go well with you and that you may be in good health, as it goes well with your soul."

How did I spend my 15 minutes of "me" time today? _____

_____

How will I spend my 15 minutes of "me" time tomorrow? _____

_____

How did I show gratitude for the ability to move my body today? _____

_____

How will I move tomorrow? _____

_____

Growth:

1 Timothy 4:15 "Practice these things, immerse yourself in them, so that all may see your progress."

What steps did I take towards my goal today? _____

_____

What did today teach me that I will bring into tomorrow? _____

_____

Reflection:

Jeremiah 29:11 "For I know the plans I have for you, declares the Lord, plans for welfare and not for evil, to give you a future and a hope."

What am I celebrating today? _____

_____

What am I grateful for today? _____

_____

What do I need to forgive myself for today? _____

_____

How did I use my gifts today?: _____

_____

Self-care:

3 John 1:2 "Beloved, I pray that all may go well with you and that you may be in good health, as it goes well with your soul."

How did I spend my 15 minutes of "me" time today? _____

_____

How will I spend my 15 minutes of "me" time tomorrow? _____

_____

How did I show gratitude for the ability to move my body today? _____

_____

How will I move tomorrow? _____

_____

Growth:

1 Timothy 4:15 "Practice these things, immerse yourself in them, so that all may see your progress."

What steps did I take towards my goal today? _____

_____

What did today teach me that I will bring into tomorrow? _____

_____

Date:_____

Reflection:

Jeremiah 29:11 "For I know the plans I have for you, declares the Lord, plans for welfare and not for evil, to give you a future and a hope."

What am I celebrating today? _____
_____

What am I grateful for today? _____
_____

What do I need to forgive myself for today? _____
_____

How did I use my gifts today?: _____
_____

Self-care:

3 John 1:2 "Beloved, I pray that all may go well with you and that you may be in good health, as it goes well with your soul."

How did I spend my 15 minutes of "me" time today? _____
_____

How will I spend my 15 minutes of "me" time tomorrow? _____
_____

How did I show gratitude for the ability to move my body today? ___
_____

How will I move tomorrow? _____
_____

Growth:

1 Timothy 4:15 "Practice these things, immerse yourself in them, so that all may see your progress."

What steps did I take towards my goal today? _____
_____

What did today teach me that I will bring into tomorrow? _____
_____

Date:_____

Reflection:

Jeremiah 29:11 "For I know the plans I have for you, declares the Lord, plans for welfare and not for evil, to give you a future and a hope."

What am I celebrating today? _____

_____

What am I grateful for today? _____

_____

What do I need to forgive myself for today? _____

_____

How did I use my gifts today?: _____

_____

Self-care:

3 John 1:2 "Beloved, I pray that all may go well with you and that you may be in good health, as it goes well with your soul."

How did I spend my 15 minutes of "me" time today? _____

_____

How will I spend my 15 minutes of "me" time tomorrow? _____

_____

How did I show gratitude for the ability to move my body today? ___

_____

How will I move tomorrow? _____

_____

Growth:

1 Timothy 4:15 "Practice these things, immerse yourself in them, so that all may see your progress."

What steps did I take towards my goal today? _____

_____

What did today teach me that I will bring into tomorrow? _____

_____

Date:_____

Reflection:

Jeremiah 29:11 "For I know the plans I have for you, declares the Lord, plans for welfare and not for evil, to give you a future and a hope."

What am I celebrating today? _____

_____

What am I grateful for today? _____

_____

What do I need to forgive myself for today? _____

_____

How did I use my gifts today?: _____

_____

Self-care:

3 John 1:2 "Beloved, I pray that all may go well with you and that you may be in good health, as it goes well with your soul."

How did I spend my 15 minutes of "me" time today? _____

_____

How will I spend my 15 minutes of "me" time tomorrow? _____

_____

How did I show gratitude for the ability to move my body today? _____

_____

How will I move tomorrow? _____

_____

Growth:

1 Timothy 4:15 "Practice these things, immerse yourself in them, so that all may see your progress."

What steps did I take towards my goal today? _____

_____

What did today teach me that I will bring into tomorrow? _____

_____

Date:_____

Reflection:

Jeremiah 29:11 "For I know the plans I have for you, declares the Lord, plans for welfare and not for evil, to give you a future and a hope."

What am I celebrating today? _____

_____

What am I grateful for today? _____

_____

What do I need to forgive myself for today? _____

_____

How did I use my gifts today?: _____

_____

Self-care:

3 John 1:2 "Beloved, I pray that all may go well with you and that you may be in good health, as it goes well with your soul."

How did I spend my 15 minutes of "me" time today? _____

_____

How will I spend my 15 minutes of "me" time tomorrow? _____

_____

How did I show gratitude for the ability to move my body today? _____

_____

How will I move tomorrow? _____

_____

Growth:

1 Timothy 4:15 "Practice these things, immerse yourself in them, so that all may see your progress."

What steps did I take towards my goal today? _____

_____

What did today teach me that I will bring into tomorrow? _____

_____

Psalms 17:15 "As for me, I shall behold your face in righteousness; when I awake, I shall be satisfied with your likeness."

As a mom, I am sure you have heard people tell you find your "mom tribe." You have been told and you have read everywhere telling you how you need to be around like-minded women who can help you through this time. Now, what if you do not have that tribe or that village. That can make you feel even more lonely I am sure. Everywhere you turn, the advice you see is to build a mom community, but what if that is something you simply do not have. I will share a story with you in hopes you do not feel alone. When I had my second child and was diagnosed with postpartum depression, I felt so alone. At that time, I would speak to other people such as my therapist or a church member about my diagnosis and how I was feeling on this journey. I repeatedly heard the same questions: "don't you have anyone who can help you with the kids?" In all honesty, no I did not. It hurt even more when this question was presented to me. The more people asked me this, the more I began to realize that everyone who was close to me had started to distance themselves. Within a few months I had even been fired from my job! FIRED! I had never even been written up a job, EVER! I was always the star employee of every job I have had. I was told I had not been the same for the past few months. So now, I have no one to lean on, my marriage was failing, I had depression, and lost my job. Yet, this question was still being asked. This is when I grew in my relationship with the Lord. It was in this time that I created my business to help other mothers. Since then, when a mother approaches me with the similar situation I went through, I never ask "do you not have any help?" Instead I say, "I am going to help you. Tell me where you need help." I realized when I stop asking if they need help, and tell the person I AM helping, the mom just cannot say no. It is only through the grace of God that I got through that time and that I am a living testimony today. Mom, if you feel you do not belong to a tribe, I urge you to lean on Him today. He has promised you hope and a future. Just focus on getting through today. Use this time to press into your relationship with Him. Take this time to make you healthy. Ask the Lord for that tribe. Have you done that yet? If not, begin that now. Again, Mom, you are never alone.

Let this serve as a reminder to you this week:

He sees you.

He hears you.

He loves you.

<u>Weekly Challenge:</u>

It's time to reflect on your entries from last week. Pray. Meditate. Celebrate.

Date:_____

Reflection:

Jeremiah 29:11 "For I know the plans I have for you, declares the Lord, plans for welfare and not for evil, to give you a future and a hope."

What am I celebrating today? _____
_____

What am I grateful for today? _____
_____

What do I need to forgive myself for today? _____
_____

How did I use my gifts today?: _____
_____

Self-care:

3 John 1:2 "Beloved, I pray that all may go well with you and that you may be in good health, as it goes well with your soul."

How did I spend my 15 minutes of "me" time today? _____
_____

How will I spend my 15 minutes of "me" time tomorrow? _____
_____

How did I show gratitude for the ability to move my body today? ____
_____

How will I move tomorrow? _____
_____

Growth:

1 Timothy 4:15 "Practice these things, immerse yourself in them, so that all may see your progress."

What steps did I take towards my goal today? _____
_____

What did today teach me that I will bring into tomorrow? _____
_____

Date:_____

Reflection:

Jeremiah 29:11 "For I know the plans I have for you, declares the Lord, plans for welfare and not for evil, to give you a future and a hope."

What am I celebrating today? _____

_____

What am I grateful for today? _____

_____

What do I need to forgive myself for today? _____

_____

How did I use my gifts today?: _____

_____

Self-care:

3 John 1:2 "Beloved, I pray that all may go well with you and that you may be in good health, as it goes well with your soul."

How did I spend my 15 minutes of "me" time today? _____

_____

How will I spend my 15 minutes of "me" time tomorrow? _____

_____

How did I show gratitude for the ability to move my body today? _____

_____

How will I move tomorrow? _____

_____

Growth:

1 Timothy 4:15 "Practice these things, immerse yourself in them, so that all may see your progress."

What steps did I take towards my goal today? _____

_____

What did today teach me that I will bring into tomorrow? _____

_____

Date:_____

Reflection:

Jeremiah 29:11 "For I know the plans I have for you, declares the Lord, plans for welfare and not for evil, to give you a future and a hope."

What am I celebrating today? _____

_____

What am I grateful for today? _____

_____

What do I need to forgive myself for today? _____

_____

How did I use my gifts today?: _____

_____

Self-care:

3 John 1:2 "Beloved, I pray that all may go well with you and that you may be in good health, as it goes well with your soul."

How did I spend my 15 minutes of "me" time today? _____

_____

How will I spend my 15 minutes of "me" time tomorrow? _____

_____

How did I show gratitude for the ability to move my body today? _____

_____

How will I move tomorrow? _____

_____

Growth:

1 Timothy 4:15 "Practice these things, immerse yourself in them, so that all may see your progress."

What steps did I take towards my goal today? _____

_____

What did today teach me that I will bring into tomorrow? _____

_____

Reflection:

Jeremiah 29:11 "For I know the plans I have for you, declares the Lord, plans for welfare and not for evil, to give you a future and a hope."

What am I celebrating today? _____

_____

What am I grateful for today? _____

_____

What do I need to forgive myself for today? _____

_____

How did I use my gifts today?: _____

_____

Self-care:

3 John 1:2 "Beloved, I pray that all may go well with you and that you may be in good health, as it goes well with your soul."

How did I spend my 15 minutes of "me" time today? _____

_____

How will I spend my 15 minutes of "me" time tomorrow? _____

_____

How did I show gratitude for the ability to move my body today? _____

_____

How will I move tomorrow? _____

_____

Growth:

1 Timothy 4:15 "Practice these things, immerse yourself in them, so that all may see your progress."

What steps did I take towards my goal today? _____

_____

What did today teach me that I will bring into tomorrow? _____

_____

Date:_____

Reflection:

Jeremiah 29:11 "For I know the plans I have for you, declares the Lord, plans for welfare and not for evil, to give you a future and a hope."

What am I celebrating today? _____

_____

What am I grateful for today? _____

_____

What do I need to forgive myself for today? _____

_____

How did I use my gifts today?: _____

_____

Self-care:

3 John 1:2 "Beloved, I pray that all may go well with you and that you may be in good health, as it goes well with your soul."

How did I spend my 15 minutes of "me" time today? _____

_____

How will I spend my 15 minutes of "me" time tomorrow? _____

_____

How did I show gratitude for the ability to move my body today? _____

_____

How will I move tomorrow? _____

_____

Growth:

1 Timothy 4:15 "Practice these things, immerse yourself in them, so that all may see your progress."

What steps did I take towards my goal today? _____

_____

What did today teach me that I will bring into tomorrow? _____

_____

Date:_____

Reflection:

Jeremiah 29:11 "For I know the plans I have for you, declares the Lord, plans for welfare and not for evil, to give you a future and a hope."

What am I celebrating today? _____

_____

What am I grateful for today? _____

_____

What do I need to forgive myself for today? _____

_____

How did I use my gifts today?: _____

_____

Self-care:

3 John 1:2 "Beloved, I pray that all may go well with you and that you may be in good health, as it goes well with your soul."

How did I spend my 15 minutes of "me" time today? _____

_____

How will I spend my 15 minutes of "me" time tomorrow? _____

_____

How did I show gratitude for the ability to move my body today? _____

_____

How will I move tomorrow? _____

_____

Growth:

1 Timothy 4:15 "Practice these things, immerse yourself in them, so that all may see your progress."

What steps did I take towards my goal today? _____

_____

What did today teach me that I will bring into tomorrow? _____

_____

Date:_____

Reflection:

Jeremiah 29:11 "For I know the plans I have for you, declares the Lord, plans for welfare and not for evil, to give you a future and a hope."

What am I celebrating today? _____

_____

What am I grateful for today? _____

_____

What do I need to forgive myself for today? _____

_____

How did I use my gifts today?: _____

_____

Self-care:

3 John 1:2 "Beloved, I pray that all may go well with you and that you may be in good health, as it goes well with your soul."

How did I spend my 15 minutes of "me" time today? _____

_____

How will I spend my 15 minutes of "me" time tomorrow? _____

_____

How did I show gratitude for the ability to move my body today? _____

_____

How will I move tomorrow? _____

_____

Growth:

1 Timothy 4:15 "Practice these things, immerse yourself in them, so that all may see your progress."

What steps did I take towards my goal today? _____

_____

What did today teach me that I will bring into tomorrow? _____

_____

Proverbs 12:15 *"The way of a fool is right in his own eyes, but a wiseman listens to advice."*

Mom, I want you to think about advice. What is one piece of advice you would give another mom? What is one piece of advice you would give yourself if you could go back in time to before you had kids? Is this advice coming from a place of regret or a place of knowledge? I remember when I was 9 months pregnant with my first born. I was so excited to be a mom soon! At that time, I was a waitress. One evening, I was waiting on a family who brought in their 1-year old boy. While they were strapping him in the highchair, they began asking me the typical pregnancy questions. You could hear the excitement in my voice with each response I gave. When I finished, they said this to me, "well the first three months are terrible!!! It gets better from there." My jaw dropped. I did not know what to say. I went home from work and cried to my husband. I said, "I cannot believe the words someone said to me today!! They ruined my idea of motherhood!" Fast forward to three months into being a mother. I looked at my husband one day and said, "the couple who came into the restaurant one day and gave me the advice about the first three months of having a baby was the best advice anyone could have given me during my pregnancy." I ended up being so grateful that someone was brutally honest with me as they were. Mom, what advice would YOU give a first-time mom? Maybe explore that advice a little deeper. Could that be a calling on your life? Think about it.

Let this serve as a reminder to you this week:

He sees you.

He hears you.

He loves you.

<u>Weekly Challenge:</u>

It's time to reflect on your entries from last week. Pray. Meditate. Celebrate.

Date:_____

Reflection:

Jeremiah 29:11 "For I know the plans I have for you, declares the Lord, plans for welfare and not for evil, to give you a future and a hope."

What am I celebrating today? _____

_____

What am I grateful for today? _____

_____

What do I need to forgive myself for today? _____

_____

How did I use my gifts today?: _____

_____

Self-care:

3 John 1:2 "Beloved, I pray that all may go well with you and that you may be in good health, as it goes well with your soul."

How did I spend my 15 minutes of "me" time today? _____

_____

How will I spend my 15 minutes of "me" time tomorrow? _____

_____

How did I show gratitude for the ability to move my body today? _____

_____

How will I move tomorrow? _____

_____

Growth:

1 Timothy 4:15 "Practice these things, immerse yourself in them, so that all may see your progress."

What steps did I take towards my goal today? _____

_____

What did today teach me that I will bring into tomorrow? _____

_____

Reflection:

Jeremiah 29:11 "For I know the plans I have for you, declares the Lord, plans for welfare and not for evil, to give you a future and a hope."

What am I celebrating today? _____
_____

What am I grateful for today? _____
_____

What do I need to forgive myself for today? _____
_____

How did I use my gifts today?: _____
_____

Self-care:

3 John 1:2 "Beloved, I pray that all may go well with you and that you may be in good health, as it goes well with your soul."

How did I spend my 15 minutes of "me" time today? _____
_____

How will I spend my 15 minutes of "me" time tomorrow? _____
_____

How did I show gratitude for the ability to move my body today? _____
_____

How will I move tomorrow? _____
_____

Growth:

1 Timothy 4:15 "Practice these things, immerse yourself in them, so that all may see your progress."

What steps did I take towards my goal today? _____
_____

What did today teach me that I will bring into tomorrow? _____
_____

Date:_____

Reflection:

Jeremiah 29:11 "For I know the plans I have for you, declares the Lord, plans for welfare and not for evil, to give you a future and a hope."

What am I celebrating today? _____

_____

What am I grateful for today? _____

_____

What do I need to forgive myself for today? _____

_____

How did I use my gifts today?: _____

_____

Self-care:

3 John 1:2 "Beloved, I pray that all may go well with you and that you may be in good health, as it goes well with your soul."

How did I spend my 15 minutes of "me" time today? _____

_____

How will I spend my 15 minutes of "me" time tomorrow? _____

_____

How did I show gratitude for the ability to move my body today? _____

_____

How will I move tomorrow? _____

_____

Growth:

1 Timothy 4:15 "Practice these things, immerse yourself in them, so that all may see your progress."

What steps did I take towards my goal today? _____

_____

What did today teach me that I will bring into tomorrow? _____

_____

Reflection:

Jeremiah 29:11 "For I know the plans I have for you, declares the Lord, plans for welfare and not for evil, to give you a future and a hope."

What am I celebrating today? _____

_____

What am I grateful for today? _____

_____

What do I need to forgive myself for today? _____

_____

How did I use my gifts today?: _____

_____

Self-care:

3 John 1:2 "Beloved, I pray that all may go well with you and that you may be in good health, as it goes well with your soul."

How did I spend my 15 minutes of "me" time today? _____

_____

How will I spend my 15 minutes of "me" time tomorrow? _____

_____

How did I show gratitude for the ability to move my body today? ____

_____

How will I move tomorrow? _____

_____

Growth:

1 Timothy 4:15 "Practice these things, immerse yourself in them, so that all may see your progress."

What steps did I take towards my goal today? _____

_____

What did today teach me that I will bring into tomorrow? _____

_____

Date:_____

Reflection:

Jeremiah 29:11 "For I know the plans I have for you, declares the Lord, plans for welfare and not for evil, to give you a future and a hope."

What am I celebrating today? _____

_____

What am I grateful for today? _____

_____

What do I need to forgive myself for today? _____

_____

How did I use my gifts today?: _____

_____

Self-care:

3 John 1:2 "Beloved, I pray that all may go well with you and that you may be in good health, as it goes well with your soul."

How did I spend my 15 minutes of "me" time today? _____

_____

How will I spend my 15 minutes of "me" time tomorrow? _____

_____

How did I show gratitude for the ability to move my body today? _____

_____

How will I move tomorrow? _____

_____

Growth:

1 Timothy 4:15 "Practice these things, immerse yourself in them, so that all may see your progress."

What steps did I take towards my goal today? _____

_____

What did today teach me that I will bring into tomorrow? _____

_____

Reflection:

Jeremiah 29:11 "For I know the plans I have for you, declares the Lord, plans for welfare and not for evil, to give you a future and a hope."

What am I celebrating today? _____

_____

What am I grateful for today? _____

_____

What do I need to forgive myself for today? _____

_____

How did I use my gifts today?: _____

_____

Self-care:

3 John 1:2 "Beloved, I pray that all may go well with you and that you may be in good health, as it goes well with your soul."

How did I spend my 15 minutes of "me" time today? _____

_____

How will I spend my 15 minutes of "me" time tomorrow? _____

_____

How did I show gratitude for the ability to move my body today? _____

_____

How will I move tomorrow? _____

_____

Growth:

1 Timothy 4:15 "Practice these things, immerse yourself in them, so that all may see your progress."

What steps did I take towards my goal today? _____

_____

What did today teach me that I will bring into tomorrow? _____

_____

Date:_____

Reflection:

Jeremiah 29:11 "For I know the plans I have for you, declares the Lord, plans for welfare and not for evil, to give you a future and a hope."

What am I celebrating today? _____

_____

What am I grateful for today? _____

_____

What do I need to forgive myself for today? _____

_____

How did I use my gifts today?: _____

_____

Self-care:

3 John 1:2 "Beloved, I pray that all may go well with you and that you may be in good health, as it goes well with your soul."

How did I spend my 15 minutes of "me" time today? _____

_____

How will I spend my 15 minutes of "me" time tomorrow? _____

_____

How did I show gratitude for the ability to move my body today? _____

_____

How will I move tomorrow? _____

_____

Growth:

1 Timothy 4:15 "Practice these things, immerse yourself in them, so that all may see your progress."

What steps did I take towards my goal today? _____

_____

What did today teach me that I will bring into tomorrow? _____

_____

Ephesians 3:20 "Now to him who is able to do far more abundantly than all that we ask or think, according to the power at work within us,"

When you think of the word "abundance," what comes
to your mind? Do you think about money and riches?
Or do you think about nothing material?

Mom, you know what is cool? God has promised us that because we live with Him in our hearts, we get to live a more abundant life. That goes BEYOND riches! That means we will be filled with joy, happiness, family, love, and we will have our needs met. Now THAT is something to praise about! Whatever is heavy on your heart today, begin to praise Him. He has made a promise to you. You may have a darkness in an area of your life, but with his promise of ABUNDANCE, He can and will bring light to that situation. Mom, you have your hands full, but how blessed are you that you are ABLE to be the mother to those children?! You are already living an abundant life. Your heart is filled with the treasures He trusted you with. Praise Him and give him your troubles today. Just watch how he will turn those into ABUNDANCE.

Let this serve as a reminder to you this week:

He sees you.

He hears you.

He loves you.

Weekly Challenge:

It's time to reflect on your entries from last
week. Pray. Meditate. Celebrate.

Date:_____

Reflection:

Jeremiah 29:11 "For I know the plans I have for you, declares the Lord, plans for welfare and not for evil, to give you a future and a hope."

What am I celebrating today? _____

_____

What am I grateful for today? _____

_____

What do I need to forgive myself for today? _____

_____

How did I use my gifts today?: _____

_____

Self-care:

3 John 1:2 "Beloved, I pray that all may go well with you and that you may be in good health, as it goes well with your soul."

How did I spend my 15 minutes of "me" time today? _____

_____

How will I spend my 15 minutes of "me" time tomorrow? _____

_____

How did I show gratitude for the ability to move my body today? _____

_____

How will I move tomorrow? _____

_____

Growth:

1 Timothy 4:15 "Practice these things, immerse yourself in them, so that all may see your progress."

What steps did I take towards my goal today? _____

_____

What did today teach me that I will bring into tomorrow? _____

_____

Date:_____

Reflection:

Jeremiah 29:11 "For I know the plans I have for you, declares the Lord, plans for welfare and not for evil, to give you a future and a hope."

What am I celebrating today? _____
_____

What am I grateful for today? _____
_____

What do I need to forgive myself for today? _____
_____

How did I use my gifts today?: _____
_____

Self-care:

3 John 1:2 "Beloved, I pray that all may go well with you and that you may be in good health, as it goes well with your soul."

How did I spend my 15 minutes of "me" time today? _____
_____

How will I spend my 15 minutes of "me" time tomorrow? _____
_____

How did I show gratitude for the ability to move my body today? _____
_____

How will I move tomorrow? _____
_____

Growth:

1 Timothy 4:15 "Practice these things, immerse yourself in them, so that all may see your progress."

What steps did I take towards my goal today? _____
_____

What did today teach me that I will bring into tomorrow? _____
_____

Date:_____

Reflection:

Jeremiah 29:11 "For I know the plans I have for you, declares the Lord, plans for welfare and not for evil, to give you a future and a hope."

What am I celebrating today? _____
_____

What am I grateful for today? _____
_____

What do I need to forgive myself for today? _____
_____

How did I use my gifts today?: _____
_____

Self-care:

3 John 1:2 "Beloved, I pray that all may go well with you and that you may be in good health, as it goes well with your soul."

How did I spend my 15 minutes of "me" time today? _____
_____

How will I spend my 15 minutes of "me" time tomorrow? _____
_____

How did I show gratitude for the ability to move my body today? _____
_____

How will I move tomorrow? _____
_____

Growth:

1 Timothy 4:15 "Practice these things, immerse yourself in them, so that all may see your progress."

What steps did I take towards my goal today? _____
_____

What did today teach me that I will bring into tomorrow? _____
_____

Date:_____

Reflection:

Jeremiah 29:11 "For I know the plans I have for you, declares the Lord, plans for welfare and not for evil, to give you a future and a hope."

What am I celebrating today? _____

_____

What am I grateful for today? _____

_____

What do I need to forgive myself for today? _____

_____

How did I use my gifts today?: _____

_____

Self-care:

3 John 1:2 "Beloved, I pray that all may go well with you and that you may be in good health, as it goes well with your soul."

How did I spend my 15 minutes of "me" time today? _____

_____

How will I spend my 15 minutes of "me" time tomorrow? _____

_____

How did I show gratitude for the ability to move my body today? _____

_____

How will I move tomorrow? _____

_____

Growth:

1 Timothy 4:15 "Practice these things, immerse yourself in them, so that all may see your progress."

What steps did I take towards my goal today? _____

_____

What did today teach me that I will bring into tomorrow? _____

_____

Date:_____

Reflection:

Jeremiah 29:11 "For I know the plans I have for you, declares the Lord, plans for welfare and not for evil, to give you a future and a hope."

What am I celebrating today? _____

_____

What am I grateful for today? _____

_____

What do I need to forgive myself for today? _____

_____

How did I use my gifts today?: _____

_____

Self-care:

3 John 1:2 "Beloved, I pray that all may go well with you and that you may be in good health, as it goes well with your soul."

How did I spend my 15 minutes of "me" time today? _____

_____

How will I spend my 15 minutes of "me" time tomorrow? _____

_____

How did I show gratitude for the ability to move my body today? _____

_____

How will I move tomorrow? _____

_____

Growth:

1 Timothy 4:15 "Practice these things, immerse yourself in them, so that all may see your progress."

What steps did I take towards my goal today? _____

_____

What did today teach me that I will bring into tomorrow? _____

_____

Date:_____

Reflection:

Jeremiah 29:11 "For I know the plans I have for you, declares the Lord, plans for welfare and not for evil, to give you a future and a hope."

What am I celebrating today? _____

_____

What am I grateful for today? _____

_____

What do I need to forgive myself for today? _____

_____

How did I use my gifts today?: _____

_____

Self-care:

3 John 1:2 "Beloved, I pray that all may go well with you and that you may be in good health, as it goes well with your soul."

How did I spend my 15 minutes of "me" time today? _____

_____

How will I spend my 15 minutes of "me" time tomorrow? _____

_____

How did I show gratitude for the ability to move my body today? _____

_____

How will I move tomorrow? _____

_____

Growth:

1 Timothy 4:15 "Practice these things, immerse yourself in them, so that all may see your progress."

What steps did I take towards my goal today? _____

_____

What did today teach me that I will bring into tomorrow? _____

_____

Date:_____

Reflection:

Jeremiah 29:11 "For I know the plans I have for you, declares the Lord, plans for welfare and not for evil, to give you a future and a hope."

What am I celebrating today? _____

_____

What am I grateful for today? _____

_____

What do I need to forgive myself for today? _____

_____

How did I use my gifts today?: _____

_____

Self-care:

3 John 1:2 "Beloved, I pray that all may go well with you and that you may be in good health, as it goes well with your soul."

How did I spend my 15 minutes of "me" time today? _____

_____

How will I spend my 15 minutes of "me" time tomorrow? _____

_____

How did I show gratitude for the ability to move my body today? _____

_____

How will I move tomorrow? _____

_____

Growth:

1 Timothy 4:15 "Practice these things, immerse yourself in them, so that all may see your progress."

What steps did I take towards my goal today? _____

_____

What did today teach me that I will bring into tomorrow? _____

_____

Matthew 11:28 "Come to me, all who labor and are heavy laden, and I will give you rest."

Mom, I know your hands are full. They are full of your little ones. They are full of your responsibilities you take on each day. They are full of work. They are full of worry. You have a big job to do. However, you do not have to do it alone. Wipe those tears. You are doing such an amazing job! This is your reminder this week that you carry it all and you do it with grace. Your reward on earth will be huge! You get to see your children grow up into God fearing men and women. You get to watch your children grow up and show kindness to those who cross their paths. You get to watch them grow up and love on those who need it most. You get to see this all because you have lit the path as an example to them of how to live a Christ like life. Your reward will be great in heaven as well. Congratulations, mom. He sees you. You are never alone.

Let this serve as a reminder to you this week:

He sees you.

He hears you.

He loves you.

Weekly Challenge:

It's time to reflect on your entries from last week. Pray. Meditate. Celebrate.

Date:_____

Reflection:

Jeremiah 29:11 "For I know the plans I have for you, declares the Lord, plans for welfare and not for evil, to give you a future and a hope."

What am I celebrating today? _____

_____

What am I grateful for today? _____

_____

What do I need to forgive myself for today? _____

_____

How did I use my gifts today?: _____

_____

Self-care:

3 John 1:2 "Beloved, I pray that all may go well with you and that you may be in good health, as it goes well with your soul."

How did I spend my 15 minutes of "me" time today? _____

_____

How will I spend my 15 minutes of "me" time tomorrow? _____

_____

How did I show gratitude for the ability to move my body today? _____

_____

How will I move tomorrow? _____

_____

Growth:

1 Timothy 4:15 "Practice these things, immerse yourself in them, so that all may see your progress."

What steps did I take towards my goal today? _____

_____

What did today teach me that I will bring into tomorrow? _____

_____

Date:_____

Reflection:

Jeremiah 29:11 "For I know the plans I have for you, declares the Lord, plans for welfare and not for evil, to give you a future and a hope."

What am I celebrating today? _____

_____

What am I grateful for today? _____

_____

What do I need to forgive myself for today? _____

_____

How did I use my gifts today?: _____

_____

Self-care:

3 John 1:2 "Beloved, I pray that all may go well with you and that you may be in good health, as it goes well with your soul."

How did I spend my 15 minutes of "me" time today? _____

_____

How will I spend my 15 minutes of "me" time tomorrow? _____

_____

How did I show gratitude for the ability to move my body today? _____

_____

How will I move tomorrow? _____

_____

Growth:

1 Timothy 4:15 "Practice these things, immerse yourself in them, so that all may see your progress."

What steps did I take towards my goal today? _____

_____

What did today teach me that I will bring into tomorrow? _____

_____

Date:_____

Reflection:

Jeremiah 29:11 "For I know the plans I have for you, declares the Lord, plans for welfare and not for evil, to give you a future and a hope."

What am I celebrating today? _____
_____

What am I grateful for today? _____
_____

What do I need to forgive myself for today? _____
_____

How did I use my gifts today?: _____
_____

Self-care:

3 John 1:2 "Beloved, I pray that all may go well with you and that you may be in good health, as it goes well with your soul."

How did I spend my 15 minutes of "me" time today? _____
_____

How will I spend my 15 minutes of "me" time tomorrow? _____
_____

How did I show gratitude for the ability to move my body today? _____
_____

How will I move tomorrow? _____
_____

Growth:

1 Timothy 4:15 "Practice these things, immerse yourself in them, so that all may see your progress."

What steps did I take towards my goal today? _____
_____

What did today teach me that I will bring into tomorrow? _____
_____

Date:_____

Reflection:

Jeremiah 29:11 "For I know the plans I have for you, declares the Lord, plans for welfare and not for evil, to give you a future and a hope."

What am I celebrating today? _____

_____

What am I grateful for today? _____

_____

What do I need to forgive myself for today? _____

_____

How did I use my gifts today?: _____

_____

Self-care:

3 John 1:2 "Beloved, I pray that all may go well with you and that you may be in good health, as it goes well with your soul."

How did I spend my 15 minutes of "me" time today? _____

_____

How will I spend my 15 minutes of "me" time tomorrow? _____

_____

How did I show gratitude for the ability to move my body today? _____

_____

How will I move tomorrow? _____

_____

Growth:

1 Timothy 4:15 "Practice these things, immerse yourself in them, so that all may see your progress."

What steps did I take towards my goal today? _____

_____

What did today teach me that I will bring into tomorrow? _____

_____

Date:_____

Reflection:

Jeremiah 29:11 "For I know the plans I have for you, declares the Lord, plans for welfare and not for evil, to give you a future and a hope."

What am I celebrating today? _____

_____

What am I grateful for today? _____

_____

What do I need to forgive myself for today? _____

_____

How did I use my gifts today?: _____

_____

Self-care:

3 John 1:2 "Beloved, I pray that all may go well with you and that you may be in good health, as it goes well with your soul."

How did I spend my 15 minutes of "me" time today? _____

_____

How will I spend my 15 minutes of "me" time tomorrow? _____

_____

How did I show gratitude for the ability to move my body today? _____

_____

How will I move tomorrow? _____

_____

Growth:

1 Timothy 4:15 "Practice these things, immerse yourself in them, so that all may see your progress."

What steps did I take towards my goal today? _____

_____

What did today teach me that I will bring into tomorrow? _____

_____

Date:_____

Reflection:

Jeremiah 29:11 "For I know the plans I have for you, declares the Lord, plans for welfare and not for evil, to give you a future and a hope."

What am I celebrating today? _____

_____

What am I grateful for today? _____

_____

What do I need to forgive myself for today? _____

_____

How did I use my gifts today?: _____

_____

Self-care:

3 John 1:2 "Beloved, I pray that all may go well with you and that you may be in good health, as it goes well with your soul."

How did I spend my 15 minutes of "me" time today? _____

_____

How will I spend my 15 minutes of "me" time tomorrow? _____

_____

How did I show gratitude for the ability to move my body today? _____

_____

How will I move tomorrow? _____

_____

Growth:

1 Timothy 4:15 "Practice these things, immerse yourself in them, so that all may see your progress."

What steps did I take towards my goal today? _____

_____

What did today teach me that I will bring into tomorrow? _____

_____

Date:_____

Reflection:

Jeremiah 29:11 "For I know the plans I have for you, declares the Lord, plans for welfare and not for evil, to give you a future and a hope."

What am I celebrating today? _____
_____

What am I grateful for today? _____
_____

What do I need to forgive myself for today? _____
_____

How did I use my gifts today?: _____
_____

Self-care:

3 John 1:2 "Beloved, I pray that all may go well with you and that you may be in good health, as it goes well with your soul."

How did I spend my 15 minutes of "me" time today? _____
_____

How will I spend my 15 minutes of "me" time tomorrow? _____
_____

How did I show gratitude for the ability to move my body today? ___
_____

How will I move tomorrow? _____
_____

Growth:

1 Timothy 4:15 "Practice these things, immerse yourself in them, so that all may see your progress."

What steps did I take towards my goal today? _____
_____

What did today teach me that I will bring into tomorrow? _____
_____

2 Corinthians 3:5 "Not that we are sufficient in ourselves to claim anything as coming from us, but our sufficiency is from God."

Mom, when is the last time you leaned on the Lord to guide your next step? I am speaking about something you have had on your heart or something you always dreamed about doing. Maybe along the road, someone told you that you would never be able to do what you always envisioned yourself doing or the way you imagined yourself serving. Maybe your resume is short. Maybe you do not have much experience in that given field, so you just brushed that dream to the side. If I told you the countless times someone told me I would never succeed in what I dreamed of doing, you would be shocked. I never pictured myself writing a planner for moms. Why? Because my resume tells me I am not qualified for that type of work. However, God's plans for my life far succeeded what a piece of paper says. A little background on me: I have a degree in architectural and interior design. I have a certification in cosmetology. I have been a behavior specialist, and direct support professional for special needs children and adults. I have owned my own cleaning business for a short time. I have been a fitness instructor. I have been a waitress and bartender. I have recently become a life coach. Now here I am writing a book for moms. One that has been on my heart. Nothing about my resume says that I should be following my heart to help mothers out who may be going through some of the same trials I have experienced. God became my resume builder. I let Him guide me and I ignored the voices of those around me. My challenge to you this week is to revisit that adventure the Lord placed on your heart. Listen to Him as He guides you through your journey. Mom, I am so proud of you.

Let this serve as a reminder to you this week:

He sees you.

He hears you.

He loves you.

Weekly Challenge:

It's time to reflect on your entries from last week. Pray. Meditate. Celebrate.

Date:_____

Reflection:

Jeremiah 29:11 "For I know the plans I have for you, declares the Lord, plans for welfare and not for evil, to give you a future and a hope."

What am I celebrating today? _____

_____

What am I grateful for today? _____

_____

What do I need to forgive myself for today? _____

_____

How did I use my gifts today?: _____

_____

Self-care:

3 John 1:2 "Beloved, I pray that all may go well with you and that you may be in good health, as it goes well with your soul."

How did I spend my 15 minutes of "me" time today? _____

_____

How will I spend my 15 minutes of "me" time tomorrow? _____

_____

How did I show gratitude for the ability to move my body today? _____

_____

How will I move tomorrow? _____

_____

Growth:

1 Timothy 4:15 "Practice these things, immerse yourself in them, so that all may see your progress."

What steps did I take towards my goal today? _____

_____

What did today teach me that I will bring into tomorrow? _____

_____

Date:_____

Reflection:

Jeremiah 29:11 "For I know the plans I have for you, declares the Lord, plans for welfare and not for evil, to give you a future and a hope."

What am I celebrating today? _____

_____

What am I grateful for today? _____

_____

What do I need to forgive myself for today? _____

_____

How did I use my gifts today?: _____

_____

Self-care:

3 John 1:2 "Beloved, I pray that all may go well with you and that you may be in good health, as it goes well with your soul."

How did I spend my 15 minutes of "me" time today? _____

_____

How will I spend my 15 minutes of "me" time tomorrow? _____

_____

How did I show gratitude for the ability to move my body today? _____

_____

How will I move tomorrow? _____

_____

Growth:

1 Timothy 4:15 "Practice these things, immerse yourself in them, so that all may see your progress."

What steps did I take towards my goal today? _____

_____

What did today teach me that I will bring into tomorrow? _____

_____

Date:_____

Reflection:

Jeremiah 29:11 "For I know the plans I have for you, declares the Lord, plans for welfare and not for evil, to give you a future and a hope."

What am I celebrating today? _____

_____

What am I grateful for today? _____

_____

What do I need to forgive myself for today? _____

_____

How did I use my gifts today?: _____

_____

Self-care:

3 John 1:2 "Beloved, I pray that all may go well with you and that you may be in good health, as it goes well with your soul."

How did I spend my 15 minutes of "me" time today? _____

_____

How will I spend my 15 minutes of "me" time tomorrow? _____

_____

How did I show gratitude for the ability to move my body today? _____

_____

How will I move tomorrow? _____

_____

Growth:

1 Timothy 4:15 "Practice these things, immerse yourself in them, so that all may see your progress."

What steps did I take towards my goal today? _____

_____

What did today teach me that I will bring into tomorrow? _____

_____

Date:_____

Reflection:

Jeremiah 29:11 "For I know the plans I have for you, declares the Lord, plans for welfare and not for evil, to give you a future and a hope."

What am I celebrating today? _____
_____

What am I grateful for today? _____
_____

What do I need to forgive myself for today? _____
_____

How did I use my gifts today?: _____
_____

Self-care:

3 John 1:2 "Beloved, I pray that all may go well with you and that you may be in good health, as it goes well with your soul."

How did I spend my 15 minutes of "me" time today? _____
_____

How will I spend my 15 minutes of "me" time tomorrow? _____
_____

How did I show gratitude for the ability to move my body today? _____
_____

How will I move tomorrow? _____
_____

Growth:

1 Timothy 4:15 "Practice these things, immerse yourself in them, so that all may see your progress."

What steps did I take towards my goal today? _____
_____

What did today teach me that I will bring into tomorrow? _____
_____

Reflection:

Jeremiah 29:11 "For I know the plans I have for you, declares the Lord, plans for welfare and not for evil, to give you a future and a hope."

What am I celebrating today? _____

_____

What am I grateful for today? _____

_____

What do I need to forgive myself for today? _____

_____

How did I use my gifts today?: _____

_____

Self-care:

3 John 1:2 "Beloved, I pray that all may go well with you and that you may be in good health, as it goes well with your soul."

How did I spend my 15 minutes of "me" time today? _____

_____

How will I spend my 15 minutes of "me" time tomorrow? _____

_____

How did I show gratitude for the ability to move my body today? _____

_____

How will I move tomorrow? _____

_____

Growth:

1 Timothy 4:15 "Practice these things, immerse yourself in them, so that all may see your progress."

What steps did I take towards my goal today? _____

_____

What did today teach me that I will bring into tomorrow? _____

_____

Date:_____

Reflection:

Jeremiah 29:11 "For I know the plans I have for you, declares the Lord, plans for welfare and not for evil, to give you a future and a hope."

What am I celebrating today? _____

_____

What am I grateful for today? _____

_____

What do I need to forgive myself for today? _____

_____

How did I use my gifts today?: _____

_____

Self-care:

3 John 1:2 "Beloved, I pray that all may go well with you and that you may be in good health, as it goes well with your soul."

How did I spend my 15 minutes of "me" time today? _____

_____

How will I spend my 15 minutes of "me" time tomorrow? _____

_____

How did I show gratitude for the ability to move my body today? _____

_____

How will I move tomorrow? _____

_____

Growth:

1 Timothy 4:15 "Practice these things, immerse yourself in them, so that all may see your progress."

What steps did I take towards my goal today? _____

_____

What did today teach me that I will bring into tomorrow? _____

_____

Date:_____

Reflection:

Jeremiah 29:11 "For I know the plans I have for you, declares the Lord, plans for welfare and not for evil, to give you a future and a hope."

What am I celebrating today? _____

_____

What am I grateful for today? _____

_____

What do I need to forgive myself for today? _____

_____

How did I use my gifts today?: _____

_____

Self-care:

3 John 1:2 "Beloved, I pray that all may go well with you and that you may be in good health, as it goes well with your soul."

How did I spend my 15 minutes of "me" time today? _____

_____

How will I spend my 15 minutes of "me" time tomorrow? _____

_____

How did I show gratitude for the ability to move my body today? _____

_____

How will I move tomorrow? _____

_____

Growth:

1 Timothy 4:15 "Practice these things, immerse yourself in them, so that all may see your progress."

What steps did I take towards my goal today? _____

_____

What did today teach me that I will bring into tomorrow? _____

_____

Proverbs 22:6 "Train up a child in the way he should go; even when he is old he will not depart"

Mom, one day your little one will be grown. One day your little one may have a family of his own and will have left your house. Maybe that day has already happened. Maybe you are becoming a grandmother soon. How many times have we been told "they grow up so fast"? In the moment you may feel as though the days are slow. One day you will look back on this day and wish you could hold our little one again.

In Proverbs, Gods promise to us is our children will NOT depart from Him if you raise them to look to Him through you journey in life. Hold tight to this promise. There may be days you find yourself on your knees for hours at a time praying the Lord hears your cries and delivers your child from evil. I pray for all my readers today. I pray your child follows the path designed for him/her. I pray the Lord helps to lighten your burden. I pray for the souls of every child who has been impacted by this planner. Mom, by taking the time to complete this planner, you have also taken steps towards becoming the mother God intended for you to be. Your children will see that. A healthier and happier you will benefit all those around you.

Today, I pray for you.

Let this serve as a reminder to you this week:

He sees you.

He hears you.

He loves you.

<u>Weekly Challenge:</u>

It's time to reflect on your entries from last week. Pray. Meditate. Celebrate.

Date:_____

Reflection:

Jeremiah 29:11 "For I know the plans I have for you, declares the Lord, plans for welfare and not for evil, to give you a future and a hope."

What am I celebrating today? _____

_____

What am I grateful for today? _____

_____

What do I need to forgive myself for today? _____

_____

How did I use my gifts today?: _____

_____

Self-care:

3 John 1:2 "Beloved, I pray that all may go well with you and that you may be in good health, as it goes well with your soul."

How did I spend my 15 minutes of "me" time today? _____

_____

How will I spend my 15 minutes of "me" time tomorrow? _____

_____

How did I show gratitude for the ability to move my body today? _____

_____

How will I move tomorrow? _____

_____

Growth:

1 Timothy 4:15 "Practice these things, immerse yourself in them, so that all may see your progress."

What steps did I take towards my goal today? _____

_____

What did today teach me that I will bring into tomorrow? _____

_____

Date:_____

Reflection:

Jeremiah 29:11 "For I know the plans I have for you, declares the Lord, plans for welfare and not for evil, to give you a future and a hope."

What am I celebrating today? _____
_____

What am I grateful for today? _____
_____

What do I need to forgive myself for today? _____
_____

How did I use my gifts today?: _____
_____

Self-care:

3 John 1:2 "Beloved, I pray that all may go well with you and that you may be in good health, as it goes well with your soul."

How did I spend my 15 minutes of "me" time today? _____
_____

How will I spend my 15 minutes of "me" time tomorrow? _____
_____

How did I show gratitude for the ability to move my body today? ____
_____

How will I move tomorrow? _____
_____

Growth:

1 Timothy 4:15 "Practice these things, immerse yourself in them, so that all may see your progress."

What steps did I take towards my goal today? _____
_____

What did today teach me that I will bring into tomorrow? _____
_____

Date:_____

Reflection:

Jeremiah 29:11 "For I know the plans I have for you, declares the Lord, plans for welfare and not for evil, to give you a future and a hope."

What am I celebrating today? _____

_____

What am I grateful for today? _____

_____

What do I need to forgive myself for today? _____

_____

How did I use my gifts today?: _____

_____

Self-care:

3 John 1:2 "Beloved, I pray that all may go well with you and that you may be in good health, as it goes well with your soul."

How did I spend my 15 minutes of "me" time today? _____

_____

How will I spend my 15 minutes of "me" time tomorrow? _____

_____

How did I show gratitude for the ability to move my body today? _____

_____

How will I move tomorrow? _____

_____

Growth:

1 Timothy 4:15 "Practice these things, immerse yourself in them, so that all may see your progress."

What steps did I take towards my goal today? _____

_____

What did today teach me that I will bring into tomorrow? _____

_____

Date:_____

Reflection:

Jeremiah 29:11 "For I know the plans I have for you, declares the Lord, plans for welfare and not for evil, to give you a future and a hope."

What am I celebrating today? _____

_____

What am I grateful for today? _____

_____

What do I need to forgive myself for today? _____

_____

How did I use my gifts today?: _____

_____

Self-care:

3 John 1:2 "Beloved, I pray that all may go well with you and that you may be in good health, as it goes well with your soul."

How did I spend my 15 minutes of "me" time today? _____

_____

How will I spend my 15 minutes of "me" time tomorrow? _____

_____

How did I show gratitude for the ability to move my body today? ____

_____

How will I move tomorrow? _____

_____

Growth:

1 Timothy 4:15 "Practice these things, immerse yourself in them, so that all may see your progress."

What steps did I take towards my goal today? _____

_____

What did today teach me that I will bring into tomorrow? _____

_____

Date:_____

Reflection:

Jeremiah 29:11 "For I know the plans I have for you, declares the Lord, plans for welfare and not for evil, to give you a future and a hope."

What am I celebrating today? _____

_____

What am I grateful for today? _____

_____

What do I need to forgive myself for today? _____

_____

How did I use my gifts today?: _____

_____

Self-care:

3 John 1:2 "Beloved, I pray that all may go well with you and that you may be in good health, as it goes well with your soul."

How did I spend my 15 minutes of "me" time today? _____

_____

How will I spend my 15 minutes of "me" time tomorrow? _____

_____

How did I show gratitude for the ability to move my body today? _____

_____

How will I move tomorrow? _____

_____

Growth:

1 Timothy 4:15 "Practice these things, immerse yourself in them, so that all may see your progress."

What steps did I take towards my goal today? _____

_____

What did today teach me that I will bring into tomorrow? _____

_____

Date:_____

Reflection:

Jeremiah 29:11 "For I know the plans I have for you, declares the Lord, plans for welfare and not for evil, to give you a future and a hope."

What am I celebrating today? _____
_____

What am I grateful for today? _____
_____

What do I need to forgive myself for today? _____
_____

How did I use my gifts today?: _____
_____

Self-care:

3 John 1:2 "Beloved, I pray that all may go well with you and that you may be in good health, as it goes well with your soul."

How did I spend my 15 minutes of "me" time today? _____
_____

How will I spend my 15 minutes of "me" time tomorrow? _____
_____

How did I show gratitude for the ability to move my body today? _____
_____

How will I move tomorrow? _____
_____

Growth:

1 Timothy 4:15 "Practice these things, immerse yourself in them, so that all may see your progress."

What steps did I take towards my goal today? _____
_____

What did today teach me that I will bring into tomorrow? _____
_____

Date:_____

Reflection:

Jeremiah 29:11 "For I know the plans I have for you, declares the Lord, plans for welfare and not for evil, to give you a future and a hope."

What am I celebrating today? _____

_____

What am I grateful for today? _____

_____

What do I need to forgive myself for today? _____

_____

How did I use my gifts today?: _____

_____

Self-care:

3 John 1:2 "Beloved, I pray that all may go well with you and that you may be in good health, as it goes well with your soul."

How did I spend my 15 minutes of "me" time today? _____

_____

How will I spend my 15 minutes of "me" time tomorrow? _____

_____

How did I show gratitude for the ability to move my body today? ____

_____

How will I move tomorrow? _____

_____

Growth:

1 Timothy 4:15 "Practice these things, immerse yourself in them, so that all may see your progress."

What steps did I take towards my goal today? _____

_____

What did today teach me that I will bring into tomorrow? _____

_____

2 Corinthians 8:11 "So now finish doing it as well, so that your readiness in desiring it may be matched by your completing it out of what you have."

MOM!!! You did it!! You made it to the last week of this planner!! Your consistency and dedication to reflection, self-care, and growth is something to be proud of! It does not stop here. Once you complete this planner, I encourage you to begin it again. See where you have improved and where you could still use guidance. It is not easy taking time for you each day while taking care of little ones. YOU DID IT!!! Praise the Lord! Mom, I will continue to keep you in my prayers daily. THANK YOU for allowing me to be an important part of your journey.

Isaiah 43:2-4 "When you pass through the waters, I will be with you; and through the rivers, they shall not overwhelm you; when you walk through fire you shall not be burned, and the flame shall not consume you. For I am the Lord your God, the Holy One of Israel, your Savior. I give Egypt your ransom, Cush and Seba in exchange for you. Because you are precious in my eyes, and honored....And I love you"

<u>Weekly Challenge:</u>

It's time to reflect on your entries from last week. Pray. Meditate. Celebrate.

Reflection:

Jeremiah 29:11 "For I know the plans I have for you, declares the Lord, plans for welfare and not for evil, to give you a future and a hope."

What am I celebrating today? _____

_____

What am I grateful for today? _____

_____

What do I need to forgive myself for today? _____

_____

How did I use my gifts today?: _____

_____

Self-care:

3 John 1:2 "Beloved, I pray that all may go well with you and that you may be in good health, as it goes well with your soul."

How did I spend my 15 minutes of "me" time today? _____

_____

How will I spend my 15 minutes of "me" time tomorrow? _____

_____

How did I show gratitude for the ability to move my body today? _____

_____

How will I move tomorrow? _____

_____

Growth:

1 Timothy 4:15 "Practice these things, immerse yourself in them, so that all may see your progress."

What steps did I take towards my goal today? _____

_____

What did today teach me that I will bring into tomorrow? _____

_____

Date:_____

Reflection:

Jeremiah 29:11 "For I know the plans I have for you, declares the Lord, plans for welfare and not for evil, to give you a future and a hope."

What am I celebrating today? _____

_____

What am I grateful for today? _____

_____

What do I need to forgive myself for today? _____

_____

How did I use my gifts today?: _____

_____

Self-care:

3 John 1:2 "Beloved, I pray that all may go well with you and that you may be in good health, as it goes well with your soul."

How did I spend my 15 minutes of "me" time today? _____

_____

How will I spend my 15 minutes of "me" time tomorrow? _____

_____

How did I show gratitude for the ability to move my body today? _____

_____

How will I move tomorrow? _____

_____

Growth:

1 Timothy 4:15 "Practice these things, immerse yourself in them, so that all may see your progress."

What steps did I take towards my goal today? _____

_____

What did today teach me that I will bring into tomorrow? _____

_____

Date:_____

Reflection:

Jeremiah 29:11 "For I know the plans I have for you, declares the Lord, plans for welfare and not for evil, to give you a future and a hope."

What am I celebrating today? _____
_____

What am I grateful for today? _____
_____

What do I need to forgive myself for today? _____
_____

How did I use my gifts today?: _____
_____

Self-care:

3 John 1:2 "Beloved, I pray that all may go well with you and that you may be in good health, as it goes well with your soul."

How did I spend my 15 minutes of "me" time today? _____
_____

How will I spend my 15 minutes of "me" time tomorrow? _____
_____

How did I show gratitude for the ability to move my body today? ____
_____

How will I move tomorrow? _____
_____

Growth:

1 Timothy 4:15 "Practice these things, immerse yourself in them, so that all may see your progress."

What steps did I take towards my goal today? _____
_____

What did today teach me that I will bring into tomorrow? _____
_____

Date:_____

Reflection:

Jeremiah 29:11 "For I know the plans I have for you, declares the Lord, plans for welfare and not for evil, to give you a future and a hope."

What am I celebrating today? _____

_____

What am I grateful for today? _____

_____

What do I need to forgive myself for today? _____

_____

How did I use my gifts today?: _____

_____

Self-care:

3 John 1:2 "Beloved, I pray that all may go well with you and that you may be in good health, as it goes well with your soul."

How did I spend my 15 minutes of "me" time today? _____

_____

How will I spend my 15 minutes of "me" time tomorrow? _____

_____

How did I show gratitude for the ability to move my body today? _____

_____

How will I move tomorrow? _____

_____

Growth:

1 Timothy 4:15 "Practice these things, immerse yourself in them, so that all may see your progress."

What steps did I take towards my goal today? _____

_____

What did today teach me that I will bring into tomorrow? _____

_____

Date:_____

Reflection:

Jeremiah 29:11 "For I know the plans I have for you, declares the Lord, plans for welfare and not for evil, to give you a future and a hope."

What am I celebrating today? _____

_____

What am I grateful for today? _____

_____

What do I need to forgive myself for today? _____

_____

How did I use my gifts today?: _____

_____

Self-care:

3 John 1:2 "Beloved, I pray that all may go well with you and that you may be in good health, as it goes well with your soul."

How did I spend my 15 minutes of "me" time today? _____

_____

How will I spend my 15 minutes of "me" time tomorrow? _____

_____

How did I show gratitude for the ability to move my body today? _____

_____

How will I move tomorrow? _____

_____

Growth:

1 Timothy 4:15 "Practice these things, immerse yourself in them, so that all may see your progress."

What steps did I take towards my goal today? _____

_____

What did today teach me that I will bring into tomorrow? _____

_____

Date:_____

Reflection:

Jeremiah 29:11 "For I know the plans I have for you, declares the Lord, plans for welfare and not for evil, to give you a future and a hope."

What am I celebrating today? _____

_____

What am I grateful for today? _____

_____

What do I need to forgive myself for today? _____

_____

How did I use my gifts today?: _____

_____

Self-care:

3 John 1:2 "Beloved, I pray that all may go well with you and that you may be in good health, as it goes well with your soul."

How did I spend my 15 minutes of "me" time today? _____

_____

How will I spend my 15 minutes of "me" time tomorrow? _____

_____

How did I show gratitude for the ability to move my body today? _____

_____

How will I move tomorrow? _____

_____

Growth:

1 Timothy 4:15 "Practice these things, immerse yourself in them, so that all may see your progress."

What steps did I take towards my goal today? _____

_____

What did today teach me that I will bring into tomorrow? _____

_____

Date:_____

Reflection:

Jeremiah 29:11 "For I know the plans I have for you, declares the Lord, plans for welfare and not for evil, to give you a future and a hope."

What am I celebrating today? _____

_____

What am I grateful for today? _____

_____

What do I need to forgive myself for today? _____

_____

How did I use my gifts today?: _____

_____

Self-care:

3 John 1:2 "Beloved, I pray that all may go well with you and that you may be in good health, as it goes well with your soul."

How did I spend my 15 minutes of "me" time today? _____

_____

How will I spend my 15 minutes of "me" time tomorrow? _____

_____

How did I show gratitude for the ability to move my body today? _____

_____

How will I move tomorrow? _____

_____

Growth:

1 Timothy 4:15 "Practice these things, immerse yourself in them, so that all may see your progress."

What steps did I take towards my goal today? _____

_____

What did today teach me that I will bring into tomorrow? _____

_____